Clothing Alterations and Repairs

BLOOMSBURY VISUAL ARTS
Bloomsbury Publishing Plc
50 Bedford Square, London, WC1B 3DP, UK
1385 Broadway, New York, NY 10018, USA
29 Earlsfort Terrace, Dublin 2, Ireland

BLOOMSBURY, BLOOMSBURY VISUAL ARTS and the Diana logo are trademarks of Bloomsbury Publishing Plc

First published in Great Britain in 2024

Copyright © Chelsey Byrd Lewallen, 2024

Chelsey Byrd Lewallen has asserted her right under the Copyright, Designs and Patents Act, 1988, to be identified as Author of this work.

For legal purposes the Acknowledgements on p. 236 constitute an extension of this copyright page.

Cover design: Eleanor Rose
Cover image © Chelsey Byrd Lewallen

All rights reserved. No part of this publication may be reproduced or transmitted in any form or by any means, electronic or mechanical, including photocopying, recording, or any information storage or retrieval system, without prior permission in writing from the publishers.

Bloomsbury Publishing Plc does not have any control over, or responsibility for, any third-party websites referred to or in this book. All internet addresses given in this book were correct at the time of going to press. The author and publisher regret any inconvenience caused if addresses have changed or sites have ceased to exist, but can accept no responsibility for any such changes.

A catalogue record for this book is available from the British Library.

A catalog record for this book is available from the Library of Congress.

ISBN: HB: 978-1-3501-6359-1
       PB: 978-1-3501-6355-3
       ePDF: 978-1-3501-6356-0
       eBook: 978-1-3501-6357-7

Typeset by Integra Software Services Pvt. Ltd.
Printed and bound in India

 Online resources to accompany this book are available at https://www.bloomsburyonlineresources.com/clothing-alterations-and-repairs. If you experience any problems, please contact Bloomsbury at: onlineresources@bloomsbury.com

To find out more about our authors and books visit www.bloomsbury.com and sign up for our newsletters.

Clothing Alterations and Repairs

Maintaining a Sustainable Wardrobe

Chelsey Byrd Lewallen

BLOOMSBURY VISUAL ARTS
LONDON · NEW YORK · OXFORD · NEW DELHI · SYDNEY

Preface vii
Introduction 1

1 How to Use This Book and Tools of the Trade 3

How to Use This Book 5
Clothing Alterations 6
Repairs 8
Tools of the Trade 9

2 Working With Alterations, Repairs, and Clients 27

Before You Get Started 28
Step One: Organizing Your Space 28
Step Two: The Logistics of Clothing Alterations and Repairs 30
Finding the Problem 32
Step Three: Working With Clients 36
Identifying Fabric 38

3 Bottom Hems 43

Shortening 44
Serge and Blind Hem: Three Methods 46
Twice Turn Hem 48
Cadet Cut Hem 49
Knitwear Coverstitch Hem 51
Knitwear Faux Coverstitch Using a Twin Needle 55
Twice-Turned Hem on Eveningwear and Formalwear 57
Napkin Roll Hem 61
Hand Stitch Hems: Cross Stitch, Vertical Hem Stitch, Prick/Pick Stitch 63
Lengthening Bottom Hems 67
Maxing Out 68
Bias Tape 69
Adding Fabric 71
Adding Lace 74

4 Top Hems 77

Shortening 77
Knitwear Coverstitch 78
Knitwear Faux Coverstitch Using a Twin Needle 80
Shirttail Hem 82
Lined Suit Jacket Hem 84
Unlined Suit Jacket Hem 86
Lengthening 88
Lengthening Suit Jacket Hem 90

5 Taking In Bottoms 93

Back Gap 94
Waistbands: Using Elastic 96
Side Seams/Outseams and Inseam Tips 98
Side Seams/Outseams 100
Inseams 102
Darts/Pleats/Tucks 105
Ease/Gathers 108
Taking in a Skirt or Pant with a Side Zipper 110

6 Letting Out Bottoms 113

Side Seams 114
Inseams 116
Waistbands: Using Seam Allowance, Elastic, or Gussets 118
Waistbands: Using Seam Allowance 119
Waistbands: Using Elastic 121
Waistbands: Using Gussets/Fabric Panels 123

7 Jeans 127
Taking In the Center Back/Back Gap 129
Jeans Hem With Option to Distress 132
Original Jeans Hem 137
Taking In the Outseams/Inseams 140

8 Taking In Tops 145
Side Seams 146
Princess Seams/Darts on Front Top 148
Princess Seams/Darts on Back Top 150
Pleats/Tucks 152
Boned Bodices in Formalwear 154

9 Letting Out Tops 157
Side Seams 158
Panels 160
Boned Bodices in Formalwear 162

10 Sleeves, Shoulders, and Armscyes 165
When to Say "No!" 166
Taking Up Shoulders 167
Taking In Sleeves or Sleeves and Side Seams 170
Lined Suit Jacket Sleeve Hems 172
Button Down Shirt Cuffs and Plackets 176

11 Crotch Seams 179
How to Measure Crotch Seams 180
Taking In Crotch Seams 183
Letting Out Crotch Seams 185
Adding Gussets 187

12 Necklines and Collars 191
Collar/Neckline Types 192
Reshaping Necklines 193
Collar Adjustments 195

13 Repairs 199
Buttons 200
Decorative Patches/Visible Mending 208
Darning 215
Zippers 219
Linings 228
Replacing or Rethreading Drawstrings 229
Hook and Loop Tape 230
Outdoor/Other Gear 231
Waterproof Gear 232

Resources 233
Glossary 234
Acknowledgements 236
Index 237

PREFACE

The moment you learn to sew you will inevitably be asked one of two things: can you make this for me, or can you fix this for me? This book is for anyone who has learned or is learning to sew and would like to dive into alterations and repairs without the use of glue, staples, or duct tape!

I vividly remember my first experience with clothing alterations and repairs when I was cast as Brigitta Von Trapp in *The Sound of Music* at age thirteen. The costume designer skillfully pinned, marked, and altered my dresses to fit beautifully. The experience made me feel and look the part. One evening, the metal zipper on my pink lace party dress broke, and another actor carefully held the back of the garment closed until the scene was over. The experience was terrifying yet thrilling! I ended up ditching acting and immediately fell in love with the costume workshop.

After graduating from college with a bachelor's degree in theater and costume technology from the University of Wyoming, I had a few part-time gigs as a stitcher in costume shops and constructed garments for freelance designers. People who knew that I could sew were constantly asking if I could hem their pants, sew on their military patches, or mend their beloved clothing. I saw the demand for alterations and repairs, so I started a clothing alterations business out of my apartment shortly after the birth of my first child. Serendipitously, I was also given the opportunity to be a teaching assistant for a patternmaking class by a former professor who was now a department director at the University of Idaho. She suggested that I get my master's degree concurrent with the teaching assistantship, so I did! After graduating with my M.S. Family and Consumer Sciences with a specialization in apparel and textiles, I launched a clothing alterations and repairs shop called Altered Ego with my business partner Sara. For four years we did oodles of alterations and repairs, moved to a larger location, taught sewing classes, and learned how to run a business. I found that teaching classes and private lessons to share my knowledge of apparel, alterations, repairs, and textiles was incredibly fulfilling. I realized it was time for me to pursue my true passion for teaching, so I sold my interest in Altered Ego to Sara. I started as an instructor in the Apparel, Textiles, and Design program at the University of Idaho in 2015 where I teach students about textiles, apparel construction, patternmaking, and textile apparel sustainability.

With twenty years of sewing, alteration, and repair experience under my belt, I am a devoted advocate for the sustainable power of maintaining one's wardrobe through mending and fitting. I hope this book helps you extend the life of beloved textile possessions and allows you slow down and enjoy the rewarding process of alterations and repairs. Happy sewing!

INTRODUCTION

SUSTAINABLE SOLUTIONS

The art of clothing alterations and repairs are not commonly known in the 21st century. At one time, this skill was passed down from generation to generation, but today sewing has become a lost art. With a growing interest in sustainability combined with online platforms and communities, there appears to be a renewed sense of wonder in sewing to make new goods. However, very little is being offered in way of repairs and alterations for clothing. With supply chain issues affecting availability of goods and the continuing problem of textile pollution, it is more important now than ever to learn how to sustain and maintain the textile products found in our homes and wardrobes.

The volume of textile waste in landfills is alarming and the way in which fast fashion has transformed the industry is not sustainable to the environment. According to the United States Environmental Protection Agency (EPA) "Landfills received 11.3 million tons of MSW textiles in 2018" which is approximately 81.5 pounds or 37 kilograms of textile waste per person per year.[1]

Sustainability isn't easy to achieve. Some sustainable solutions that would require a real shift in the apparel industry and economy lie within the concept of slow fashion. Slow fashion considers the long game of every part of apparel including the design process, textile manufacturing, fiber content selection, packaging and shipping, and considering the wellbeing of the workers who create the apparel.

We can't fix this problem entirely, but we can take small steps to move forward in a new direction and clothing alterations and repairs are the ideal first steps to maintaining our textile goods. I hope this book helps you keep at least one article of clothing out of landfill and will leave you with a few suggestions for keeping your wardrobe sustainable.

1. Plan ahead and purchase life-long garments—quality over quantity
2. Choose natural fibers when possible
3. Thrift
4. Upcycle
5. And my favorite option—alter and repair!

I recommend reading chapters 1 and 2, especially pages 30–38 before starting any alteration to set a solid foundation before diving in, especially if you are new or relatively new to sewing/mending. "An ounce of prevention is worth a pound of cure," says Benjamin Franklin (and my dad)!

This book will guide you with general written and illustrated step-by-step instructions for common alterations and repairs. The garments that you alter may not look like the illustrations depending on seam/hem finishes, what techniques and machinery were used when the garment was created, varying styles/cuts of garments, and the type of fabric used. While you do not need to have sewing experience prior to doing most repairs and alterations, it is helpful! Use your creative solving skills, bounce questions and ideas off of other sewists, and use your references to determine the best course of action. Be willing to make some mistakes, take your time, and become best friends with your seam ripper!

[1] "Textiles: Material-Specific Data." *EPA*, Environmental Protection Agency, https://www.epa.gov/facts-and-figures-about-materials-waste-and-recycling/textiles-material-specific-data

CHAPTER 1

How to Use This Book and Tools of the Trade

It is always good to identify and define what you are doing before you get started with any new skill. This chapter discusses what clothing alterations and repairs are as well as how to use this book. Each chapter covers a category of alterations or repairs as it relates to garment types and locations of the alteration/repair. After your initial journey into alterations and repairs, you may also choose to dub yourself as one or any of the following:

Sewist
Alteration Specialist
Soft Form or Organic Form Engineer
Stitcher

Beware of a common homonym should you choose to call yourself a sewer!

HOW TO USE THIS BOOK

There are a variety of methods that can be used to achieve your desired alterations and repairs, and each task will have various tools, materials, and notions or trims needed to complete the project. I hope to provide you with achievable options for most alterations and repairs no matter your skill level or access to machinery.

On each page you will see a key that will let you know the skill level/project as well as an estimated time commitment required for that specific alteration. The key is a fast way for you to determine whether you have the time and skill to complete the alteration or repair at hand. Each project will have a triangle that correlates the project skill level from beginner, intermediate to advanced and an estimated time commitment. Use it as a guide, but not a hard and fast rule! There is more than one way to any task and this book is full of my suggestions, but do what works best for you!

Beginner/ Easy

Intermediate/ Moderate Difficulty

Advanced/ Challenging

1.1 Skill Level Key

CLOTHING ALTERATIONS

Clothing alterations are adjustments that are made to custom fit a garment to an individual body. The goal of an alteration is to make a garment functional as well as to have a fit that makes the wearer feel positive about their appearance in it. Garments can be taken in (made smaller) and let out (made larger) as well as shortened or lengthened.

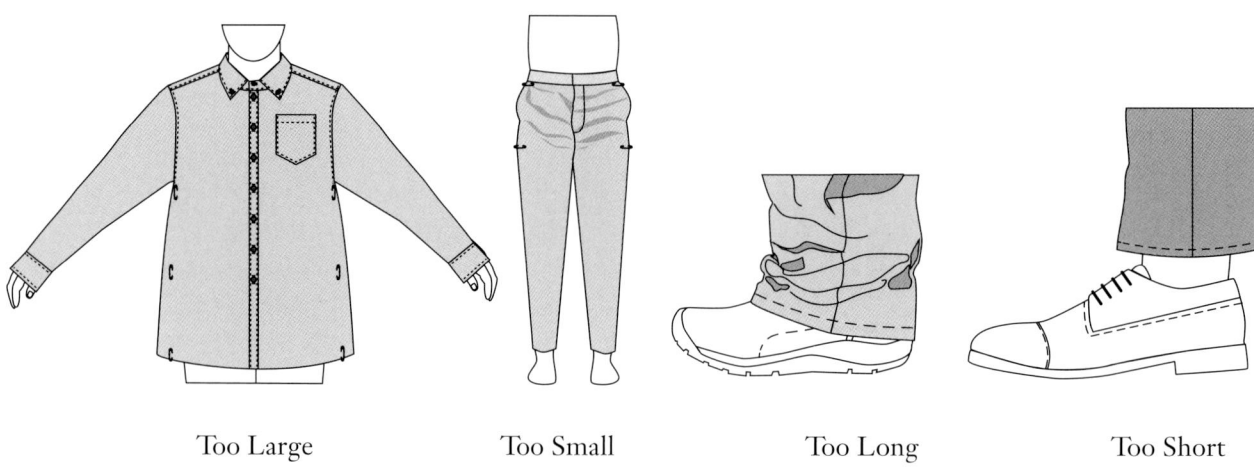

Too Large Too Small Too Long Too Short

1.2

There are multiple ways that you can alter garments. The following illustrations are some general examples of methods that can be used to accomplish similar tasks. This section is a small sample platter of some of the techniques you can use to make adjustments to customize or repair apparel.

- Taking In: Making a garment smaller or more fitted to a body: Darts, seams, pleats, tucks, adding elastic

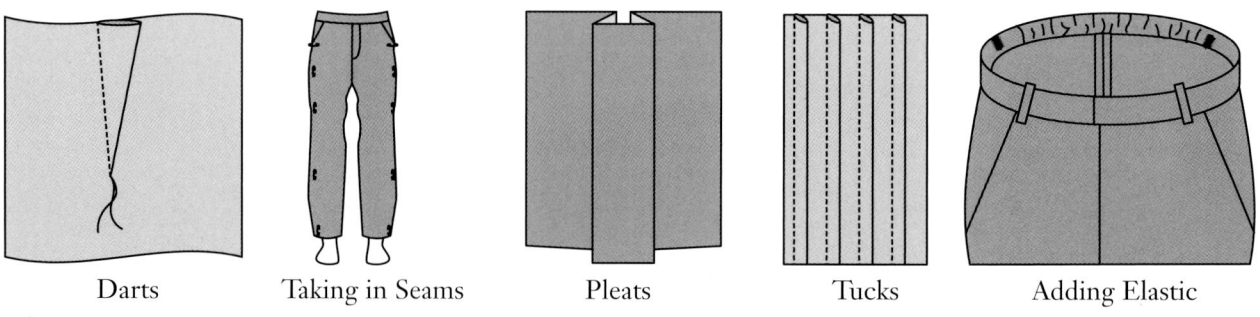

Darts Taking in Seams Pleats Tucks Adding Elastic

1.3

- Letting Out: Making a garment larger to fit the body via stitching closer to the seam allowance/maxing out, adding gussets

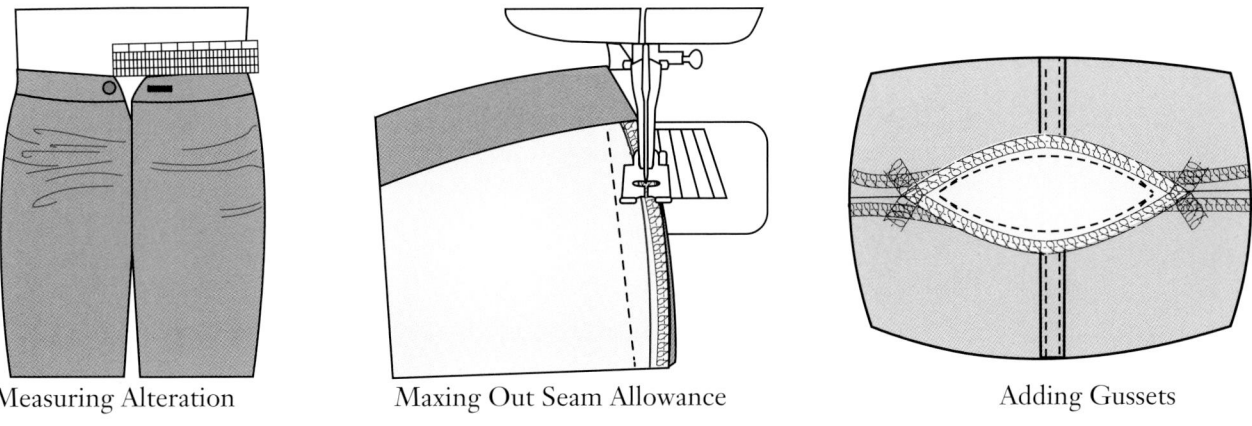

Measuring Alteration | Maxing Out Seam Allowance | Adding Gussets

1.4

- Shortening: Making a garment shorter via hemming, cutting, pleats, tucks

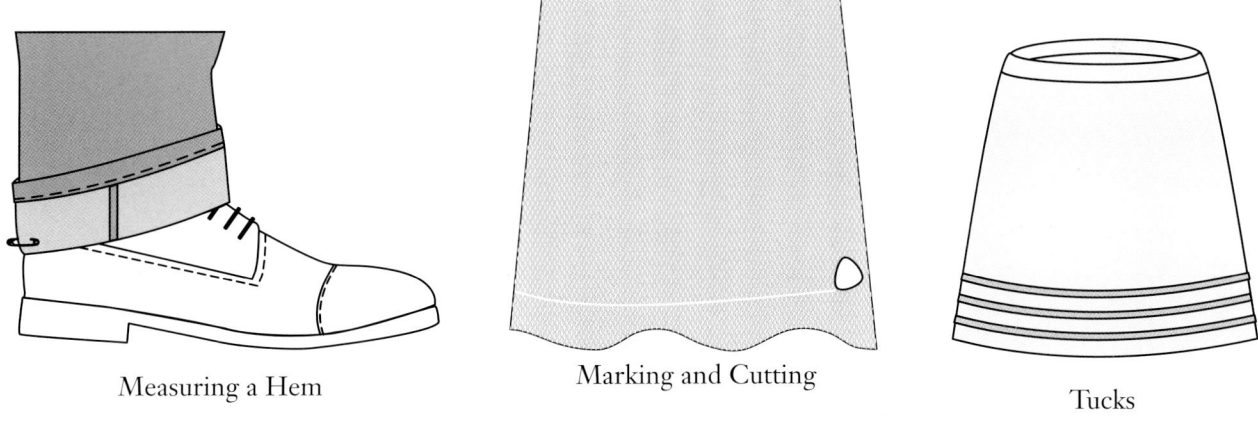

Measuring a Hem | Marking and Cutting | Tucks

1.5

- Lengthening: Making a garment longer by maxing out seam allowance or adding fabric/trims

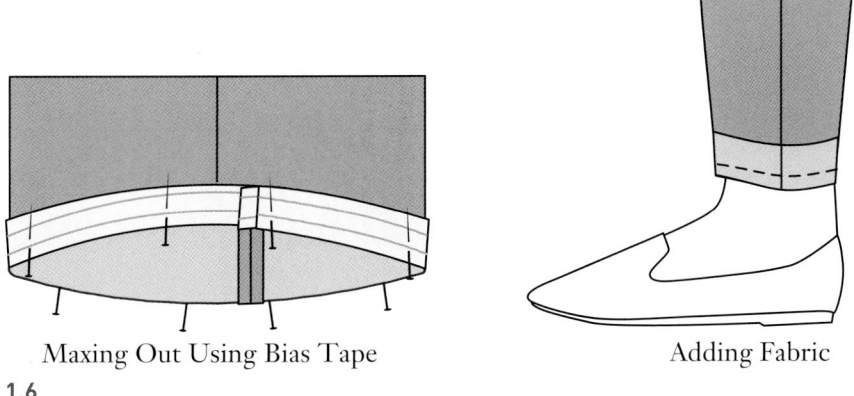

Maxing Out Using Bias Tape | Adding Fabric

1.6

REPAIRS

Repairs are a way to extend the life of our clothing by darning, mending, patching, or fixing/replacing hardware.

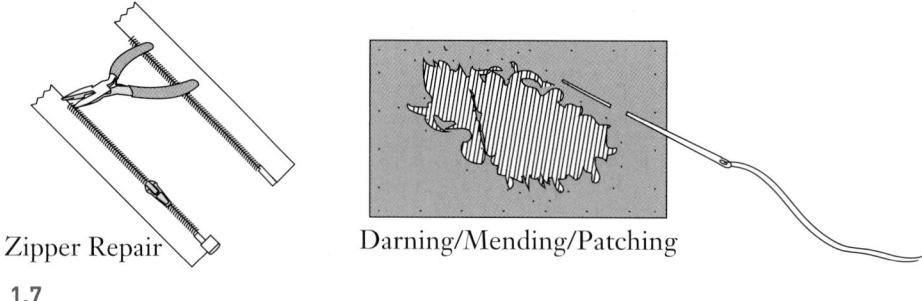

Zipper Repair

Darning/Mending/Patching

1.7

- Darning: Mending a hole by interweaving yarn on fabric

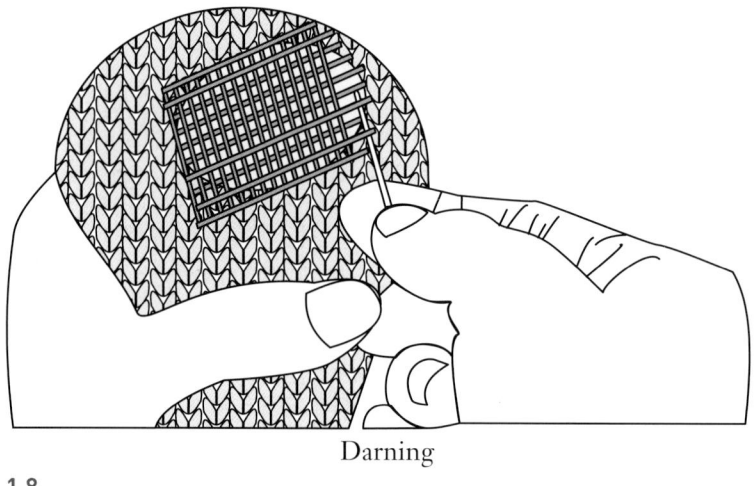

Darning

1.8

- Patching: Applying fabric or a patch to mend a hole

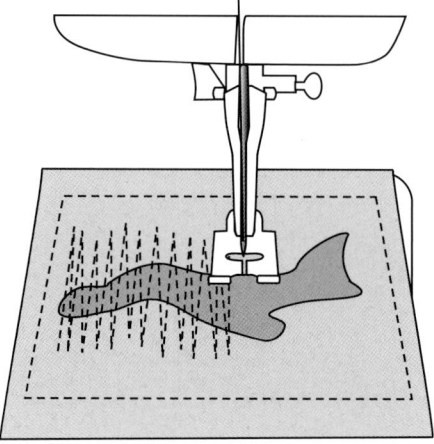

Machine Darning/Patching/Mending

1.9

TOOLS OF THE TRADE

Pinning, Measuring, and Marking

I suggest using safety pins to mark alterations and repair locations on most fabrics because they do not fade, rub off, or fall out. I once had a colleague use a double-sided disappearing ink pen to mark alterations on a wedding dress where blue ink disappears when exposed to water and the purple ink disappears with exposure to oxygen over time. She used the purple side and then didn't get to the alterations for a couple of weeks and when she went in to start the adjustments, all her markings had vanished! Weddings and deadlines will not wait for second fittings, so be sure to do it right the first time! Stick with good quality safety pins and dispose of pins that do not easily go through fabric into a sharps container.

With delicate fabric or non-healing fabric like leather, special care must be taken when pinning and marking. Thread marking or a long hand baste stitch works well for delicate fabrics and binder clips or small clamps work well with leather.

Do NOT put pins in your mouth! They can easily be inhaled and can spread germs. If you need pins close by, use a pin magnet or pin cushion.

Types of Pins

a. **Dorcas Pins:** My favorite pins! They are sharp, strong, and do not easily bend or melt.
b. **Ball Point:** Ball point pins are used for knits and have a blunt tip that separates the fibers rather than piercing through. I do not use these often, but they are excellent for knitwear.
c. **Ball Head:** These are helpful pins for beginners because they are easy to remove. Be mindful if you are pressing apparel with these pins in the fabric as the plastic ball will melt under an iron.
d. **T-Pin:** T-pins are incredibly useful for holding fabric in place if you are working with stretching out elastic on a garment and have a table that you can pin into. Do not use these on delicate fabrics as they can permanently damage the cloth.
e. **Glass Head:** These pins are extra fine and leave very small holes in the fabric. They are desirable if you need to iron fabric with pins in as they will not melt.
f. **Silk:** Extra fine pins that should be used on silk fabrics that do not self-heal or spring back.
g. **Flat Head Pins/Decorative Head Pins:** Pins with fun flat head shapes like buttons, hearts, bows, etc. … These can be helpful for children and people with limited hand dexterity and can be easier to pick up than other pins.
h. **Safety:** Pins with a spring mechanism and clasp. Great to use in fittings and come in a variety of sizes and metal types.

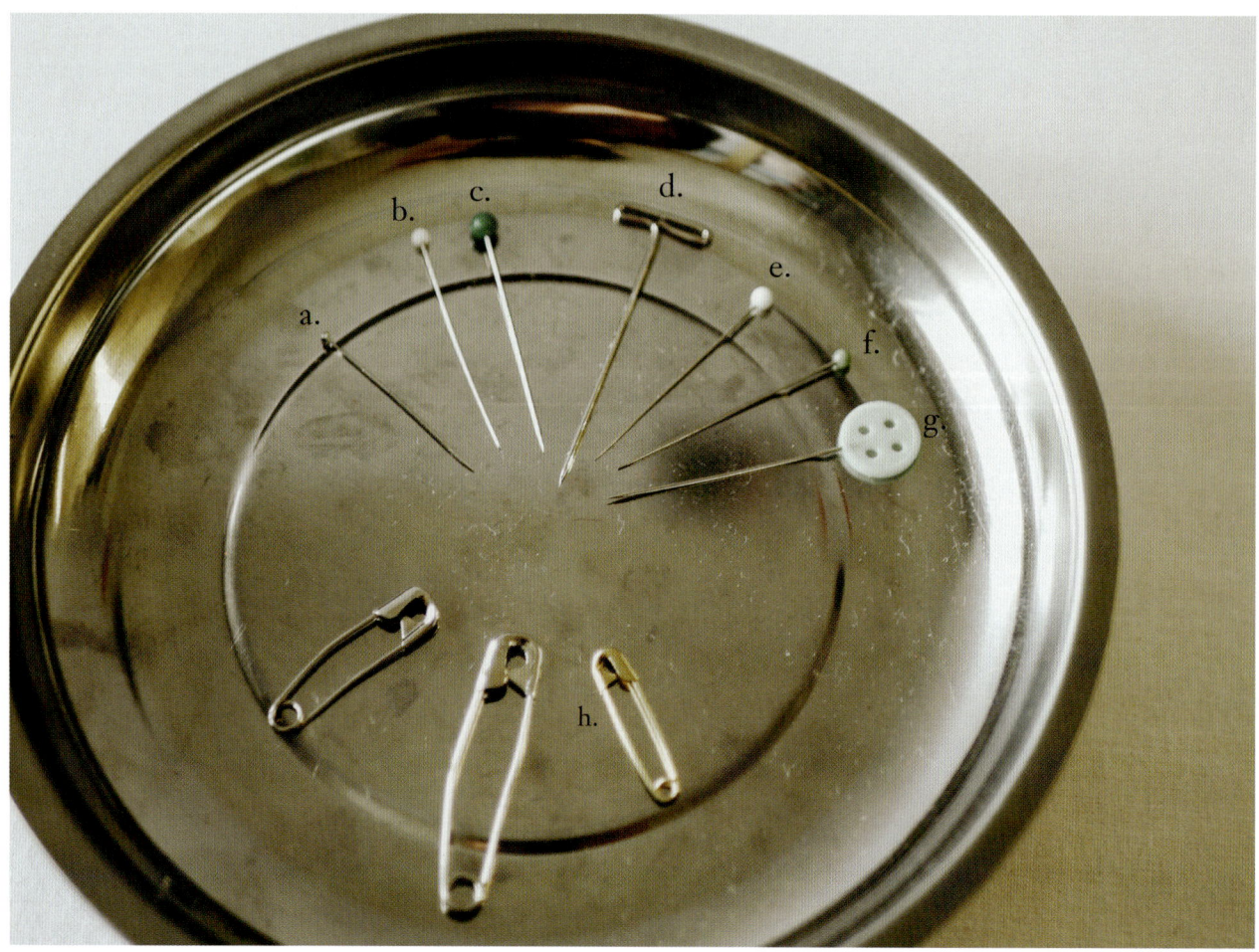

Types of Rulers

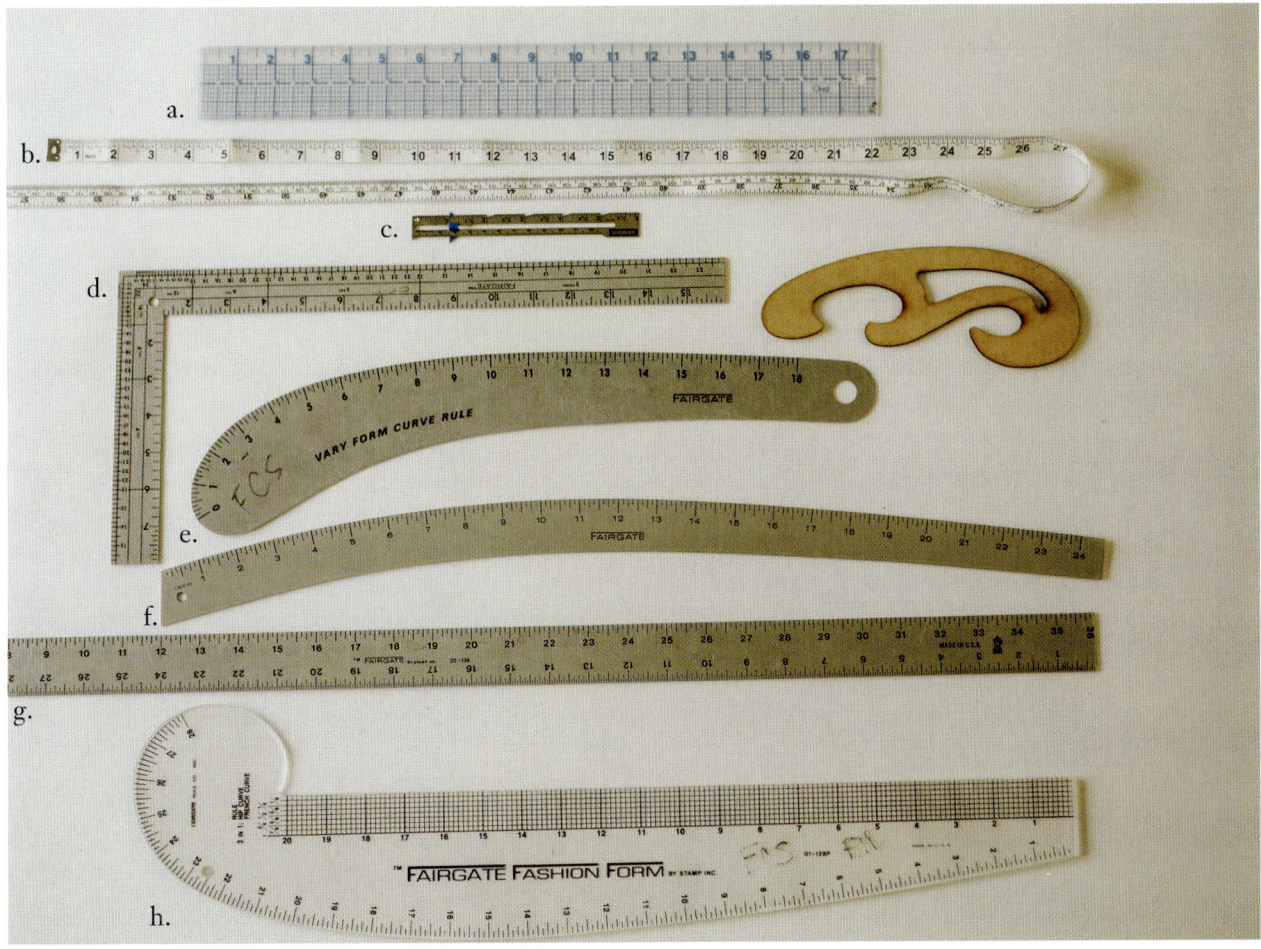

a. **2" × 18" Clear Plastic Ruler:** This is my absolute favorite ruler. I prefer blue rulers over red or black because they are easier to see on most fabrics, but whatever works best for you is fantastic.
b. **60"/150 cm Tape Measure:** These handy tape measures are great for taking body measurements and are usually made from fiber glass. It is helpful to have one that has both metric and imperial measurements.
c. **Seam Gauge:** Helpful for measuring out consistent seam allowances, especially on hems.
d. **L Square:** These can be used in pattern drafting, while marking a hem from the floor, or anytime you need a right angle.
e. **French Curve:** Good for creating smooth lines for longer contours of the body, necklines, collars, and armscyes.
f. **Hip Curve:** Helpful for subtle curves including inseams, lapels, sleeves, hiplines, and some hems.
g. **Yard Sticks:** Perfect for when you need to make long, straight lines, and can be used while marking a hem from the floor.
h. **Fashion Rulers:** These rulers have a straight and curved edge and are commonly used in patternmaking and can be helpful for armscyes, necklines, collars, out seams, and hems.

Marking Tools

When selecting marking tools, always test a sample in an inconspicuous area of the fabric before using. Only use white or off-white chalk when working with white or light colored fabrics so you do not accidentally and permanently stain the fabric.

- a. **Wax Chalk:** Tailors wax chalk usually comes in small rectangular shapes and is my marking tool of choice for most fabrics. Some wax chalks will disappear when ironed, but they cannot be used on polyester and silk because they will melt and leave a permanent mark on the fabric.
- b. **Clay Chalk:** Comes in small rectangles or triangles and works well on wool. You can rub or brush this chalk off with fabric. It does not glide well, but is great for fabrics with a little texture.
- c. **Fabric Markers and Pencils:** The most common fabric marker is a dual-purpose pen with blue ink on one side that disappears with water and purple that disappears with air. Be careful with these as sometimes they disappear and then after heat is applied, they can permanently stain the fabric. Test in an inconspicuous area before using fabric markers on a project.
- d. **Thread Marking:** This method can be used on fabrics that you do not want markings on like bridal gowns or heirloom items. Simply use a basting stitch to mark cut and/or alteration lines.

Needles

Having the correct needle is half the battle of sewing! Whether you are sewing by hand or machine, use this section as a guide to make your sewing experience a pleasant one!

a. **Hand Sewing Needles:** There are a vast array of hand sewing needles. My go-to for most projects is a size 9 sharps needle. Occasionally, you may need specialty needles for the project you are working on. For example, you may need curved or milliners'/straws needles for items like hats, quilting/betweens needles for quilting, ball point needles for knits, darners for darning, or a leather/glover needle for leather (watch out, these are SHARP!). The sizing on hand sewing needles is a little confusing, so be sure to reference needle guides when purchasing your needles. If you are using a sharps hand needle, low numbers mean a shorter needle with a smaller eye, and larger number sized needles will be longer with a larger eye, and the opposite is true of quilting needles.

b. **Thimbles:** Thimbles can be used to protect your finger when pushing the needle through thicker fabrics. Some people claim there is a "correct" finger to use a thimble on, usually the middle finger, but I think you should do whatever feels intuitive for you and your hand sewing. They come in many shapes and sizes for various projects from cross-stitch to leather work.

c. **Needle Threaders:** Needle threaders are incredibly helpful tools if it is challenging for you to see the eye of the needle and can be used with hand and machine needles. Simply place the open/flexible end of the needle threader through the eye of your needle, then place the thread at least 1" (2.5 cm) through the needle threader, finally pull the needle threader back out through the eye of the needle and your needle will be threaded!

d. **Beeswax/Thread Conditioner:** Thread treatment materials helps to strengthen thread and prevents thread from getting tangled. You can use beeswax or thread conditioner.

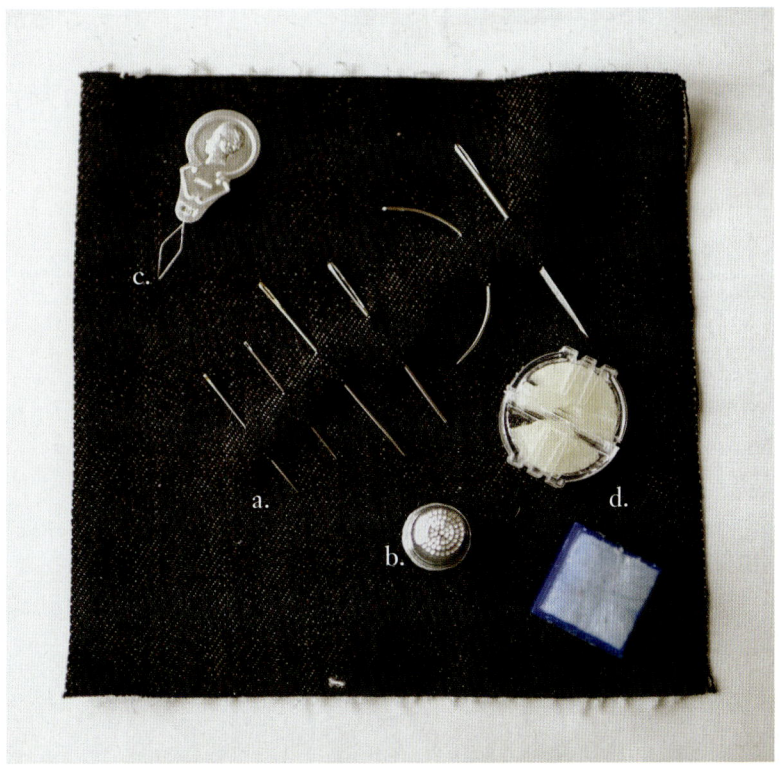

Machine Needles

The first step in selecting a needle for your machine is determining whether the needle is for a home or industrial machine. Home machine needles have a flat back and a round front on the shank, and industrial needles have a completely round shank. All home needles are the same length. Industrial machines require different needle lengths depending on the machine's needle bar height so be sure to reference your user manual or read the needle size letters and numbers to determine the correct size for your machine.

a. **Industrial Machine Needles:** These needles can be used on industrial sewing machines including lockstitch, coverstitch, overlock/sergers, chainstitch, flatlock, and specialty machines.
b. **Home Machine Needles:** Home needles can be used on classic mechanical machines, home overlock/sergers, home coverstitch machines, and home embroidery machines.
c. **Denim/Jeans Needles:** These needles are used to sew through denim, canvas, and fabric that has a heavier weight. The eye in a denim needle is larger so that thicker thread can pass through it easily without splitting up on the back side of the needle.
d. **Twin Needles:** Twin needles are used on home sewing machines as a way of creating a "faux coverstitch" with two parallel lines or for decorative purposes.
e. **Other Specialty Needles:** There are many other types of specialty needles including hemstitch/wing needles for decorative or heirloom stitching that produce lace-like designs, microtex needles for fine fabrics or densely woven fabrics like silk, and leather needles that are extra sharp for sewing on leather.
f. **Curved Machine Needles:** Curved needles are used for blind hem and some overedge machines.

Needle Sizes: Needles come labeled with two numbers that represent sizing systems. The first number represents the European size via diameter of the needle blade in hundredths of a millimeter and typically range from 60 to 180. The second number represents the American needle size typically ranging from 8 to 25. The larger the number needle, the thicker the needle diameter and the larger the eye. If you are using thicker thread, you will need a needle with a large enough eye for the thickness/Tex of the thread to avoid a thread caterpillar wadding up in the back of your machine needle!

Needle Size	Use/Fabric Type
60 (8) 65 (9)	Lightweight fabrics
70 (10) 75 (11)	Light to mediumweight fabrics
80 (12) 90 (14)	Mediumweight fabrics, most commonly used
100 (16) 110 (18)	Heavyweight fabrics and thicker thread

- **Universal Versus Ball point Needles:** Universal needles are the best to be used on woven fabrics because they have a sharper tip that pierces through the fiber. Ballpoint/jersey/stretch needles work best on knits because the tip of the needle is slightly rounded which separates the knit fibers rather than piercing them.

Needles and Woven Fabrics

- When working with weaves, use a universal needle when sewing. If the woven fabric has stretch due to the presence of elastane, Spandex, Lycra®, etc. … test to see if waves in the fabric form when you sew. If so, try a ball point or stretch needle to eliminate fabric distortion.

Needles and Knit Fabrics

- When working with knits, use ball point, stretch, or jersey needles. Because the needle is rounded at the tip, it separates the fibers rather than piercing a hole in the fabric.
- **Notes about Needles:** One of the biggest causes of issues with sewing machines is that people don't regularly change the machine needle. Needles have a short, but powerful life and should be changed between projects or after 6–8 hours of use. If your needle is bent, broken, or has a burr, it will not sew well or at all. If you do not remember the last time you changed your machine needle, go ahead and put in a fresh needle. Check for burrs by running your fingernail up against the side and tip of the needle and if it isn't smooth that means it is time to change that needle. When in doubt, throw that needle out!

Thread

Types of Thread: There are several types of thread that you can use during alterations and repairs. I have outlined the most common threads you might use including hand, machine, jeans/topstitching, cone, and bulky nylon thread.

   a. **Hand Sewing Thread:** You can use just about any thread you like for hand sewing, but whatever type of thread you choose it needs to be pre-treated. There are a few ways to treat thread so that it doesn't easily get knotted up while you are working, and it can also strengthen the thread to avoid it breaking while you work. You can treat hand sewing thread with wax or a thread conditioner like Thread Magic by running the thread over the wax/thread conditioner. Alternatively, you can use good ol' fashioned spit or colorless lip gloss by running the thread through your mouth/on your lips a couple of times (beware, it tickles!)
   b. **Silamide/2-Ply Waxed Nylon Thread:** Silamide is pre-waxed hand sewing thread. I highly recommend getting this if you do a lot of hand sewing. If you purchase this, you will simply cut through the bottom loop of the threads to get perfect lengths of thread for stitching. The first time my business partner opened a Silamide package she did not know about cutting the bottom loops and made a mess resembling what a cat might do with a bunch of string!
   c. **Machine Sewing Thread:** If you are working on smaller projects, smaller spools of thread can be an excellent choice. I often use Tex 30 all-purpose thread or polyester wrapped/poly core machine thread which lasts longer than cotton or cotton core spun thread. Keep in mind that when it comes to thread, you often get what you pay for. Inexpensive thread is tempting, but beware, it will break and "fuzz" faster which leads to having to clean your machine more often as well as having to rethread your machine often.

d. **Cone Thread:** My favorite alternative to small spools of thread is cone thread! You can save a lot of money and trips to the store by purchasing cones instead of small spools of thread. You get more bang for your buck and the thread is ideal for sergers. If you use this on a home machine, you will need to get a thread stand to hold the cone for sewing. I like to use Tex 27 spun polyester thread for sergers and Tex 30 or greater for everyday apparel use.
e. **Bulky/Woolly Nylon or "Fluff" Thread:** This is used for stretch or knit fabrics on the bobbin or lower loopers of sergers and coverstitch machines so that the fabric and stitches can expand and contract. Take a peek at your knit underwear—most likely it was sewn using this thread! If you are working on activewear or swimwear, this thread is a must so that the thread won't snap when you put fitted garments over feet, hands, and heads.
f. **Jeans/Topstitching Thread:** If you are working on hemming denim, regular Tex thread will look unprofessional on jeans. I like to use a minimum thickness of a Tex 80 poly wrapped poly core thread in a matching color. If you are in a bind, you can double or triple your thread by winding bobbins of the thread and then feeding them all through the machine and eye of the needle to create a thicker thread. I've even gone so far as to carefully unpick the hem thread, wind it on a bobbin, and reuse it to match the color and thread thickness!

***Note that there is a difference between overlock thread and regular 3 ply thread. Overlock/serger thread is weaker and will break easily if used for lockstitch seams.

Testing Strength and the Fuzz Factor: Wooden spools and bags of discount thread from garage sales are tempting, but they won't last long! Most thread on those beautiful spools is too old for use. You can test it out by trying to break the thread with your hands. If it breaks easily, the thread has reached its expiration date and needs to be used for a very creative craft (not sewn) or discarded. If you notice fuzz on your thread, there is a good chance it is going to gunk up your machine and can also be a sign of thread that is disintegrating.

Thread Thickness/Tex: Thread is measured by the weight in grams per 1,000 meters of thread. Therefore, the larger the Tex number, the thicker the thread. For example, if you are hand sewing a delicate silk chiffon, you will want to use a smaller Tex thread (Tex 27) and if you are sewing a pair of triple layer canvas work pants, you will need to use a larger Tex (Tex 80). Be mindful of the thickness of your thread as it relates to the project/fabric you are working on.

Machines

When someone asks me for a sewing machine recommendation, I always ask them two questions: what is your budget and what is the intended use of your machine? Many sewists can do beautiful work with a simple, inexpensive home sewing machine and others have individualized machines with very specific functions. Before you purchase or request a machine, think about what your budget is and what you will realistically be doing. As with most purchases, you get what you pay for, and anything sold at a thrift store or garage sale will almost certainly require servicing which often costs around $90 and may be more depending on the year that you read this book! Below I have outlined some basic machine types and valuable information about troubleshooting machines when you, inevitably, run into issues!

- **Home:** Home sewing machines should have backstitch, straight stitch, and zigzag capabilities. They often come with a variety of useful presser feet or attachments.
- **Industrial:** Machines that have one purpose, typically come with a table, and do their one job really well. Types of industrial machines include flatlock, sergers/overlock, coverstitch, bartack, and many more! It may take a little bit of time to figure out how to thread them, but once you master that, industrial machines are a dream to work with—especially when dealing with heavier weight fabrics! Some industrial machines connect to compressed air and can even cut the thread for you at the end of a seam with the tap of your foot! If you choose to purchase an industrial machine, I highly recommend getting one with a servo motor so you can control the speed of the machine as you are learning rather than to diving into a machine with one speed: FAST!
- **Serger/Overlock Machine:** Sergers can finish the raw edges of fabric and are used for knit construction and decorative hemming. If you are serious about sewing, you'll need one of these. If you dabble, it won't be necessary to purchase one of these so long as you have a seam finishing technique that works for you.
- **Coverstitch:** A machine used to hem knits and some wovens. They can also serve as binders for finishing raw edges with bias tape or making belt loops. I do NOT recommend getting one that has other purposes (a serger/coverstitch combo) as it is challenging to switch the functions over and, in my experience, does two jobs poorly. This is helpful if you do a lot of work with knits and activewear/swimwear but is not necessary for basic repairs and alterations. A great alternative to the coverstitch machine is serging the raw edge of fabric and then using a twin needle to create the coverstitch aesthetic. You can create a faux flatlock seam (the stitching you see on flat seams in activewear) using a coverstitch machine if you flip the fabric over so the technical back of the fabric (wrong side) is facing up.

Industrial Sewing Machine

Home Sewing Machine

TOOLS OF THE TRADE

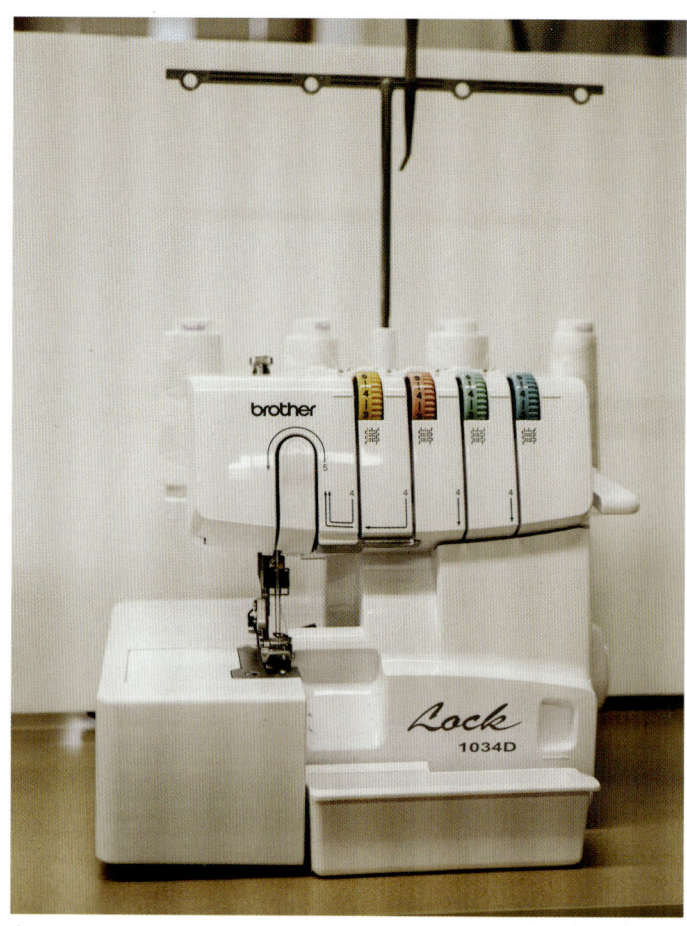
Overlock Machine

Coverstitch Machine

Pressing/Ironing

It is not uncommon to want to fast forward through a project and skip pressing and ironing a garment. In reality, pressing/ironing is often just as important to alterations and repairs as the stitching! Make sure you have your ironing station set up before any alteration or repair that requires some heat and/or steam!

- **Pressing Versus Ironing:** Ironing and pressing are two different motions. When fabric is unfinished (has not been made into a garment) you should aim to *press* the fabric by setting the iron onto the crease or wrinkle on the textile, steaming it, and lifting up the iron without moving it back and forth. This prevents the warping of the fibers which will make your fabric shift and off grain, or as my favorite sewing instructor would say, "woodgie." When a fabric is finished in the form of a garment or textile good, you can use back and forth motions to *iron* out wrinkles.
- **Heat + Steam = Success:** Dry pressing works to set dye/paint on fabric, but in order to eliminate wrinkles, you need the winning combination of heat and steam. Be sure to keep your fingers away from the tip of the iron where most of the steam escapes.

- **Home Irons:** Home irons are a necessity for the household and should come with the ability to add distilled water and a range of heat settings. When purchasing a home iron, look for one that has adjustable temperature and steam settings.
- **Gravity Feed Irons:** If you have the ability to put a hole in your ceiling or in a wooden ceiling beam, ditch the home iron and get one of these! The water reservoir hangs from the ceiling and a tube pulls water down using gravity to force steam out of the iron. These irons are powerful and highly effective. They often come with filtration beads called rapid steam iron resin to purify the water before it passes through the iron. If you don't get the beads, be sure to use distilled water so that minerals don't build up in the iron and damage/stain garments. I also recommend getting a "shoe" for the iron which will help distribute steam evenly on your fabric. Once you try one of these, you won't want to go back to a home iron!
- **Ironing Board or Table:** You can get a variety of standing boards, table boards, mats, build a table with a topper of batting and muslin, or use a towel on top of a surface in your home. Whatever fits your workspace and desired outcome is fantastic.
- **Steaming:** A steamer is really helpful for delicate and historic/older fabrics as a way to release wrinkles. You can also hang a garment in the bathroom while taking a hot shower to help relax the fibers.
- **Pressing Tools:** Ham, sausage, point turner, clapper, sleeve/leg board, and a needle/velvet board can be incredibly helpful for pressing curves and points as well as challenging fabrics.

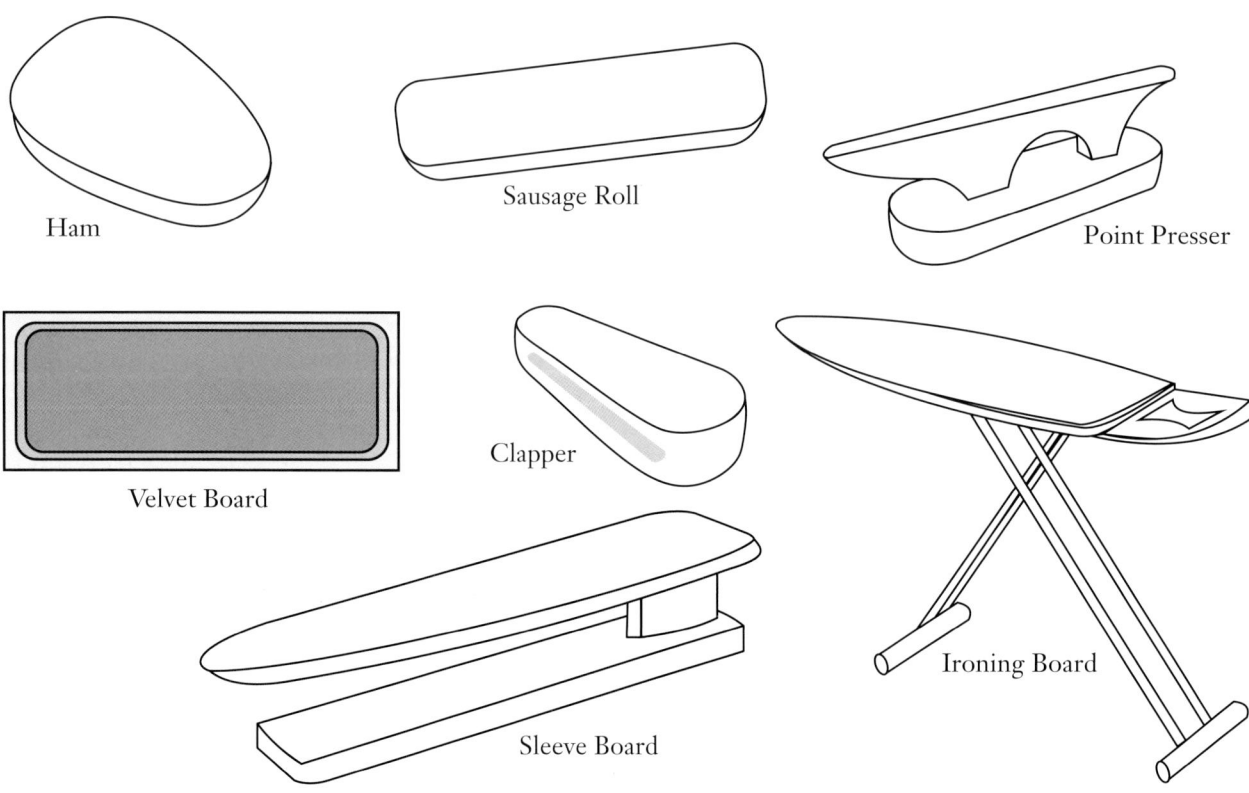

1.10

Hardware and Tools

Hardware and hand tools are most common when performing repairs. Whether you are sewing a missing button back onto a shirt, replacing a zipper head on a jacket, or fixing the buckle slider on a pair of overalls, having the correct size and type of hardware is essential.

- **Zipper Repair Kit:** You can purchase pre-made zipper repair kits or make your own custom kit based on what type of apparel you are working with. Kits should include a variety of zipper slider types (metal, coil, molded plastic, invisible, reverse coil, reversable molded plastic), sizes 3–10, and colors. You can also add top stops and bottom stops in a variety of sizes and colors, zipper lubricant, a toothbrush for cleaning dirty zippers, small pliers for removing stops and teeth, and a lighter to melt the ends of zipper tape so it doesn't fray. Zipper repair is fun, fast, easy, and rewarding when you have all your tools and hardware in one place!
- **Hammers, Sandpaper, Rasps, and Awls:** If you are struggling to stitch over thick layers of fabric, on a belt loop on heavy canvas pants for example, you can use a hammer to reduce the bulk of the fabric by hammering directly onto it. You can also add distressing to jean hems with hammers, sandpaper, and rasps. Hammers and awls are helpful when resetting jean tack buttons, or adding/marking the placement of grommets or eyelets.
- **Grommets, Buckles, Eyelets, etc.:** Whether you are adding grommets to a back panel on a formal gown, repairing a lace-up corset, or replacing broken hardware you will need to determine the correct size before ordering your supplies. Some hardware is measured by inside circumference, like grommets and eyelets, or strap size for things like buckles. When in doubt, order a couple of sizes so you don't lose time if you order the wrong size, color, or material type.

- **Buttons:** There are many types of fantastic buttons in all shapes and sizes. The main types that you will encounter are two-hole, four-hole, shank, and suspender buttons. Button sizing is determined based on the diameter of the button and is represented by a number following the letter L which stands for ligne. One ligne (pronounced like the word lean) is equivalent to 0.025 inches or 0.635 mm. For example, a button with a 1" or 2.5 cm diameter equals 40 lignes and is labeled as 40L. So, if you are trying to determine what size of button you need and a measurement isn't included, you can do the math! You must also consider the height of the button as it will determine whether or not a button will be able to fit through a button hole.

- **Fasteners:** Skirt/pant bar and hooks, hook and eyes, hook and bars, sew on snaps, Anorak snaps, jersey snaps, camping snaps, magnetic snaps, and metal prong snaps can all be useful to have on hand in your sewing kit. Some of these fasteners are hand sewn on while others require a snap tool or press to be set. If you work with outdoor gear or formal gowns, some of these fasteners will be absolutely necessary as they can fall off apparel and gear easily.
- **Point Turners:** A point turner is a tool that can be used to push out fabric to create a sharp point in items like collars, cuffs, and sharp/square necklines. Point turners can also be used to help turn fabric tubes right side out for things like straps. The easiest point turner to access is a chopstick, but you can also purchase turners like the white tool in the image below.

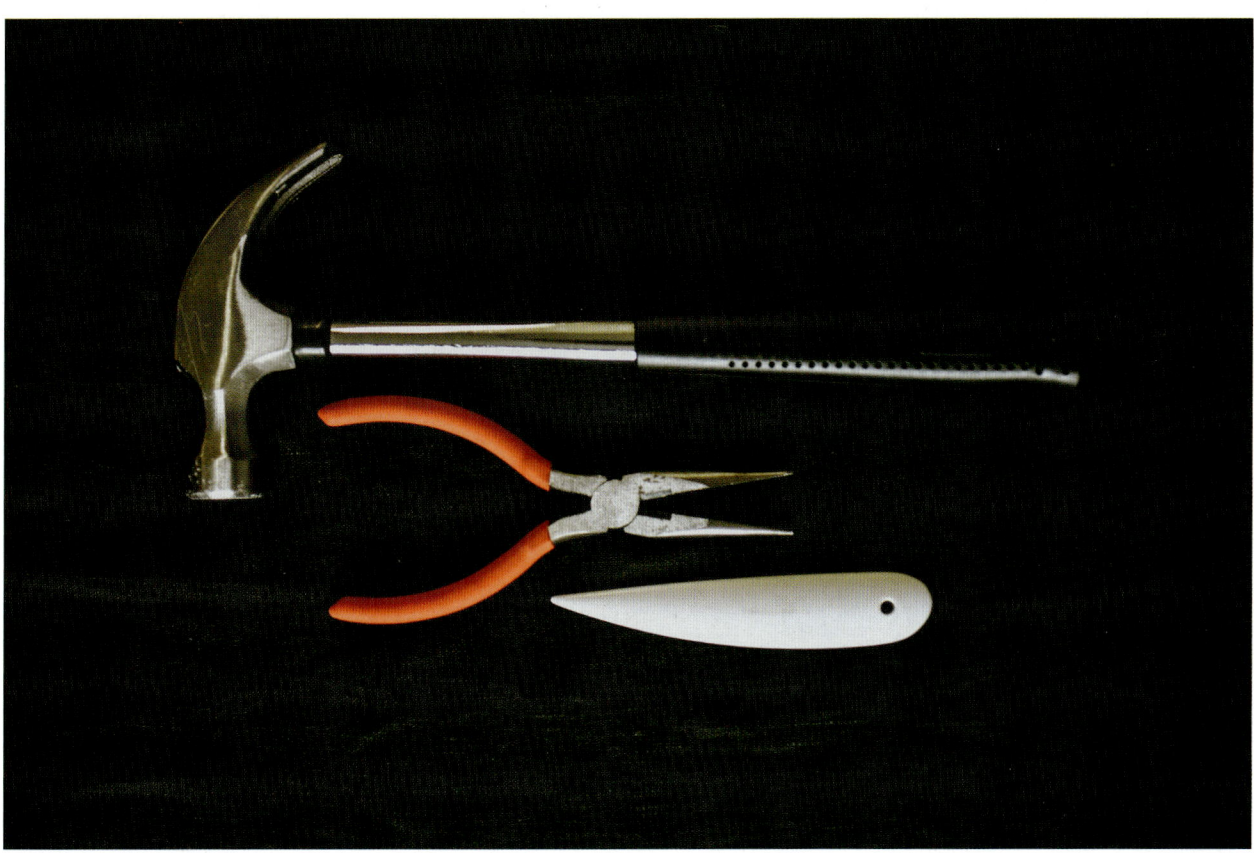

CHAPTER 2

Working With Alterations, Repairs, and Clients

This chapter will go over what to do before, during, and after your work on a project including setting up your space, working with clients, and the logistics of clothing alterations and repairs.

BEFORE YOU GET STARTED

This book is your all-in-one guide to successfully repair and alter your textile goods professionally, practically, and beautifully. Some alterations can be done by a novice; others will require a great deal of patience, time, and practice. The following chapters offer step-by-step written and illustrated instructions, and you may also choose to utilize the online resources for detailed, no-nonsense video tutorials. This section will include how to pin and mark fabric, tips on sewing even hems, pre-washing garments, wearing appropriate shoes and undergarments, taking notes, and pinning/marking options.

STEP ONE: ORGANIZING YOUR SPACE

Before you begin sewing, prepare your "mise en place"—gather and organize your materials in a way that will allow you to be efficient and successful in your alterations and repairs. You don't need a gorgeous studio or a ton of space. Work with what you have, get creative, don't feel like you need to get too fancy, and you will quickly figure out what configuration works best for your circumstances. Here are some suggestions for getting your sewing space organized and efficient:

The Bare Necessities Sewing Space

- A comfortable **chair**. I prefer armless, rolling office, or sturdy wooden chairs for sewing at a machine. Rolling chairs are my favorite, but they do gather thread! Hand sewing is more flexible, and can be done on a cozy couch or bed.
- A **sewing caddy, pegboard, or toolbox**. Keep your scissors, snips, thread, beeswax or thread conditioner, needles, marking tools, and rulers together in one place.
- An **iron and ironing board**. If you can't fit a full-sized ironing board in your space, you can purchase small table-top boards. At a pinch you can simply iron over a terry towelling cloth on a surface of your choice, being very careful not to hold the iron on the fabric/towel for too long. Make sure your iron has steam capabilities and adjustable heat settings.

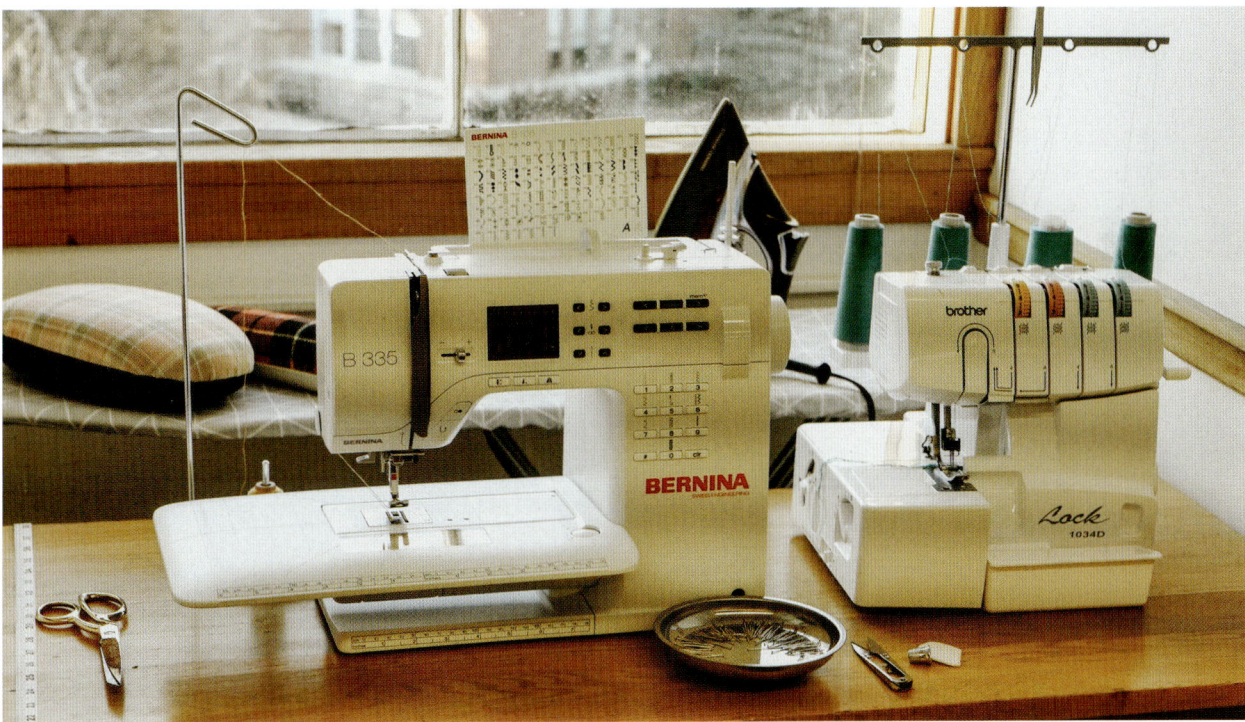

The Deluxe Sewing Space

- A **sewing machine**. If possible, get something that can do a straight stitch, backstitch, and zigzag. It's an added bonus if your machine has a darning stitch!
- A **serger/overlock machine**. This is how most raw edges of fabric are finished, especially on knitwear. Having a serger isn't mandatory, but you will benefit immensely from having one.
- A **coverstitch machine**. This machine is used to finish the hems of most knitwear. This is really helpful if you are doing a lot of alterations, but won't be necessary for most sewists. You can also use a twin needle/serged edge on a sewing machine if you choose not to purchase one of these machines.
- **Ironing tools**: a sleeve board, ham, sausage roll, and clapper.
- A darning egg or other **darning tool**.
- A **zipper repair kit** with pliers, zipper ease, top/bottom stops, and various sliders.

STEP TWO: THE LOGISTICS OF CLOTHING ALTERATIONS AND REPAIRS

***Please read this section prior to making any alterations!

- Confirm that the client has washed, dried, and prepressed any garments that need to be hemmed. Depending on the fabric, textiles can shrink enough to eliminate the need for hemming, so make sure that the garment has been laundered prior to the fitting. The length of a garment can be different if a garment is very wrinkled or is pinned for hemming prior to pressing.
- Be sure the client is wearing any undergarments, belts, and shoes that they will wear with the apparel as they can change the length of the hem, tightness of a bodice, etc.
- While you are pinning a garment, have something for the client to look at on the wall, like a painting or piece of art. Be sure to tell them to look straight ahead with their arms down by their side in a neutral position. If the client is looking down, folding their arms, or twisting it will change the way the hem falls on the body or floor.
- Human bodies are not typically even or perfectly aligned. Most of us have one arm or leg that is longer, or rests lower than the other. Some people have medical conditions such as scoliosis that might make one side of the body longer or they may have an injury that has relocated the position of their joints. Moral of the story: do not assume that just because you are hemming one leg of a pant 1" (2.5 cm) that the other side will be equal.
- Garments are not manufactured perfectly. Despite the best efforts of manufacturers, there are deviations in the construction and cutting processes that may make garment measurements different. If you are curious, go to your closet and grab a pair of pants. Without stretching the fabric, measure one outseam from the top of the waistband to the hem and then measure another with a tape measure. Are they the same, slightly different, or very different? In many cases, the measurements are slightly different so be sure to measure twice, cut once!

- When pinning/marking hems, there are a few ways you can accurately mark the desired alteration:
  a. Mark from the floor up using a hard stick or hem puffer
  b. Mark from the floor up an equal height, pin, and then measure down from that reference point OR the calf/elbow down to the hem
  c. Mark to/at the floor
  d. Mark from a reference point/index. For example, the top of the sole of a shoe

STEP TWO: THE LOGISTICS OF CLOTHING ALTERATIONS AND REPAIRS

FINDING THE PROBLEM

- Some alterations and repairs can be perplexing, and there can be several solutions to the issue. Here are some general rules you can use to find the answers to your questions:

1. **Drag lines point to the problem**. When you see drag lines/cat whiskers/or areas where fabric is pulling, the lines usually point to the problem. In the image below, the drag line indicates that the shirt needs to be larger at the center front or side seam.

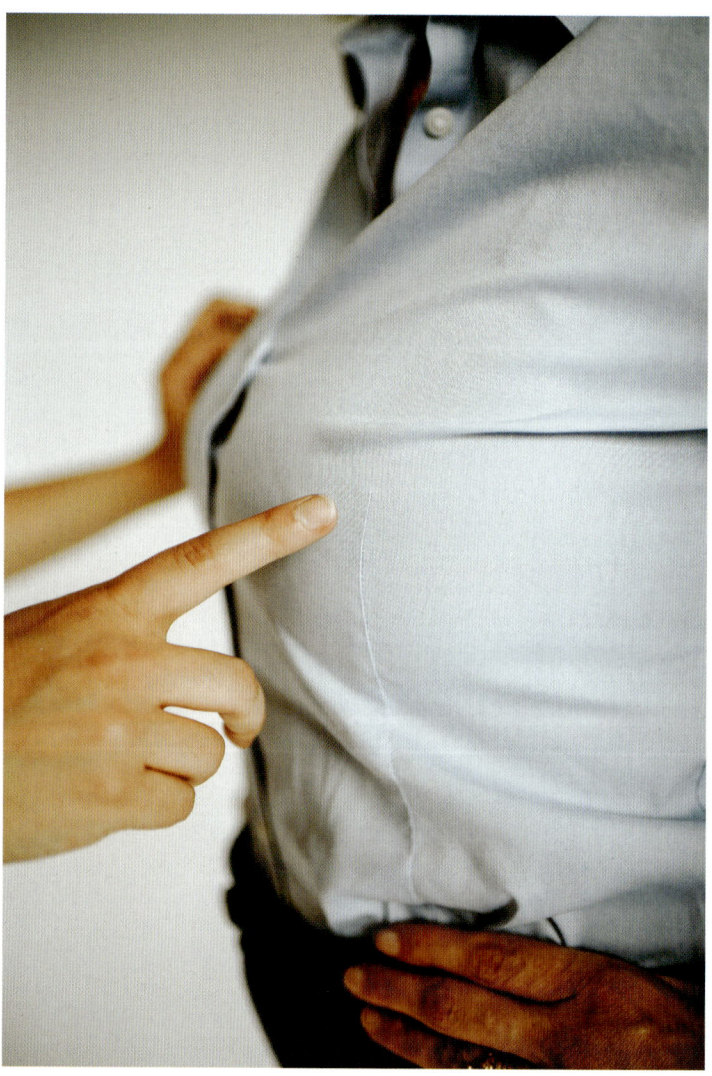

2. **Start from the top and work your way down**. If the shoulders of a dress need to be taken up and you also need to hem the garment, you must start at the top and work your way down. Raising the shoulders will also raise the hem.

3. If the garment is too small, start by **"maxing out"** or letting the seam out as much as possible. If the garment is still too small, you can add fabric to enlarge and strengthen the garment in the form of panels or shaped fabric pieces called gussets.

4. **Play**. If you are really struggling, play around by pinning the problem in a few ways, the best course of action is typically clear! For example, you could start by pinning side seams, then try creating darts, and then experiment with doing both.

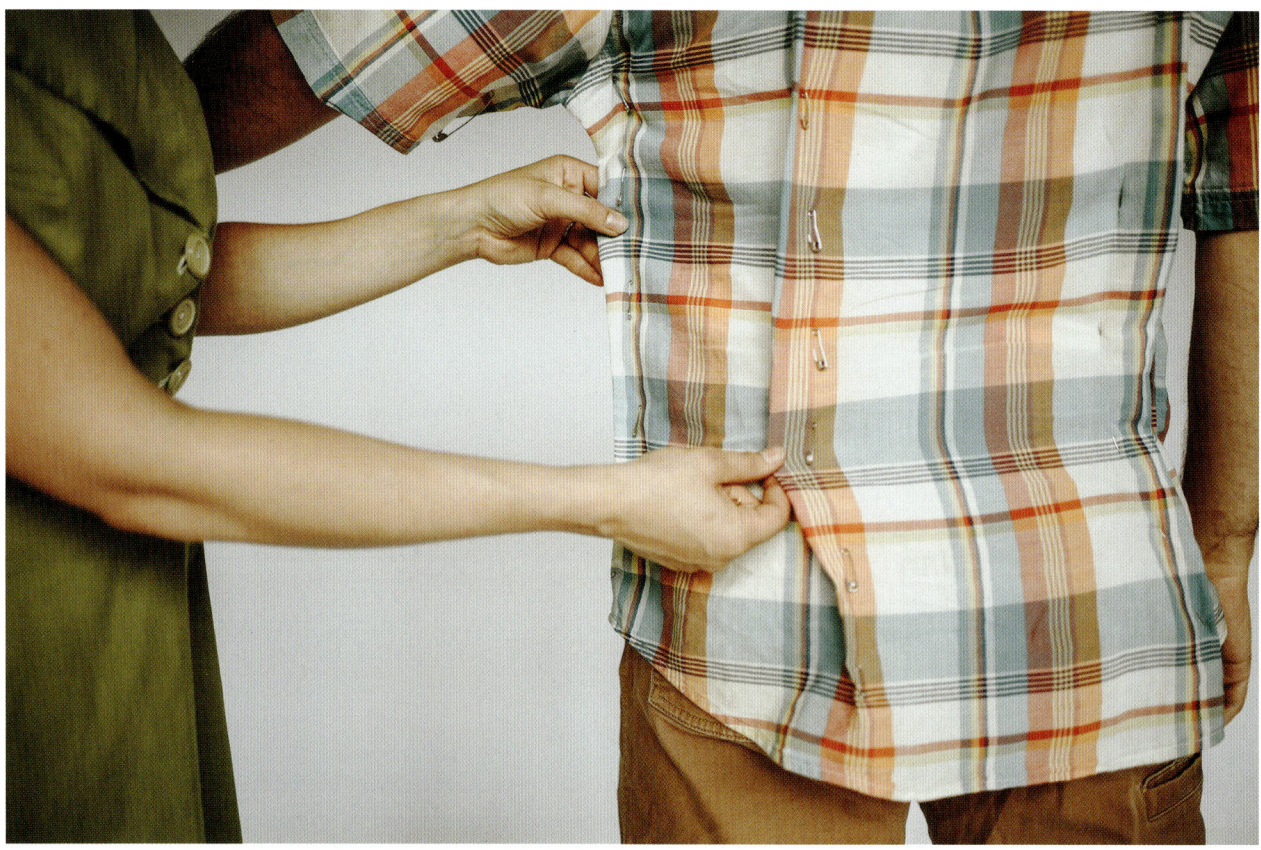

5. **Seam allowance**
    - Seam allowance is the space between the raw/finished edge of fabric and the stitch line. If we don't have seam allowance and stitches at the very edge of the fabric, our garments would come apart at the seams!
    - Generous seam allowance is given in formalwear, while there is little to none whatsoever in active wear. If a client mentions that their weight fluctuates regularly, suggest that they purchase knits that can expand and contract with their body, or select garments that can easily be altered with at least ½" (1.2 cm) of seam allowance.
    - Examine and really get to know the ins and outs of a garment so that you can gauge whether you have extra fabric to work with.

STEP THREE: WORKING WITH CLIENTS

The way clothing fits our bodies can sometimes be a sensitive subject. It is incredibly important to be mindful and respectful of each individual and their body. Refrain from commenting on appearance and weight both in and out of the fitting room. The following points cover what to do if you are doing work for payment.

- Give an estimate before a client leaves and know that it is common for them to only hear the smaller number. I suggest only saying the higher end of an estimate knowing that they will be pleasantly surprised if the cost is less than they had anticipated. For example, instead of saying: "Your alterations will cost between $30 and $50" say "Your alteration will cost about $50."
- Collect the client's first and last name, phone number, email address, and desired date of pick up.
- Communicate with clients if you run into issues and remember that honesty is the best policy. We are all human and understand that life happens and communicating clearly to your customer will almost always be a positive experience. If you don't communicate, the client may not be so forgiving.
- Accidents and bad reviews happen. Some people are impossible to please and it isn't your job to do that type of repair on a human! If you make a big mistake, imagine what you would want if the tables were turned and try to make things right with your customer in a way that would feel fair to you.

IDENTIFYING FABRIC

In textiles courses, the most important lesson we learn is to identify fabric by two properties: **Structure and Fiber Content**. Many people will ask me what type of fabric I think their garment is made of and suggest that they think it is something like "satin." Satin is not a fiber, but rather a type of woven structure and can be made with a variety of fibers like silk, polyester, or cotton. This common misunderstanding can also apply to fiber content when someone says that a fabric structure is "linen." Linen is a fiber that comes from the flax plant and is not a textile structure. You can have knit linen, plain weave linen, non-woven linen paper, or even use the word to categorize sheets and tablecloths! You must know the *structure and content* of the fabrics you are working with so you can launder, alter, pin, mark, and cut them appropriately.

Fiber Content

Fiber properties and fiber blends are limitless! This makes the world of textiles exciting and challenging. While fiber content is more important for selecting the end use of a garment and laundering/care, it is still helpful to know what you are working with so that you do not damage the garment. If the garment does not have a label to identify the fiber, test marking tools, pressing, applying heat, and pins in an inconspicuous area to make sure you aren't damaging the fabric.

Natural
Fibers that come from plants and animals such as linen (flax), cotton, silk (silkworms), wool (sheep, goats, and rabbits), and hemp.

Semi-Synthetic
Natural fibers that require synthetic, organic, or chemical processes in order to be spun into yarn. These include acetate and all the rayons (wood pulp) including: bamboo, Lyocell/Tencel® (eucalyptus), HWM Rayon/Lenzing Modal®, Bemberg®, and Lenzing Viscose®.

Synthetic
Manufactured fibers that are created using chemical processes including: polyester, acrylic, nylon, PLA, Elasterell-p/Lycra®, and Spandex.

Structure: Wovens, Knits, and Nonwovens

Like fiber content, the fabric structure of garments is also limitless! The most important part of identifying the structure of the fabric you are working with will be needle selection. Reference pages 14–15 for details on proper needle selection.

- Woven fabrics are created on a loom with perpendicular lines called a warp (straight of grain = selvedge) and a weft (cross grain). Here is a silly way you can remember the difference between the two: the warp goes orp/up and down and a weft goes weft/left to right. The true bias of a woven fabric is at a 45 degree angle from the warp and weft and has natural stretch. A 30 degree or 60 degree bias may also be used in some garments. If you have ever had a shirt or pair of pants that wraps around your body in an unusual way, it most likely was not cut on the straight of grain, cross grain, or proper bias.

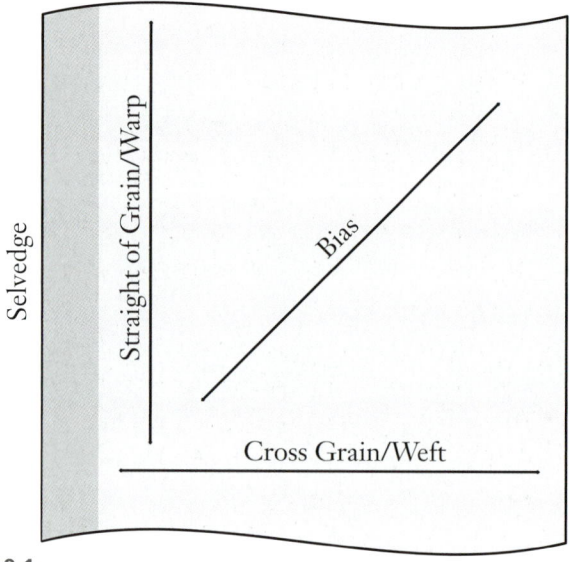

2.1

- Knits are structures that use a continuous yarn and are created by forming a series of loops with knitting needles by hand or machine. They have knit stitches that look like Vs or hearts and purl stitches that look like Cs or waves. Most knits are naturally stretchy, but some knits that are created by machine are not!

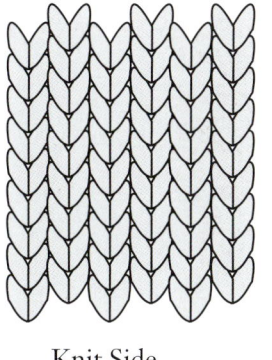
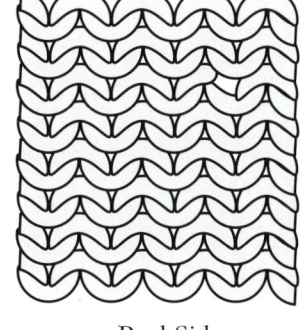

Knit Side   Purl Side

2.2

- Nonwovens are fabrics are created by bonding or interlocking fibers to create a web of fibers. They can be felted, spun laced, melt blown, needle punched, laminated, tufted, embroidered, etc. If you have ever seen a white, cream, grey, or black bit of fabric that shreds if you pull on it, it is most likely that interfacing or stabilizer was used to stiffen or strengthen the fabric.
- Other textiles include items such as fur and leather and behave differently than knits and wovens. Special care needs to be taken when working with either as both can be permanently damaged and messy!

CHAPTER 3

Bottom Hems

Garments worn on the bottom half of the body: pants, shorts, skirts, dresses, etc.

SHORTENING:
- Measuring pants, shorts, skirts, and dresses for hemming
- Serge and blind hem
- Twice turn hem
- Cadet cut hem
- Knitwear coverstitch hem
- Knitwear faux coverstitch using a twin needle
- Twice-turned hem on eveningwear and formalwear
- Napkin roll hem
- Hand stitch hems
  - Cross stitch
  - Vertical hem stitch
  - Prick/pick stitch

LENGTHENING:
- Lengthening bottom hems
- Maxing out
- Bias tape
- Adding fabric
- Adding lace

SHORTENING
MEASURING PANTS, SHORTS, SKIRTS, AND DRESSES FOR HEMMING

Prior to hemming a garment, it is important to note the hem depth, seam allowance/turn of the cloth, hemming method, thread type/color size, and general aesthetic of the hem so it can be replicated. These initial instructions will help you set a strong foundation for all the hemming methods in this book.

1. Ensure that the garment has been pre-washed, dried, and pressed if necessary.
2. Check that the client is wearing the undergarments, belt, suspenders, and/or shoes that they will wear with the bottoms. This is especially important in formalwear so that the garments lie as they will when the client wears the garment.

    a. For Pants: Use a reference point by either using (3.1a) the floor, (3.1b) the base of the sole of the shoe, or by (3.1c) measuring with an L or T square and marking a reference point at the calf and then measuring the new hem length down from the reference point. You can turn the hem under to see a basic idea of what the pants will look like at a certain length, but this may cause undesirable bunching.

    b. For Shorts/Mid-Length Pants: Use a reference point from the (3.1d) waistband down, from the floor up, or (3.1e) using a hem puffer.

    c. For Skirts and Dresses: Pin to the floor (3.1f) as it falls from the waist without twisting the fabric (you can measure up or down from there) or use a hem puffer.

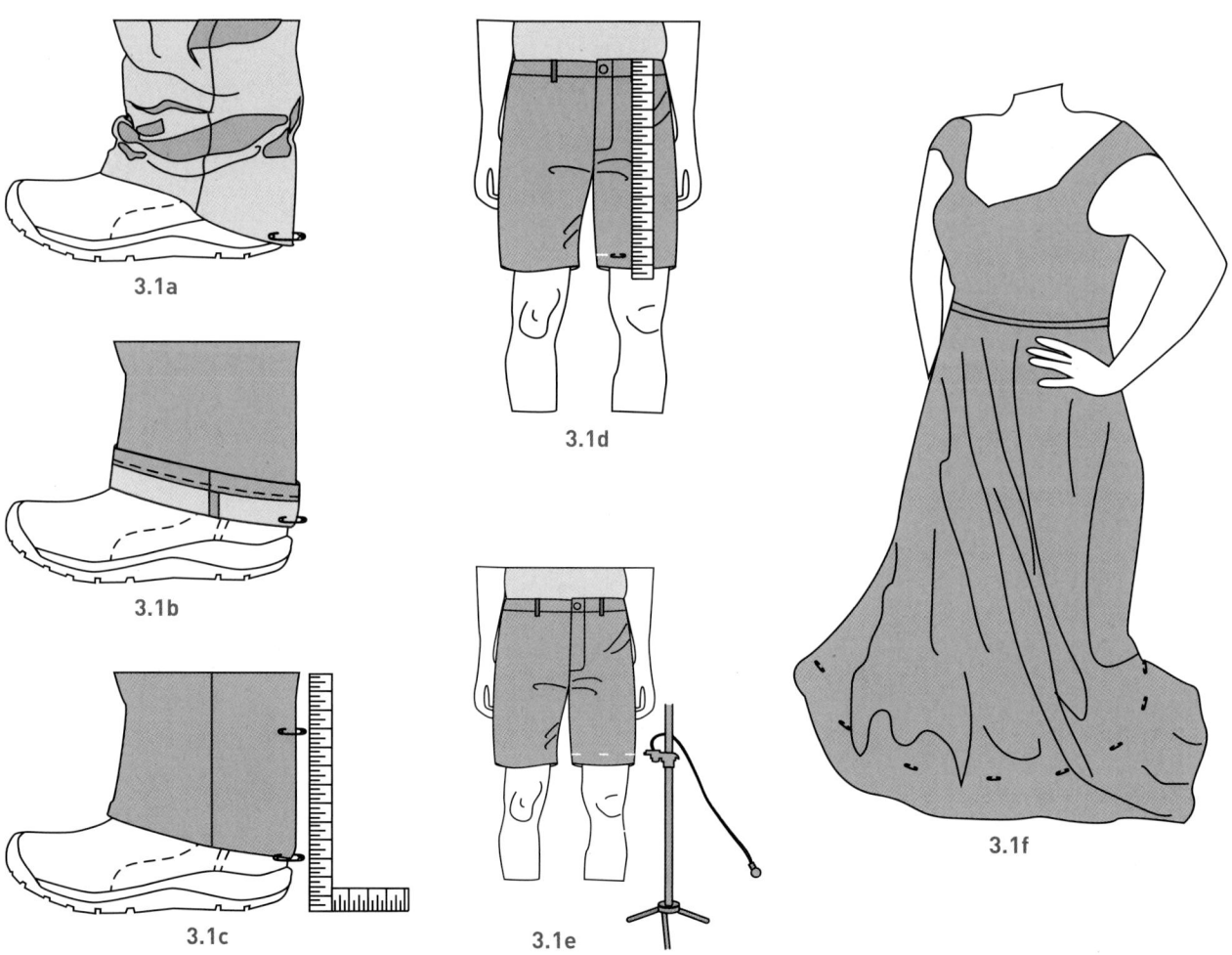

3.1a

3.1b

3.1c

3.1d

3.1e

3.1f

CHAPTER 3 BOTTOM HEMS

3. Decide on the depth of hem you would like to have and determine how much seam allowance you need or how much was used (3.2a.) See example 3.2b for a twice turned hem, example 3.2c for a narrow roll/narrow twice turned hem, and example 3.2d for an example of a serge and stitch hem.

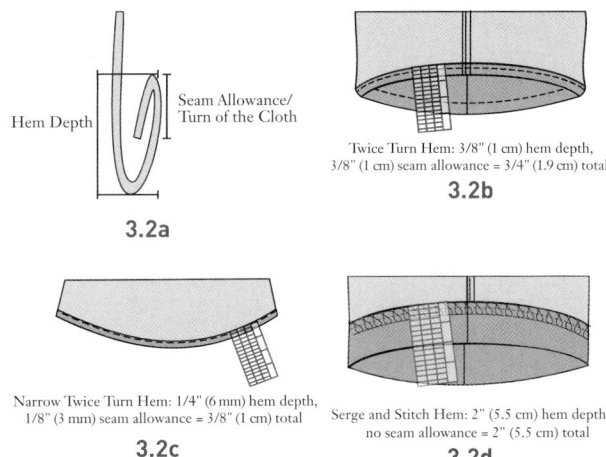

4. Mark the turn of the hem based on the safety pin mark. Measure your desired hem depth down and mark that line. Next, measure and mark the seam allowance below the first line you drew (3.2e) which will become the cut line. Note that if the new cut line is below the original hem/stitching that you will need to unpick the hem with a seam ripper before proceeding (3.2f). All the following hemming instructions will only show two chalk markings: one for the new hem line and then another for hem depth plus the seam allowance which will be the new cut line.

5. Continue on to a hem method that is appropriate for the garment.

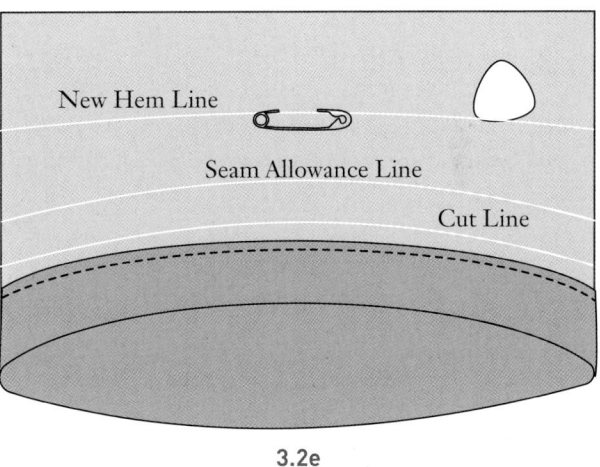

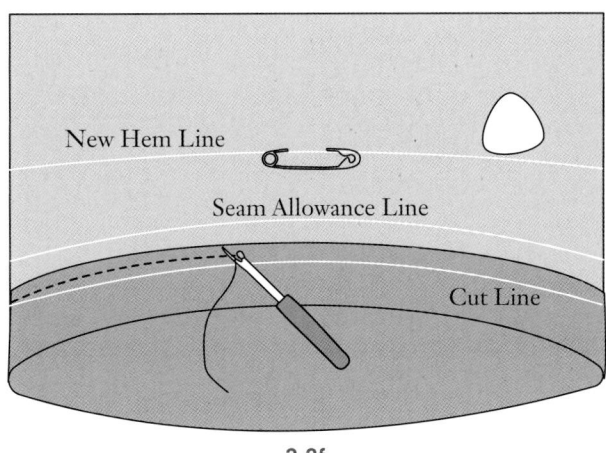

SHORTENING | 45

SERGE AND BLIND HEM: THREE METHODS
Blind Hemming Machine, Home Machine Blind Hem, or Hand Stitch

30 minutes–1 hour ⚠

Use: most common in dress pants, skirts, and dresses.

1. For all three methods the initial steps are the same. First measure and mark the hem (3.3a) (see pages 44–5).

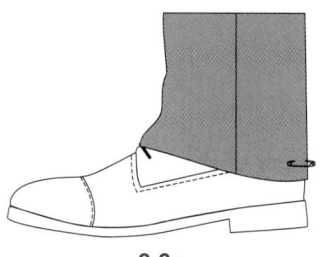

3.3a

2. Decide on the depth of hem you would like to have and determine how much seam allowance you need or how much was used. Replicate the distance that was used originally as a guide if possible (3.3b).

3.3b

3. Mark the new hem line and cut line based on the safety pin mark and the measurements you took for the hem depth and seam allowance. Seam rip the hem if the cut line extends below the original stitching (3.3c).

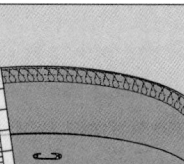

3.3c

4. Cut the excess fabric off on the cut line (3.3d).

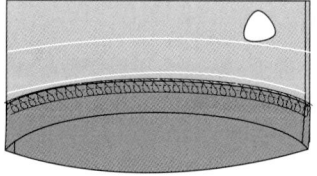

3.3d

5. Serge on the cut line (3.3e).

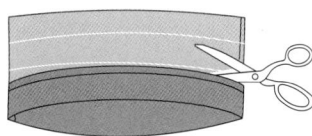

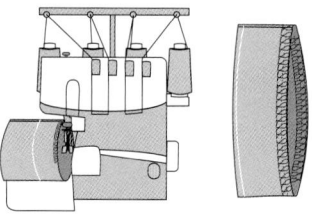

3.3e

6. Press at the turn mark (3.3f). Now go to step A for a blind hem machine, step B for a home machine blind hem, or step C for hand stitch.

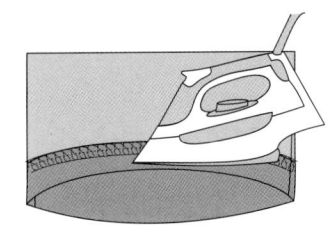

3.3f

A. *Blind Hem Machine:* Test your machine for appropriate tension to stitch directly above the serge line to take a minimally visible "bite" on the public side of the garment. Begin stitching around the inside hem and then end by stitching directly over where you began blind stitching to lock the hem. Check by running your finger between the two layers of fabric to ensure that the blind hem caught the outside fabric (3.4a).

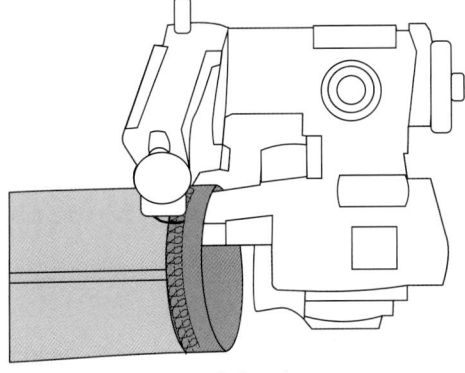

3.4a

B. *Home Machine Blind Hem:* Set your machine stitch length, zigzag width, and attach the blind hem presser foot according to your user manual. Place pins every 2" (5 cm) directly below the bottom of the serge line. Roll the hem in up towards the top of the garment, the pins will flip down and there should be one layer of fabric (the serged edge) and three layers of fabric that will take the "bite" for the blind hem. The blind hem will take several stitches on the right side (serge only) and a zigzag (bite) on the left side. Check by running your finger under the stitch to ensure that the blind hem caught (3.4b).

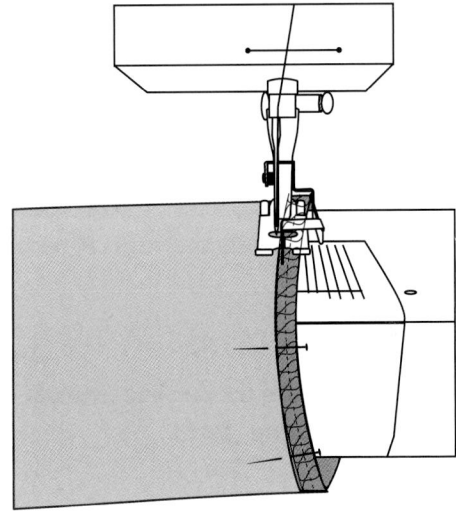

3.4b

C. *Hand Stitch:* Use a vertical hemstitch, a prick/pick stitch, or a cross-stitch to stitch to complete the hem (see pages 63–6 for details on hand stitching) (3.4c).

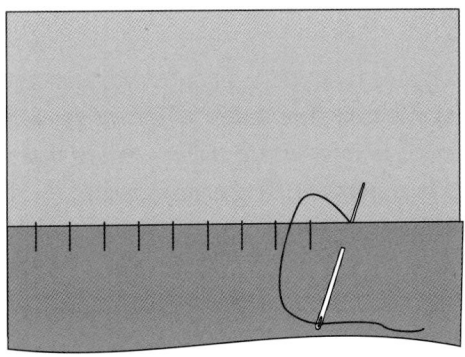

3.4c

TWICE TURN HEM

1 hour

1. Measure and mark the hem (3.5a) (see pages 44–5).

3.5a

2. Decide on the depth of hem you would like to have and determine how much seam allowance you need or how much was used. Replicate the distance that was used originally as a guide if possible (3.5b).

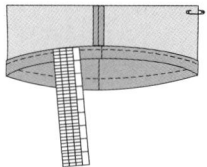

3.5b

3. Mark the new hem line and cut line based on the safety pin mark and the measurements you took for the hem depth and seam allowance (3.5c).

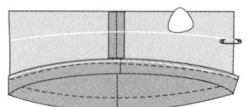

3.5c

4. Seam rip the hem if the cut line extends below the original stitching (3.5d).

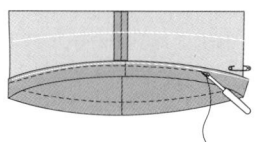

3.5d

5. Cut the excess seam allowance (3.5e).

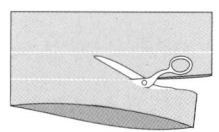

3.5e

6. Press the turn line under and then press the seam allowance under and evenly so that the hem is consistent all the way around (3.5f).

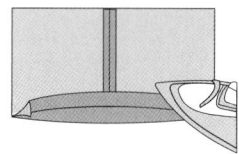

3.5f

7. Stitch the hem and replicate the SPI/SPC (stitches per inch/centimeter), thread color, and thread weight if possible. Begin stitching ½" (1.2 cm) past the inseam on the back leg so that your backstitch is inconspicuous. You may backstitch first for 2–3 stitches or simply stitch over the original stitches and backstitch at the end to secure the hem (3.5g).

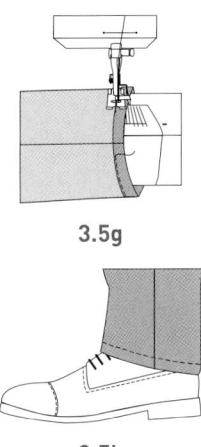

3.5g

3.5h

8. Clip your threads. Press the hem. Check the fit (3.5h).

CADET CUT HEM

1 hour

Cadet cut hems are the type of hem that many formal military uniforms use and are characterized by being shorter in the front and longer in the back. This hem type is great if you want to eliminate a break in the fabric on the top of the shoe and have the back hem long enough to cover the wearers socks.

1. Measure and mark the hem on the client. The front of the pant leg should rest just on top of the shoe without a break. The back should generally be ⅞" (2.2 cm) longer than the front. Check the official standards for specific guidelines if doing this for someone in the military. Pin in the front at the shoe line. You only need to pin the back if the client is looking for something specific, otherwise you will simply measure ⅞" (2.2 cm) down from the front hem (3.6a).
2. Unpick the hem (3.6b).
3. Fold the pants inside out and in half so that the inseam and outseam are touching. Press so that you have a crease on the center front and center back if it isn't already pressed. Mark on the inside the center front and then with the ruler lined up with the inseam or outseam line as a guide, mark ⅞" (2.2 cm) down from the front OR as pinned. This step is helpful for getting your lines laid out (3.6c).
4. Mark a diagonal line with chalk on the line you just pressed for the new hem line. Next, mark 1"–2" (2.5–5 cm) below the fold line and mark. This is your cut line (3.6d).

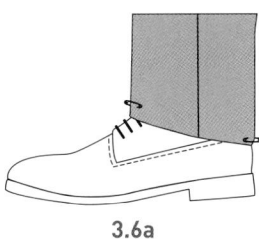

3.6a

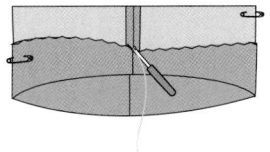

3.6b

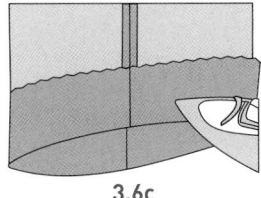

3.6c

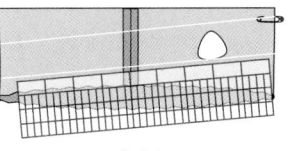

3.6d

5. Check that you are cutting on the second line (not the top one) and cut the pants on the fold with both layers together at once or mark both sides and cut separately. If you use pinking shears on this step you can skip the next step (3.6e).

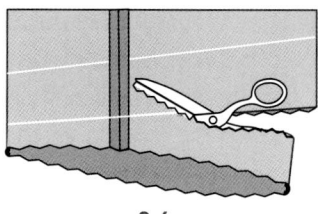

3.6e

6. Restitch the bottom of the inseam and outseam.

7. Serge the raw edges of the fabric if you have not already pinked them.

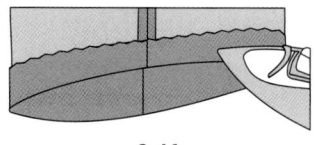

3.6f

8. Re-press the hem up (3.6f).

9. Using pinking shears, cut the center front to ½"– ¾" (1.2–1.9 cm) above the turn of the hem. This allows the fabric to lay flat so that it doesn't pucker when you stitch around it (3.6g).

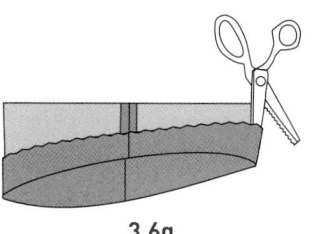

3.6g

***If you do not have pinking shears you can carefully cut the fabric and then use a fabric glue like Fray Check to keep the raw edges from unraveling. You must let the glue dry completely before moving to the next step.

10. Using a blind hem machine, blind hem stitch on a home machine, or a hand stitch of your choice (see pages 63–6 for blind hem tips), stitch the hem being sure that you cannot see the "bite" of thread on the public side of the garment (3.6h).

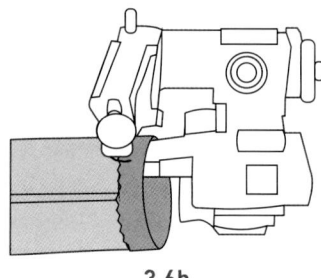

3.6h

11. Press the pants right side out, clip loose threads, and check the fit (3.6i).

3.6i

***If the turned edge is too small and tucks when you try to hem it there are a few steps you can take to make it fit.

- Max out the side seam and inseam to widen the circumference of the bottom hem.
- Clip the center back as you did for the center front with pinking shears.
- Trim the seam allowance down if you used more than 1" (2.5 cm).

KNITWEAR COVERSTITCH HEM

30 minutes–1 hour

1. Measure and mark the hem on the client (see pages 44–5) (3.7a).

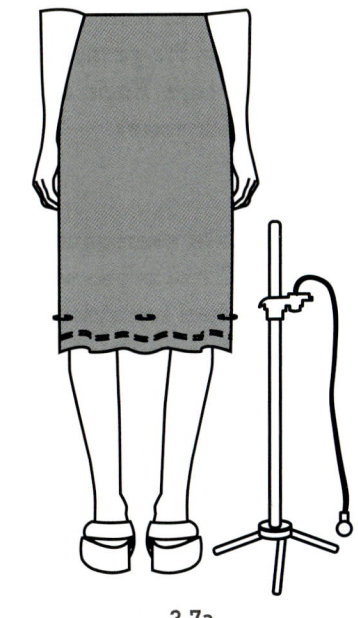

3.7a

2. Mark, press, and pin the new hemline and seam rip the original hem ONLY if it extends beyond the original seam allowance (3.7b). As you are pressing the hem up, let the fabric go where it wants to go and try not to worry about it going exactly where you pinned it in the fitting.

3. Use all-purpose thread in the needles and woolly nylon/bulky nylon in the lower looper of your coverstitch machine, if possible, although all-purpose thread will also work. You can use regular thread for the entire machine if your garment is woven. Test the machine tension, stitch length, and whether the distance between the needles is wide or narrow enough to match the original garment.

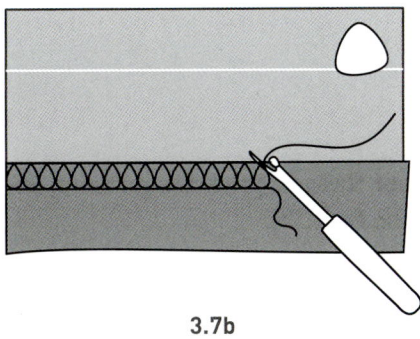

3.7b

4. You have two options for how to proceed with stitching the hem (3.7c). Each comes with a bit of work. If you are a beginner, I would recommend option a.

   a. Stitch around the entire hem and carefully cut the excess seam allowance after stitching. Begin your stitching 1" (2.5 cm) away from the side seams as starting directly on seam allowance can be challenging (3.7d).

   OR

   b. Cut the seam allowance to the desired length, check that the position of the seam is correct and aligned with the needles and then stitch around the garment being sure to catch the raw edge. Begin 1" (2.5 cm) away from the side seams.

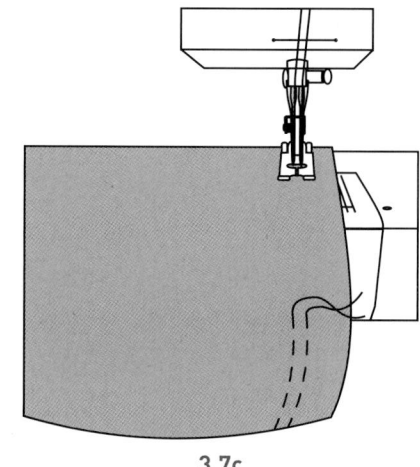

3.7c

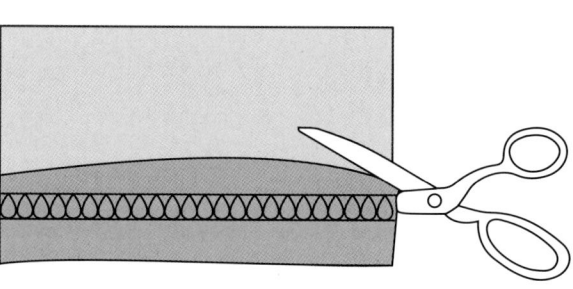

3.7d

5. Complete the stitch by overlapping by about 8 stitches or ½" (1.2 cm) as you will have to crank the handwheel back/clockwise 3–4 stitches to release the tension on most home coverstitch machines.

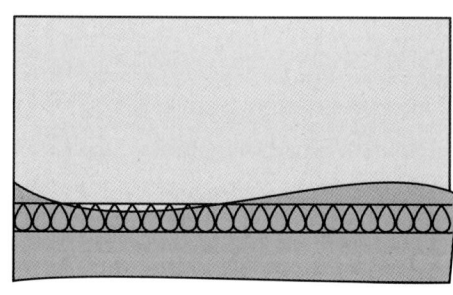

3.7e

6. Check that you caught all raw edges of the garment. If you didn't, know that this alteration commonly requires a couple of practice rounds and that you may need to unpick the stitch and try again. (3.7e).

7. Clip your threads, press the garment, and check the fit (3.7f).

3.7f

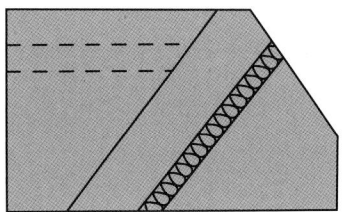

***Notes on the coverstitch machine: practice on your coverstitch for an hour or more before sewing something permanent. Practice sewing on knits with woolly/bulky nylon in the lower looper only and wovens with regular thread. I've noticed that sometimes the coverstitch doesn't like to go over side seams/bulk. If you take a deep breath, believe, and give yourself a running start so that you don't stop on the seam—it works! Be sure to stitch directly over your original starting stitches to lock the stitches in place. Thankfully and unfortunately, the coverstitch has a magic thread that will chain off the entire hem if you pull it. This is wonderful when you want to re-do a hem and really frustrating when you accidentally pull on it. You can find the magic spot on the thread chain by pulling about ½" (1.2 cm) of the double needle threads out on the face of the garment and then tugging on the lower looper thread going in the reverse direction of your stitching.

3.7g Example of the face and back of a coverstitch

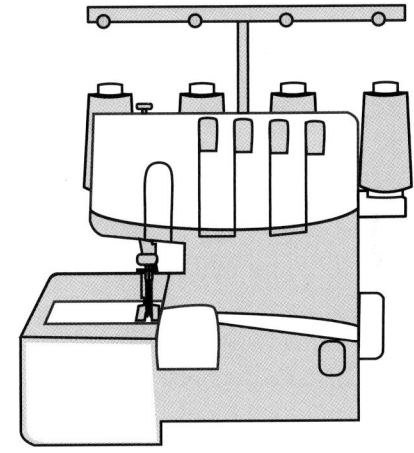

3.7h Example of a coverstitch machine

***Notes on woolly nylon/bulky nylon/fluff thread: this magical thread is used in swimwear, activewear, and knits. When you tug on it, it stretches and becomes tight, and when you release it, it relaxes. It is difficult to thread, so you will need a needle threader to get it through the eye of a looper, but its stretching properties make it a dream for your knits (see page 17 for more information on this thread).

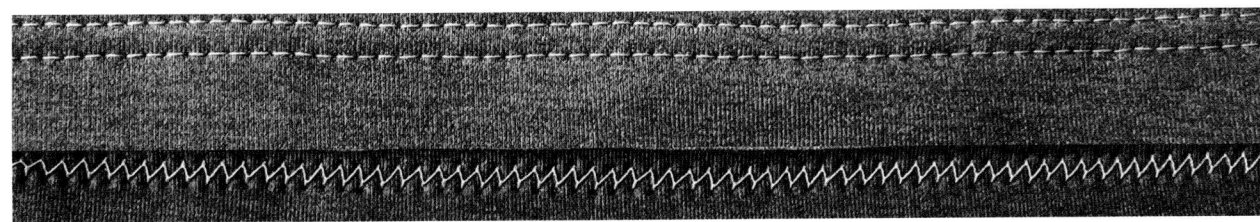

KNITWEAR FAUX COVERSTITCH USING A TWIN NEEDLE

30 minutes–1 hour

If you do not have access to a coverstitch machine, you can easily recreate a coverstitch using a twin needle in your home sewing machine. For more information on twin needles, see page 56.

1. Measure and mark the hem on the client (see pages 44–5) (3.8a).

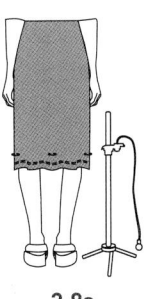

3.8a

2. Mark, press, and pin the hem and seam rip the original hem if it extends beyond the original seam allowance (3.8b). Let the fabric go where it wants to go and try not to worry about it going exactly where you pinned.

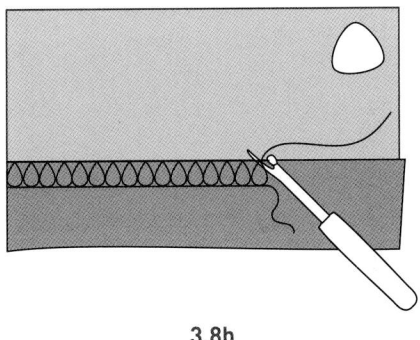

3.8b

3. Use all-purpose thread in the needles (one spool on the horizontal spool holder, the other on the vertical) and woolly nylon/bulky nylon in the bobbin if you are sewing on a knit. Winding a bobbin of woolly nylon often requires a thread stand as the cones the thread comes on do not work with home machines. You can use regular thread if your garment is woven. Test the machine tension, stitch length, and whether the distance between the needles is wide or narrow. Twin needles come in various widths and can be ball point or universal.

4. You have two options for how to proceed to stitching the hem. Each comes with a bit of work. If you are a beginner, I would recommend option a.

   a. Stitch around the entire hem and carefully cut the excess seam allowance after stitching. Begin 1" (2.5 cm) away from the side seams (3.8c).

   OR

   b. Cut the seam allowance to the desired length, check that the position of the seam is correct and aligned with the needles and then stitch around the garment being sure to catch the raw edge. Begin 1" (2.5 cm) away from the side seams (3.8d).

5. Complete the hem with a backstitch.
6. Check that you caught all raw edges of the garment. If you didn't, know that this alteration commonly requires a couple of practice rounds! (3.8e).
7. Clip your threads, press the garment, and check the fit (3.8f).

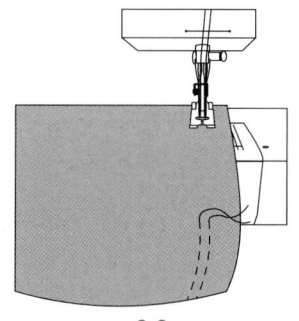

3.8c

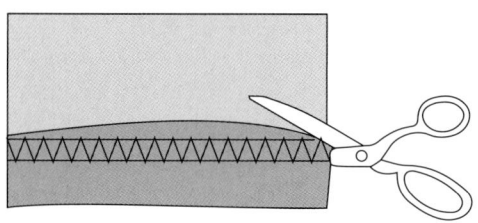

3.8d

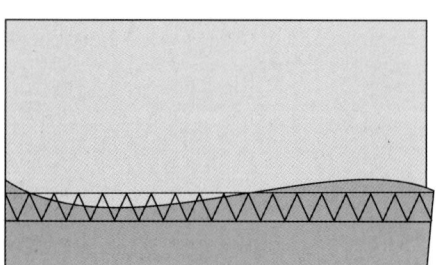

3.8e

***Notes on twin needles (3.9): twin needles come in a variety of widths and can be universal or ball point. Try to get a ball point twin needle for knits, if possible, but if you cannot source them, universals will often work as well. The needle will produce two rows of stitching on the public/top side of the garment and a zigzag on the bottom. DO NOT SET YOUR MACHINE TO A ZIGZAG, keep it on a straight stitch with a longer length to mimic the SPI/ SPC and to allow for stretch. Wind a bobbin of the thread you will be using for the needle threads rather than purchasing two spools.

***Notes on woolly nylon/bulky nylon/fluff thread: see page 17 for more information on this thread.

3.8f

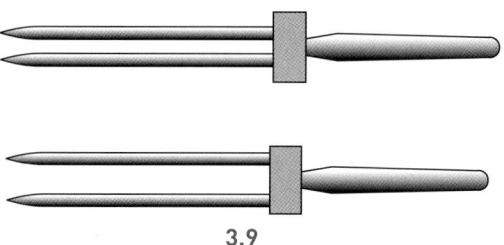

3.9

TWICE-TURNED HEM ON EVENINGWEAR AND FORMALWEAR

1+ hours

1. Measure and mark the hem on the client (see pages 44–5). If working with multiple layers, begin by pinning up the outer layers out of the way at the center back. Pin all layers to the floor or at the desired length of the outer most layer and then you can determine how much shorter to make the linings. Typically, linings are 1–2" (2.5–5 cm) shorter than the outer layer. This is based on preference and functionality. Most of the time clients do not want to see the lining extend past the outer layer and it is also best that the lining is shorter so that the wearer does not trip on it (3.10a).

3.10a

2. If the hem needs to be shortened ¾" (1.9 cm) or more, proceed to step 4.

3. If the hem needs to be shortened less than ¾" (19 mm) you will need to seam rip the hem at all areas that are ¾" (1.9 cm) or shorter (3.10b).

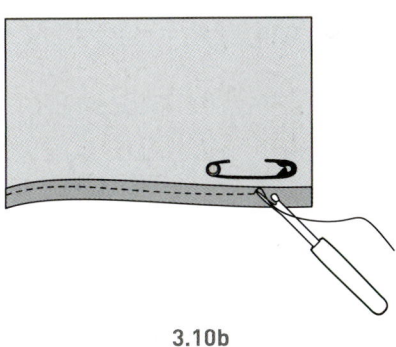

3.10b

4. There are two methods that can be used for the next step.

   a. The first method is to mark the hem using a non-permanent marking tool and a hip curve or curve ruler to mark ¼" (6 mm) to ½" (1.2 cm) below the pins all the way around the garment and then remove the safety pins once you have the cut line marked. If you would like to have an ⅛" (3 mm) hem you will mark ¼" (6 mm) down, if you would like a ¼" (6 mm) hem, mark ½" (1.2 cm) down. Next, you will have two options to either cut, press, and stitch OR stitch, cut, and stitch. I am a big fan of stitching and then cutting as it is really challenging to twice turn most eveningwear/formalwear fabric like chiffon and organza, for example.

b. The second method is to let the fabric "mark" itself. This is my favorite method of hemming bridal dresses and other formalwear. I've found that it looks fantastic and takes half the time! Fold the fabric ⅛"–¼" (3–6 mm) below the pins with the right side/technical face up. Use a blind hem/edge presser foot and move the needle position over to the left (or use any presser foot of your choice that allows you to easily stitch 1/16" (1.5 mm)–⅛ (3 mm)" away from the edge, and stitch around the hem to create an easy turn line (3.10c).

Next, carefully cut as close to the stitch line as you can, 1/16"–⅛" (1.5–3 mm) away without cutting the thread, or the other layer of fabric, all the way around the hem (3.10d).

This takes a little bit of time and concentration, but completely eliminates the need to fuss with the challenge of stitching curves with varying circumference. Last, fold the hem again so that the sliver of seam allowance you left from the cut is folded under (3.10e).

Move your needle position to the right if you are using a blind hem/edge foot and stitch directly on top of the previous stitch (3.10f). No pinning is necessary here, just use your fingers to roll the fabric and it should happen like magic!

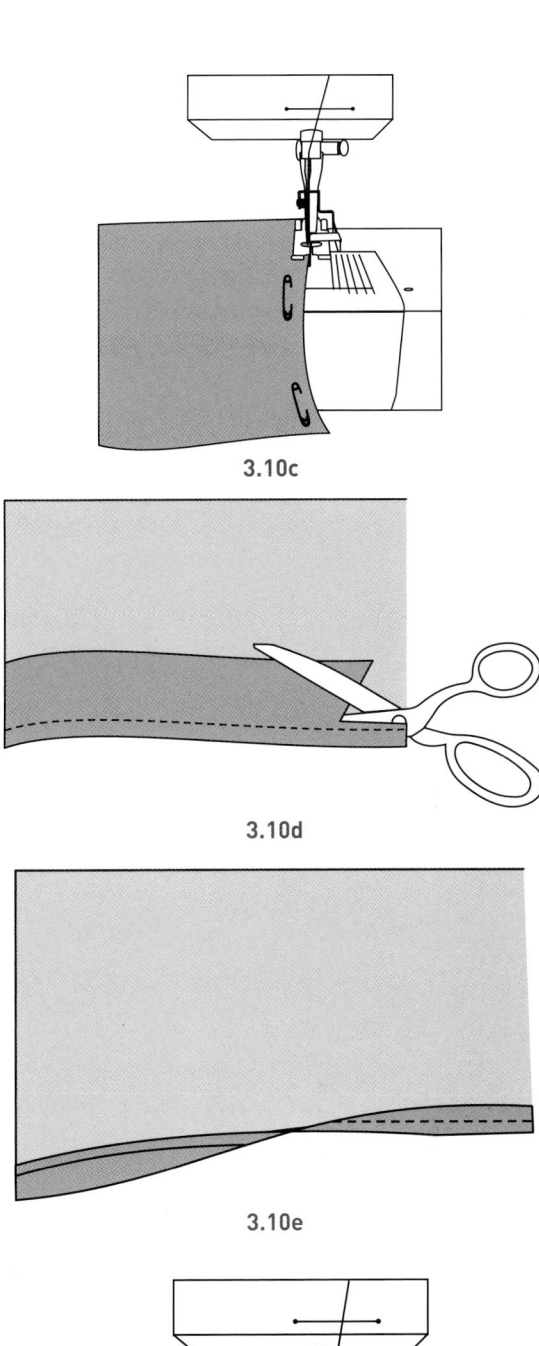

3.10c

3.10d

3.10e

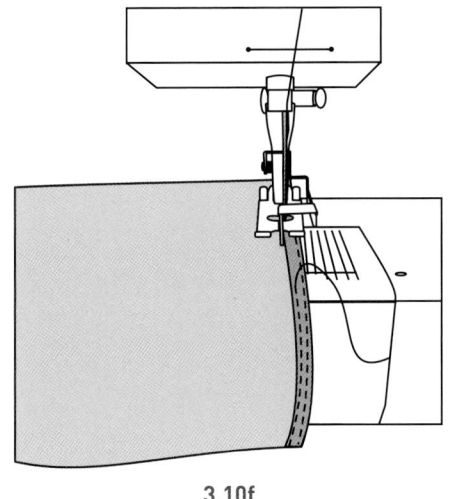

3.10f

TWICE-TURNED HEM ON EVENINGWEAR AND FORMALWEAR

5. Continue this process with the lining layers but make sure to stitch and/or mark them up the desired amount which is usually 1"–2" (2.5–5 cm). If the lining was attached by swing tacks, you will create 2"–3" (5–7.5 cm) long thread chains to attach the lining to the outer fabric at the seam allowances/side seams.
6. Press the hem, clip your threads, and check the fit (3.10g).

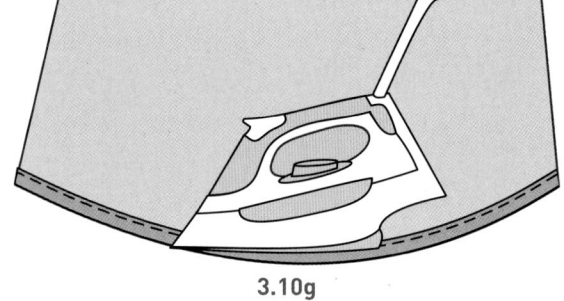

3.10g

NAPKIN ROLL HEM

30 minutes–1 hour

This technique is most commonly used on napkins, but can also be used in knit and eveningwear. Typically, a serger is used to achieve this hem finish, but you can also use the zigzag feature on your sewing machine for similar results!

1. Measure and mark the hem on the client (see pages 44–5) (3.11a).
2. Set up the serger according to your user manual. If you do not have a manual, you should do the following:

   a. Use woolly or bulky nylon in the upper and lower looper. Clip the thread that was previously on your serger by the spool and tie off the woolly nylon to pull the thread through. Have a needle threader in your hand in case you are struggling to get the thread through the eyes of the needles.
   b. Use all-purpose thread in the right needle. Remove the left needle.
   c. Set the cutting width to the lowest setting.
   d. Set the stitch length to 1.
   e. Sew out a thread chain without fabric in the machine to begin. Doing this will reduce the risk of the machine getting stuck on the fabric and creating a giant "thread caterpillar." Test a scrap sample of your fabric if possible.

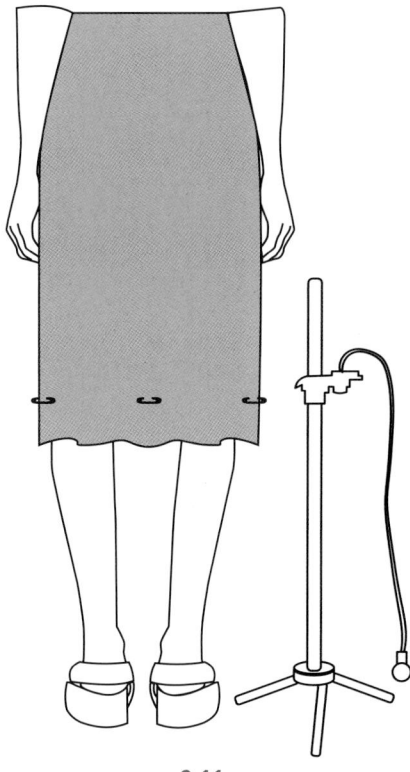

3.11a

NAPKIN ROLL HEM | 61

3. Mark your hem with a marking tool and curve ruler that are appropriate for the textile you are working with ⅛" (3 mm) below your hem line. I like to mark the hem ⅛" (3 mm) lower because the fabric tends to shrink up slightly with the pull of the serger or zigzag (3.11b).

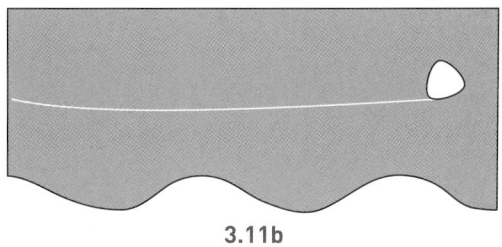

3.11b

4. Clip up the side seam to the new desired hem line so you can place the fabric under the serger easily. There is no need to pre-cut the fabric if you are using a serger with a blade. If you are using a zigzag on a home machine, you will now need to cut the hem.

5. Serge the hem placing the blade on the cut line. This stitch is very small and tends to move slowly, but if you get stuck in one area for more than a couple of seconds, STOP! The thread can get caught in the feed dogs and will create a thread caterpillar that is very hard to seam rip (3.11c).

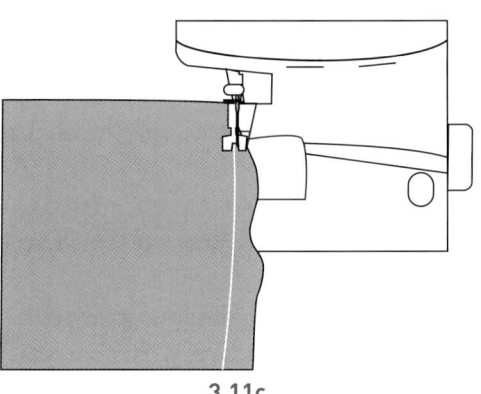

3.11c

6. If using a zigzag stitch, stitch as close to the edge as you can to avoid having too many thread slivers poking out of the hem.

7. To end the hem, stitch over the first stitch for ½" (1.2 cm) and then veer off the hem to create a long thread chain. Thread the chain in a tapestry needle and feed the chain into the back side of the hem for ¼" (6 mm) and cut the remaining tail (3.11d).

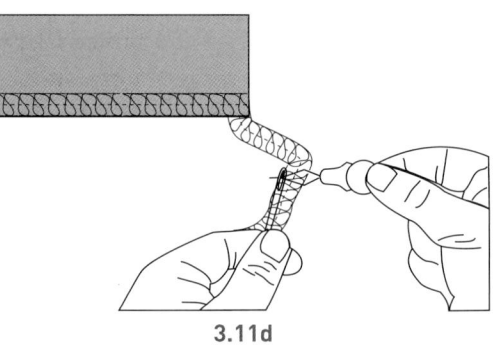

3.11d

8. Press the hem and check the fit (3.11e).

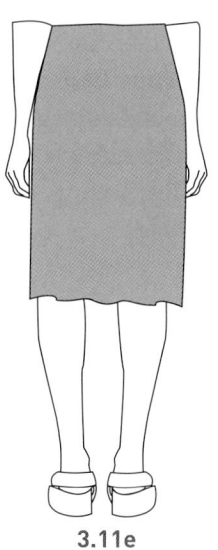

3.11e

62 | CHAPTER 3 BOTTOM HEMS

HAND STITCH HEMS: CROSS STITCH, VERTICAL HEM STITCH, PRICK/PICK STITCH

30 minutes–1 hour △

Each of the following hand stitch options are fantastic, discrete, and have varying applications for hemming and beyond! Follow the chart below to determine what stitch will work best for your project.

Cross/Catch Stitch	Best for full skirts/dresses in medium to heavyweight fabrics
Prick/Pick Stitch	Best for lightweight and delicate fabrics
Vertical Hem Stitch	Best for pants and narrow hems. Especially good if garment is worn with heels.

Cross Stitch

1. Treat (wax, thread conditioner, or saliva) or use a length of hand sewing thread the length of your suprasternal notch/center of your collar bone, to your pointer finger. Use a sharps hand needle size 8, 9, or 10 and double thread for fabrics that are heavier OR a single thread for mediumweight fabrics. Tie a knot at the end of the thread tail(s) and clip down to ⅛" (3 mm).
2. Begin by hiding the tail of the thread ¼" (6 mm) below the top of the turned hem fabric at a seam by taking a bite out of the seam allowance and pulling the thread all the way through.
3. Next, take a bite out of the technical back (wrong side) of the main fabric ¼" (6 mm) away from your first stitch with the needle going right to left if you are right-handed/sewing clockwise or left to right if you are left-handed/sewing counterclockwise. The direction of your needle will oppose the direction of your hem stitch.
4. Stitch a bite of the seam allowance ¼" (6 mm) away from the last stitch you made and ¼" (6 mm) down from the edge of the seam allowance. You will start to create something that looks like a series of Xs.
5. Continue this around the entire hem until you reach the end. If you begin to run out of thread with about a 3" (7.5 cm) tail, take a bite out of the seam allowance at your last stitch, wrap the thread around the needle twice, and pull the needle through to secure the knot. Begin again with your new length of thread near your last seam allowance stitch and continue around the hem.
6. Finish the hem by securing the last stitch with a bite in the seam allowance, wrapping the thread around the needle twice, and pulling the needle through. Press the hem and clip loose threads to ~ ¼" (6 mm).

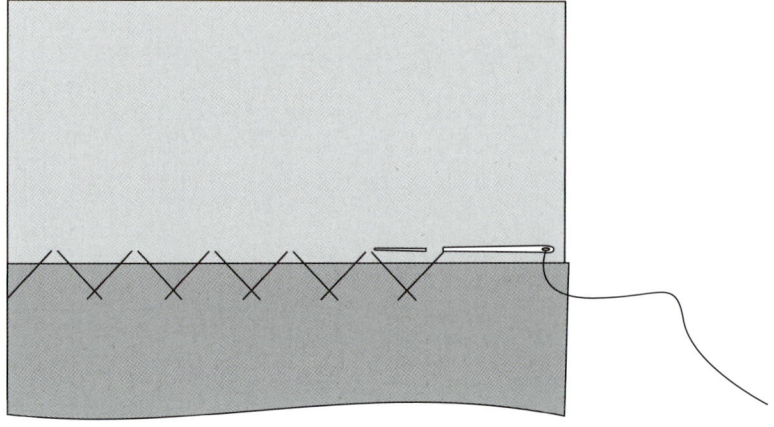

3.12

Vertical Hem Stitch

1. Treat (wax, thread conditioner, or saliva) or use a length of hand sewing thread the length of your suprasternal notch/center of your collar bone to your pointer finger. Use a sharp hand needle size 8, 9, or 10 and double thread for fabrics that are heavier OR a single thread for medium or lightweight fabrics. Tie a knot at the end of the thread tail(s) and clip down to ⅛" (3 mm).
2. Begin by hiding the tail of the thread ¼" (6 mm) below the top of the turned hem fabric at a seam by taking a bite out of the seam allowance and pulling the thread all the way through.
3. Next, take your stitch vertically up onto the main garment, take a bite from the left down to the right and angle the needle down ¼" (6 mm) to the right of the first stitch into the seam allowance.
4. Push the needle through the back of the seam allowance and up vertically to repeat the last step. The outside of the garment will have vertical stitches like a picket fence with a forward slash between the layers.
5. Continue this around the entire hem until you reach the end. If you begin to run out of thread with about a 3" (7.5 cm) tail, take a bite out of the seam allowance at your last stitch, wrap the thread around the needle twice, and pull the needle through to secure the knot. Begin again with your new length of thread near your last seam allowance stitch and continue around the hem.
6. Finish the hem by securing the last stitch with a bite in the seam allowance, wrapping the thread around the needle twice, and pulling the needle through. Press the hem and clip loose threads to ~ ¼" (6 mm).

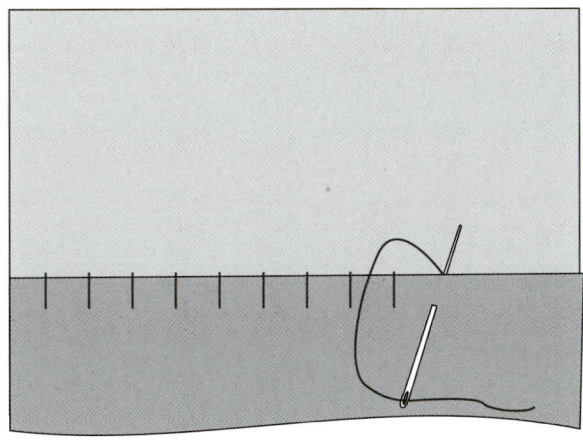

3.13

HAND STITCH HEMS: CROSS STITCH, VERTICAL HEM STITCH, PRICK/PICK STITCH

Prick/Pick Stitch

1. Treat (wax, thread conditioner, or saliva) or use a length of hand sewing thread the length of your suprasternal notch/center of your collar bone to your pointer finger. Use a sharps hand needle size 8, 9, or 10 and use a single thread unless you want the prick stitch to be decorative, in which you can use a double or thicker thread. Tie a knot at the end of the thread tail(s) and clip down to ⅛" (3 mm).
2. Begin stitching through all the layers from a seam through to the public side of the garment.
3. If you are right-handed, you will go directly behind the stitch the right to make your small "pick/prick" if you are left-handed, you will go directly behind the last stitch to the left.
4. Pull the thread through the back side catching the main fabric and seam allowance. Come back up to the public side of the garment and continue the process.
   ***If you would like your stitch to be even more invisible, you can do this process on the back side of the garment by only catching a few threads of the fabric. This is not as secure, but works well if you need something to be concealed.
5. Continue this around the entire hem until you reach the end. If you begin to run out of thread with about a 3" (7.5 cm) tail, take a bite out of the seam allowance at your last stitch, wrap the thread around the needle twice, and pull the needle through to secure the knot. Begin again with your new length of thread near your last seam allowance stitch and continue around the hem.
6. Finish the hem by securing the last stitch with a bite in the seam allowance, wrapping the thread around the needle twice, and pulling the needle through. Press the hem and clip loose threads to ~ ¼" (6 mm).

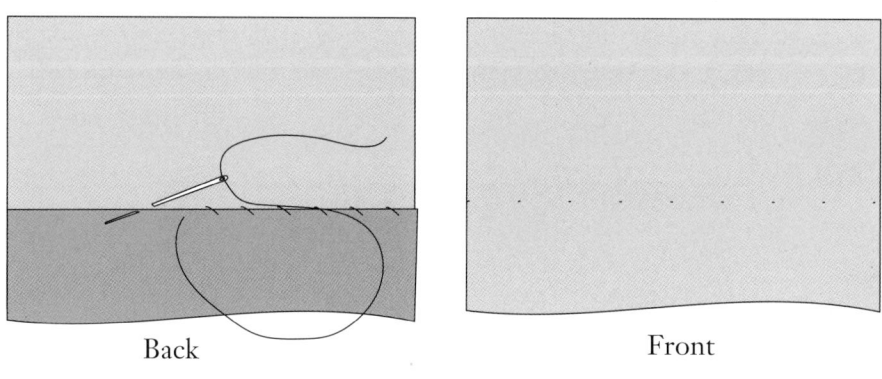

Back   Front

3.14

LENGTHENING BOTTOM HEMS

Lengthening garments can be key for growing children, making that thrift store purchase work to your advantage, or to fix any accidental mistakes in the shortening/hemming process. I vividly remember hemming a dear friend's non-traditional wedding dress and I second guessed my pin marks and made the dress about ¼" (6 mm) too short. I used to have a bad case of impostor syndrome when doing work for the people I was close to/for really important occasions. It's normal if you experience this as well! We found a creative solution to the problem by adding some lovely lace to the dress which ended up making it even more special. Fabric doesn't grow back like hair does, but when something is too short you have the opportunity to be a creative problem solver and, in some cases, make the garment really special and individualized!

MAXING OUT

1+ hours

To "max out" a garment means to let out the seam allowance as much as possible. This method is ideal when possible so that you don't have to match or add fabric. Woven skirts, formalwear, and dress pants typically have 1"–2" (2.5–5 cm) of seam allowance at the hem which makes for easy alterations! If a hem only needs to be let out a little or there is enough seam allowance to make the garment work, this method is your best option!

1. Measure the desired amount that the client would like the bottoms to be let out (3.15a).
2. Unpick the hem and clear all loose threads (3.15b).
3. Press the hem (3.15c). If the creases are hard to iron out, use a spray bottle with water or a spray bottle with a vinegar water solution (1 part vinegar, 3 parts water) to dampen the wrinkle and then press it out.
4. Use the desired hemming method from the beginning of this chapter OR
   a. Serge the edge of the fabric (3.15d). You can either leave the serged edge plain or you can single turn the hem and stitch the edge down (3.15e).
   b. Leave the raw edge to naturally fray for a distressed look.
   c. Serge, turn, and stitch for a narrow hem (see figure set 3.10).
   d. Use bias tape (see next hem method).
5. Press the hem, clip loose threads, and check the fit (3.15f).

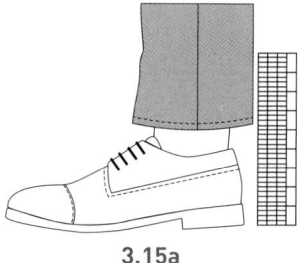
3.15a

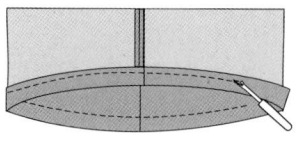
3.15b

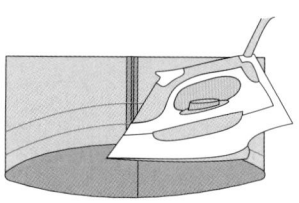
3.15c

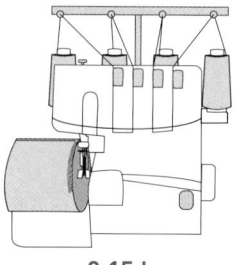
3.15d

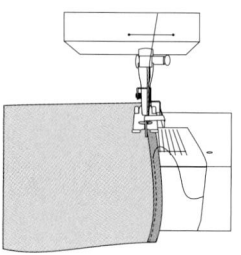
3.15e

3.15f

BIAS TAPE

1+ hours

If using this method, you will let out the hem/max out the hem and will need at least ¼" (6 mm) of seam allowance for a bias-faced hem or cut at your desired hem for the bias-covered edge.

1. Measure the desired amount that the client would like the bottoms to be let out.

2. Unpick the hem and clear all loose threads (3.16a).

3. Press the hem (3.16b). If the creases are hard to iron out, use a spray bottle with water or with a vinegar water solution (1 part vinegar, 3 parts water) to dampen the wrinkle and then press it out.

4. With the technical front (right sides) together, fold and pin the bias tape back on itself ¼" (6 mm), beginning just to the back of the inseam on pants or just behind one of the side seams on skirts/dresses. Pin around the entirety of the hem adding bias tape lengths if needed. When you reach the end, lay the raw edge of the end of the bias tape over the ¼" (6 mm) fold. This will create a clean finished edge (3.16c).

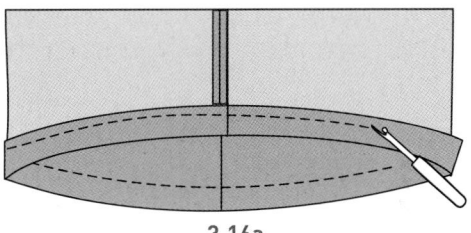

3.16a

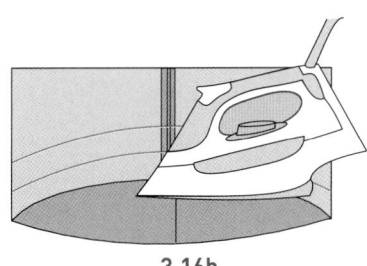

3.16b

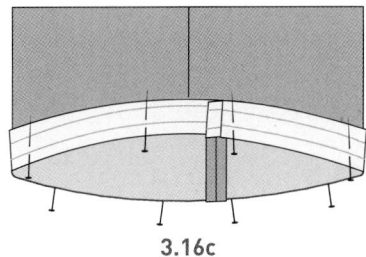

3.16c

5. Stitch the bias tape to the hem in the fold line closest to the edge of the fabric (3.16d).

6. Press the bias tape and seam allowance away from the garment making sure you don't press out the fold of the bias tape.

7. Optional: Understitch the seam allowance to the bias tape using an edge foot and stitching ⅛" (3 mm) away from the ditch. This will create a natural roll so that the bias tape does not peek out from the hem.

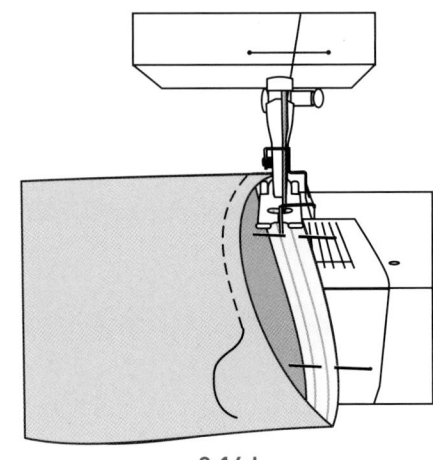

3.16d

8. Press the bias tape up and flat so that there is ⅛" (3 mm) of the hem rolled under the bias tape (3.16e).

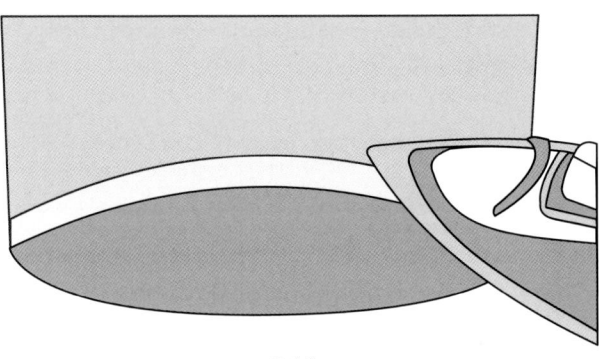

3.16e

9. Use the edge foot, or stitch as close to the turned edge of the bias tape as possible, around the hem beginning and ending with a backstitch just to the back of the inseam (pants) or just to the back of the side seams (skirts/dresses). Keep in mind that the bobbin thread will be on the public side of the garment, so choose your thread wisely! (3.16f).

10. Clip your threads, press the hem, and check the fit.

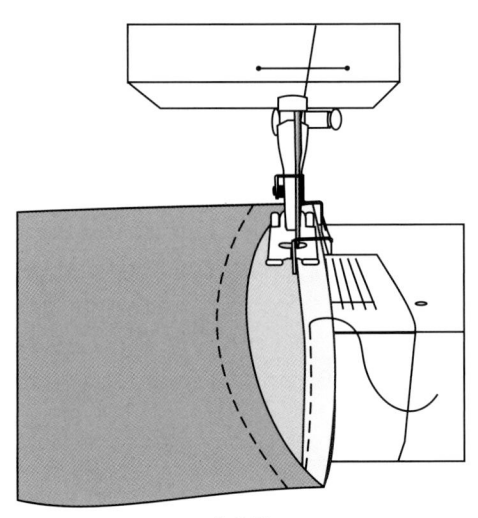

3.16f

ADDING FABRIC

1+ hours

1. Measure the length of the desired hem extension and the circumference of the bottom of the hem (3.17a).
2. Find a fabric that has a similar weight, weave/knit, and fiber content. You may choose to have the color match closely, accent the garment, or go wild and do something different/loud/quirky. It is best to select woven fabrics for woven garments and knit fabrics for knit garments. (See pages 40–1 if you need a refresher on knits versus wovens.) Pre-wash, dry, and press the extension fabric. Determine the extra length you will need and add ¼"–½" (6 mm–1.2 cm) of seam allowance to the top of the fabric and ¼"–2" (6 mm–5 cm) of seam allowance to the bottom of the fabric for a total of ½"–2½" (1.2–6.2 cm) of seam allowance in addition to your desired length. Measure the amount of width you will need and add ¼"–½" (6 mm–1.2 cm) seam allowance for all seams (left and right) (3.17b).

   Cutting out a simple rectangle of fabric will work for some garments, but often the hem will come out at angle (flare) or come in (skinny jeans/pencil skirts) and you will need to follow your garment as a guide. If your garment was cut on the bias or is very curvy, you will want to cut your extra fabric on the bias. (See page 40 for information on the bias of fabric.)

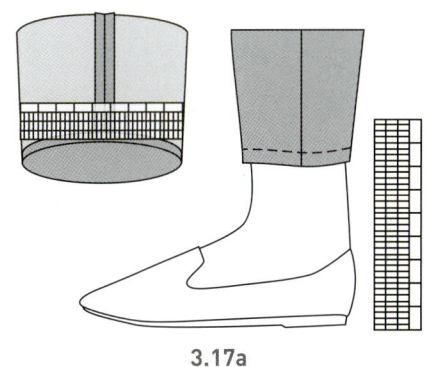

3.17a

3.17b

3. If necessary, unpick the hem of the garment to reduce bulk prior to attaching the extension (3.17c).

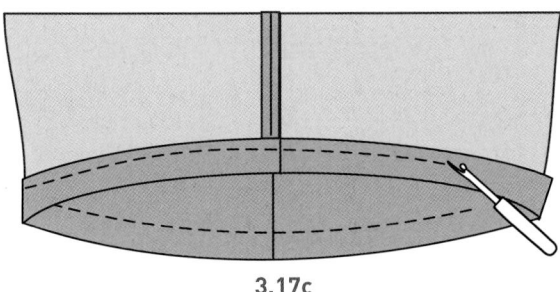

3.17c

4. Press the hem flat. If the creases are hard to iron out, use a spray bottle with water or a spray bottle with a vinegar water solution (1 part vinegar, 3 parts water) to dampen the wrinkle and then press it out (3.17d).

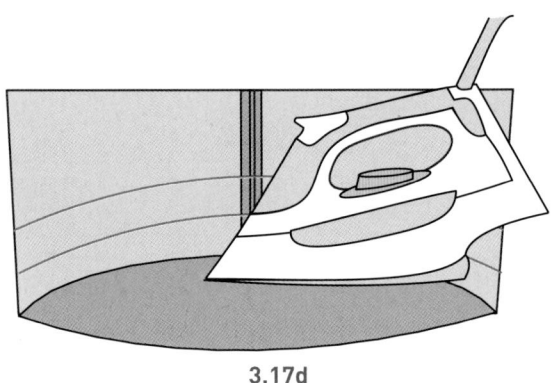

3.17d

5. Once your extension pieces are cut, you will connect them at one side seam replicating the method used on the original garment. For example, the side seams may be stitched and serged or French seamed (3.17e).

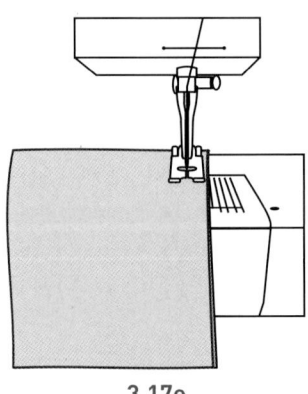

3.17e

6. Press the new side seams open (3.17f).

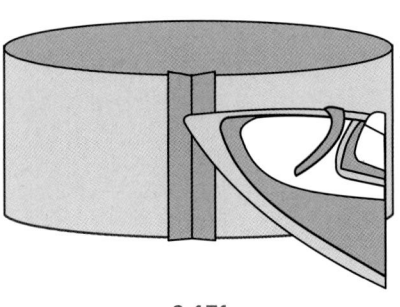

3.17f

7. With your pants right side out and your hem extension inside out, match the side seams by pinning in the ditch and stitch all the way around the hem to stitch the two pieces using ¼"–½" (6 mm–1.2 cm) seam allowance (3.17g).

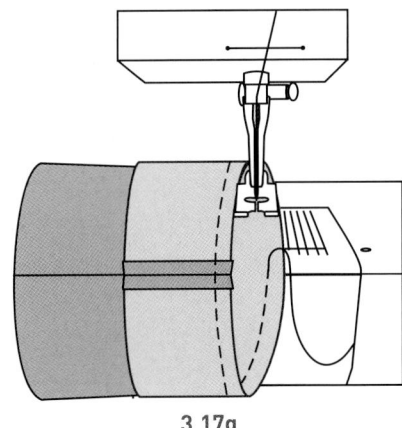

3.17g

8. Pull the extension down and press the seam. You may need to serge the raw edges together or separately to prevent fraying (3.17h).

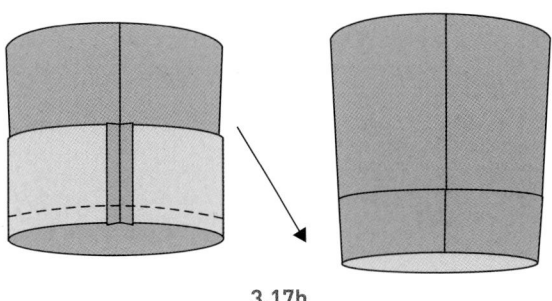

3.17h

9. Finish the new hem using a hem method of your choice from this chapter that most closely replicates the original garment hem. Press the hem, clip your threads, and check the fit (3.17i).

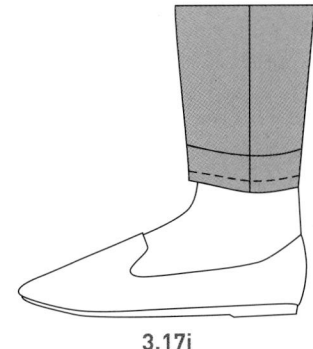

3.17i

ADDING FABRIC | 73

ADDING LACE

1+ hours

Use this method if you are adding lace to a finished hem that needs to be lengthened equally around the hem.

1. Select your desired lace. Consider the length, width, fiber content, pattern, weight, and color. Lace can come as a trim (narrow) or in yardage like fabric. If you select the trim, you may not have enough for something that needs to be lengthened substantially, if you select fabric, you may need to spend more time finishing the raw edges. Also note that you will often stitch the top portion of the lace under the hem, so be sure to purchase something that is at least ½" (1.2 cm) wider than you need for your hem.

2. Measure the circumference of the garment hem and add 2" (5 cm) to determine your cut length (hems tend to magically shrink and you will need some seam allowance for overlap) (3.18a).

3. Measure, mark, and cut your lace (3.18b).

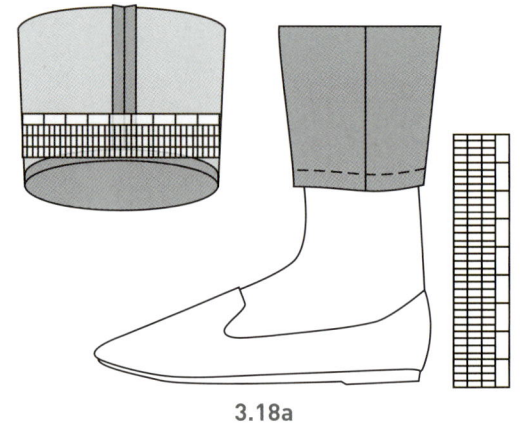

3.18a

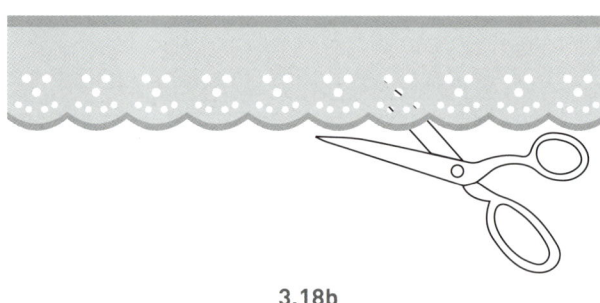

3.18b

4. You may attach the lace to your hem by topstitching or stitch/press/topstitch.
5. Pin hem on the front of the garment (public side) to the lace as desired 1" (2.5 cm) behind the back of the inseam on pants or 1" (2.5 cm) behind one of the side seams on skirts/dresses with 1" (2.5 cm) of unpinned seam allowance. Pin around the entirety of the hem to determine where your seam should go (3.18c). When you get to the first portion of the raw edge of the lace you can either:
   a. Line up the lace to stitch with right sides together and press open to create a seam (3.18d).

   OR

   b. Overlap the lace and use a lycra stitch/elastic attaching stitch or if you do not have a stitch that looks like this, using a zigzag. Trim the excess seam allowance (3.18e).

3.18c

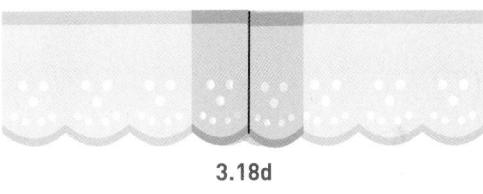

3.18d

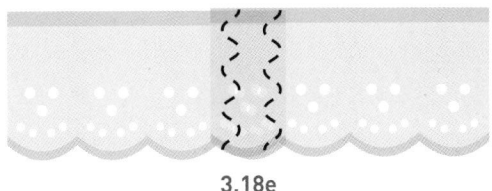

3.18e

6. Pin the remainder of the hem and stitch on the public side of the garment ensuring that you catch the top of the lace (3.18f).

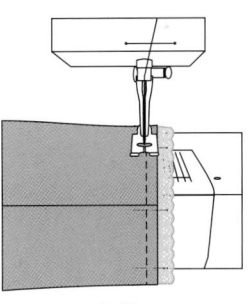

3.18f

7. Clip your threads, press the hem, and check the length (3.18g).

3.18g

ADDING LACE | 75

CHAPTER 4

Top Hems

Garments worn on the top half of the body: shirts, vests, sleeves, jackets, etc.

SHORTENING:
- Knitwear coverstitch
- Knitwear faux coverstitch using a twin needle
- Shirttail hem
- Lined suit jacket hems
- Unlined suit jacket hems

LENGTHENING:
- Maxing out seam allowance
- Suit jacket hems

KNITWEAR COVERSTITCH

30 minutes–1 hour

1. Measure and mark the hem on the client at the center front, center back, and both side seams (see pages 44–5) (4.1a).

2. Mark the new hem and the desired seam allowance line, replicating the original design, when possible. If the fabric below the pins is ½" (1.2 cm) or greater, you will not need to unpick the hem. If there is less than ½" (1.2 cm) below the pin, unpick the hem (4.1b).

3. Next, you will prepare to stitch the hem. Use woolly nylon/bulky nylon in the lower looper if working with a knit garment. You have two options for the next step:
   a. Option A: Best for experienced coverstitch users. Press the fabric up on the new hemline, then measure down and cut the fabric on the seam allowance line.
   b. Option B: Best for new coverstitch users. Press the fabric up on the new hemline and leave the seam allowance and trim it after stitching.

4. Press the hem at the pin lines. Make sure the seam allowance is equal all the way around, this will be very important especially if you cut any excess fabric (4.1c).

5. Test your coverstitch machine to ensure it is functioning. Check the placement of the garment on the seam allowance guides so that it catches the hem if you cut it.

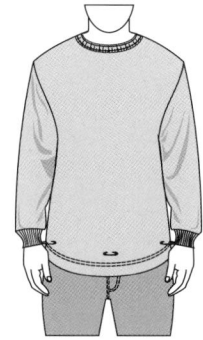

4.1a

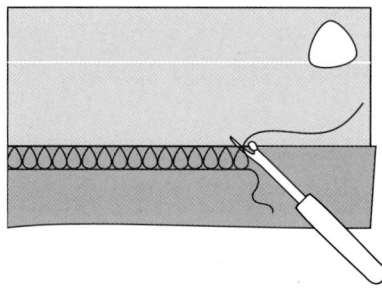

4.1b

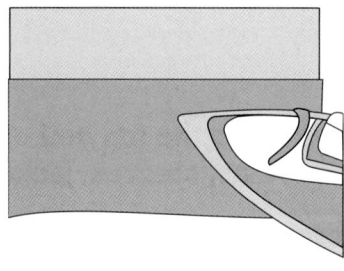

4.1c

6. Begin your coverstitch 1" (2.5 cm) behind one of the side seams. I usually need to take a breath and plow over the seam allowances—this varies from machine to machine! To secure your coverstitch, stitch directly over your beginning stitching for 1" (2.5 cm). Hand crank the wheel 1–4 times to release the tension (4.1d).

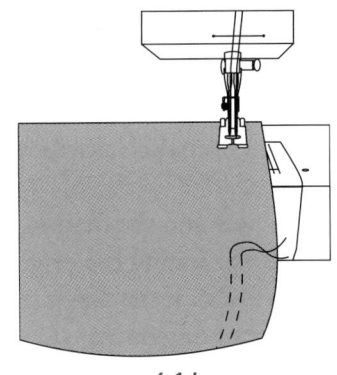

4.1d

7. If you have not cut your excess seam allowance yet, carefully do so now (4.1e). Make sure you are only cutting the excess fabric and not the technical face of the garment.

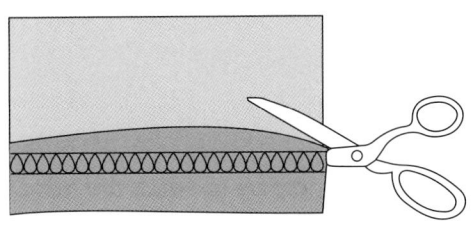

4.1e

8. Unpick and re-do the coverstitch if you have parts of the hem that did not get caught in the stitch (4.1f).

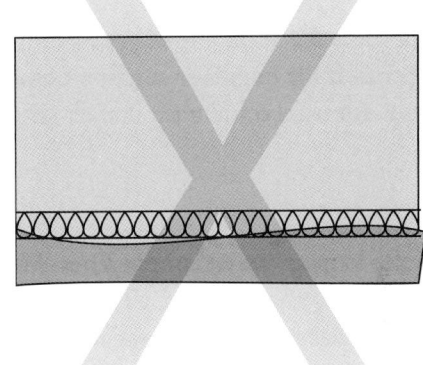

4.1f

9. Press the hem and check the fit (4.1g).

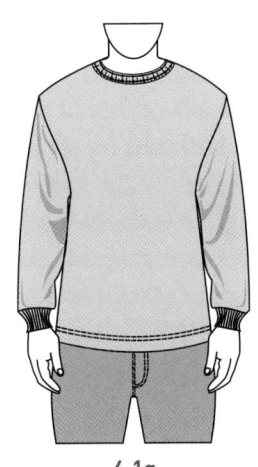

4.1g

KNITWEAR COVERSTITCH

KNITWEAR FAUX COVERSTITCH USING A TWIN NEEDLE

30 minutes–1 hour

If you don't have a coverstitch machine, this option replicates the stitch beautifully!

1. Mark the new hem and the desired seam allowance line, replicating the original design, when possible (4.2a). If the fabric below the pins is ½" (1.2 cm) or greater, you will not need to unpick the hem. If there is less that ½" (1.2 cm) below the pin, unpick the hem (4.2b).

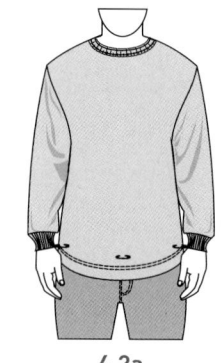

4.2a

2. Next, you will prepare to stitch the hem. Use woolly nylon/bulky nylon in the lower looper if working with a knit garment. You have two options for the next step:
   a. Option A for experienced sewists: Cut the fabric on the seam allowance line.
   b. Option B for beginner sewists: Leave the seam allowance and trim it after stitching.

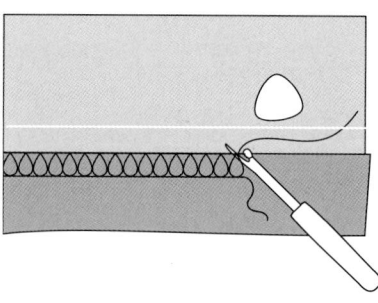

4.2b

3. Press the hem at the safety pin lines. Make sure the seam allowance is equal all the way around, this will be very important especially if you cut any excess fabric (4.2c).

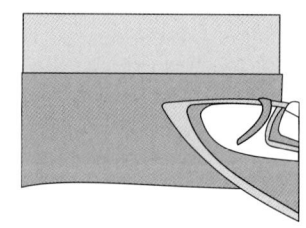

4.2c

4. Insert the twin needle into your machine. Thread two spools of thread through the top thread guides and then have one thread go through the right needle, and one in the left. Use woolly nylon/bulky nylon in the bobbin if working with a knit garment. Adjust the stitch length to a longer stitch to allow for stretching and aesthetics (4.2d).

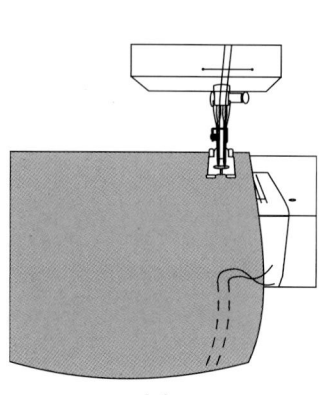

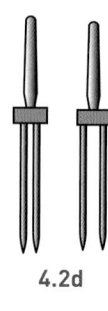

4.2d

4.2e

5. Check the placement of the garment on the seam allowance guides so that it catches the hem if you cut it.

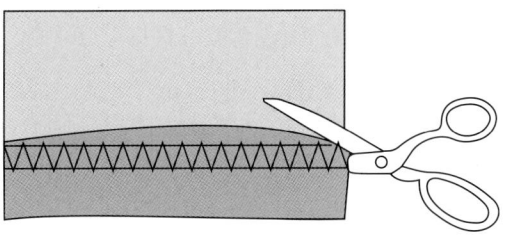

4.2f

6. Begin your twin needle faux coverstitch 1" (2.5 cm) behind one of the side seams (4.2d). To secure your coverstitch, stitch directly over your beginning stitching and backstitch 2–4 stitches (4.2e).

4.2g

7. If you have not cut your excess seam allowance yet, do so now carefully. Make sure you are only cutting the excess fabric and not the technical face of the garment (4.2f).

8. Unpick and re-do the coverstitch if you have parts of the hem that did not get caught in the stitch (4.2g).

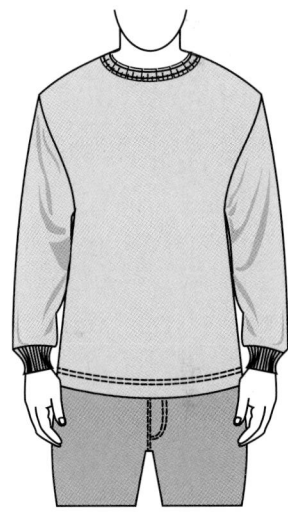

9. Press the hem and check the fit (4.2h).

4.2h

KNITWEAR FAUX COVERSTITCH USING A TWIN NEEDLE

SHIRTTAIL HEM

30 minutes–1 hour

1. Measure and mark the hem on the client at the center front, center back and both side seams (see pages 44–5) (4.3a). Note that the hem may be curved or straight and the client can decide what style they would like.

4.3a

2. If the fabric below the pins is ½" (1.2 cm) or greater, you will not need to unpick the hem. If there is less that ½" (1.2 cm) below the pin, unpick the hem (4.3b).

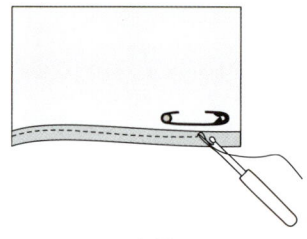

4.3b

3. Mark the hem line using a hip-curve or straight ruler (4.3c).

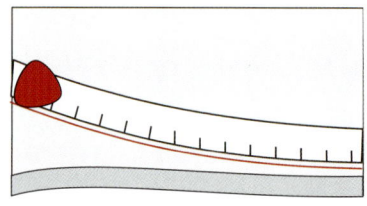

4.3c

4. You have two options for the next step to hem the shirt.

   a. Fold the fabric up ¼" (6 mm) below the hem line that you drew towards the inside of the shirt. Use an edgefoot or ⅛" (3 mm) seam allowance to stitch the turn of the hem (4.3d). Cut the excess seam allowance as close to the stitch line as possible taking great care not to cut any other layers (4.3e). Fold the hem on the line that you originally drew (4.3f), ¼" (6 mm) turn, and stitch on top of the stitchline that you just stitched (4.3g). This is the easiest, fastest way to stitch a shirttail hem.

   b. Cut the excess seam allowance ½" (1.2 cm) below the desired hem line. Fold the hem ¼" (6 mm), press, and then fold again ¼" (6 mm) and press. If you are working on a curve, you will want to stitch at ¼" (6 mm) using a basting stitch so you can pull in the fabric on the curves to ease the fabric in. After pressing, stitch using the edgefoot or ⅛" (3 mm) away from the turn of the cloth (4.3g).

5. Press the hem, clip your threads, and check the fit (4.3h).

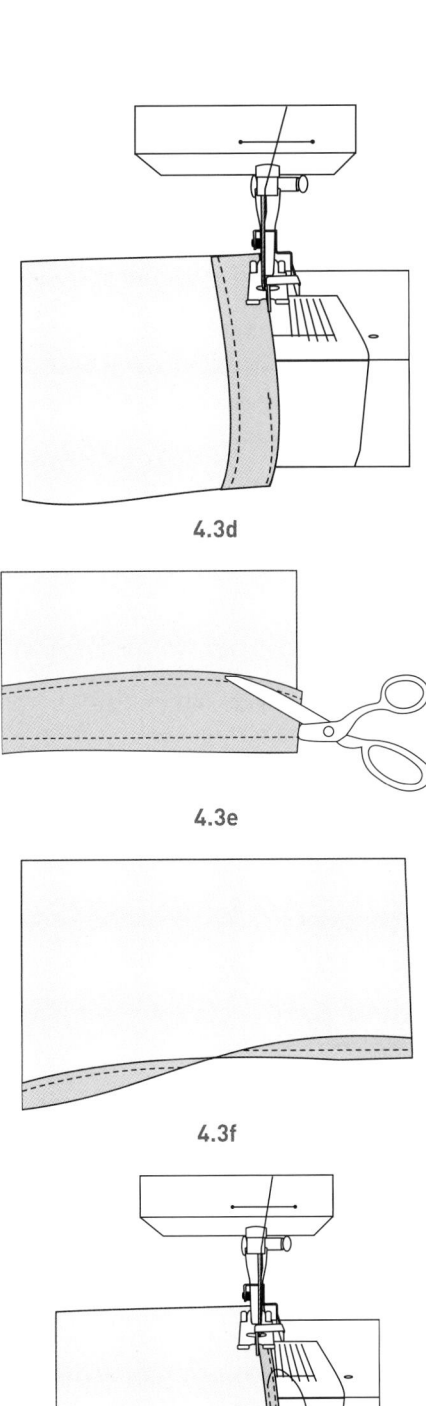

4.3d

4.3e

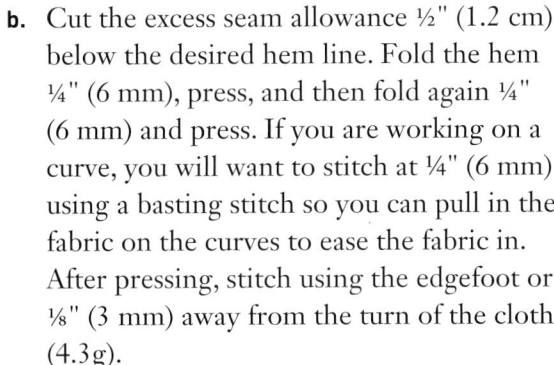

4.3f

4.3g

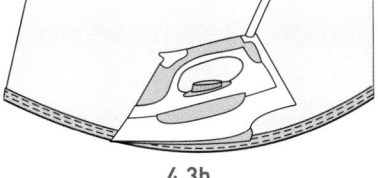

4.3h

SHIRTTAIL HEM

LINED SUIT JACKET HEM

1+ hours

1. Measure and mark the hem on the client at the center front, center back, and both side seams (see pages 44–5). Note that the jacket may be straight or curved and may or may not have a vent. The measurement from the hem to the pin should be about the same all the way around, if it is slightly off, average the measurements or go with the longer measurement (4.4a).

4.4a

2. Unpick the center back seam on the lining. Turn the jacket inside out (4.4b).

4.4b

3. Unpick the tacks that hold the lining to the main jacket fabric. Note the amount that the fabric has been turned under as you will mimic this after sewing. Press the lining flat so that the fabric is flat on the stitch line. (The lining will be pressed down ½"–1½" (1.2–3.7 cm) for movement.) (4.4c).

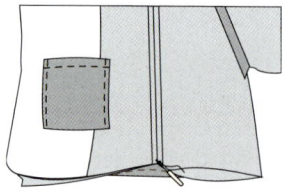

4.4c

4. Mark the new hemline. If the center front of the jacket is curved, use a curved ruler to taper the new hem line into the front of the jacket to avoid removing fullness from the center front of the jacket (4.4d).

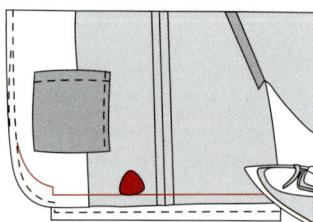

4.4d

5. Stitch the new hemline and make sure to begin the stitch directly on the original stitch line and begin and end with a backstitch. If your jacket has a vent, you will need to do the left and right side of the jacket separately (4.4e).

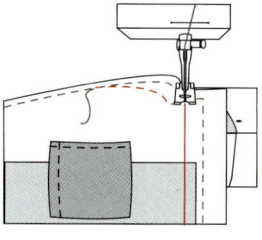

4.4e

6. Trim the excess fabric to the seam allowance allotted in the jacket originally (4.4f).

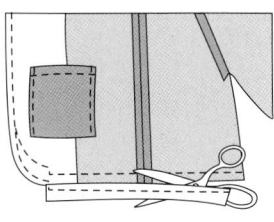

4.4f

7. Press the fabric up the amount recorded in step 3 and tack the bottom lining seam allowance to the seam allowance in the jacket at the side seam, center back, and/or center back vent (4.4g).

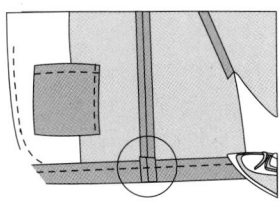

4.4g

8. Hand or machine sew the side and back seam allowances up so that the outer fabric is pressed under how it was originally and so that the lining does not show (4.4h).

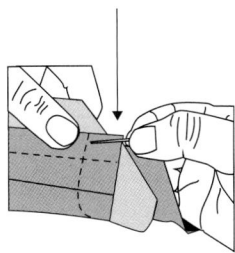

4.4h

9. Turn the jacket right-side out and press the hem. Note that the lining should be pressed down ½"–1½" (1.2–3.7 cm) below the stitching for movement.

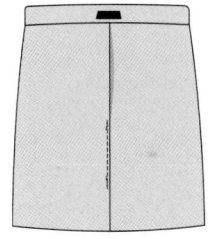

10. Stitch the center back opening (4.4i).

11. Press the hem, clip your threads, and check the fit.

4.4i

LINED SUIT JACKET HEM

UNLINED SUIT JACKET HEM

1+ hours

1. Measure and mark the hem on the client at the center front, center back, and both side seams (see pages 44–5). Note that the jacket may be straight or curved. The measurement should be about the same all the way around, if it is slightly off, average the measurements or go with the longer measurement (4.5a).

4.5a

2. Mark the new hemline using an appropriate marking tool (4.5b).
   ***Often, bias bound edges are used in these jackets. You may replicate this or use a different method. Depending on how much seam allowance you have, you may not even need to trim the excess fabric. If you have excessive seam allowance, more than 2" (5 cm), you will most likely need to trim the excess fabric. Try to replicate the hem finish when possible.

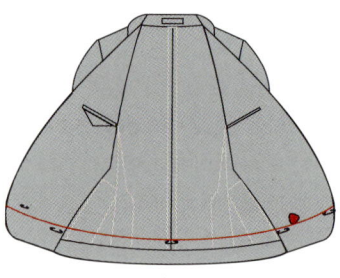

4.5b

3. Unpick the hem, the topstitching on the curve of the front jacket, and tacks that are holding the facing to the jacket (4.5c).

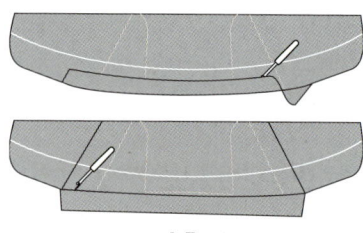

4.5c

4. Press the fabric up to the new seam allowance on the back of the jacket and re-mark the front curve. The front curve usually has a bit of facing that is sewn to the front of the jacket before the fabric is hemmed around the side seams and center back (4.5d).

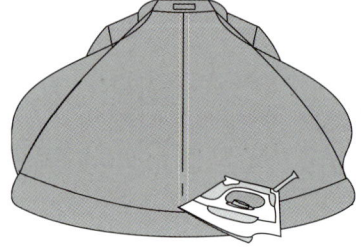

4.5d

5. Stitch the curves first on the left and right center front jacket using a sewing machine (4.5e).

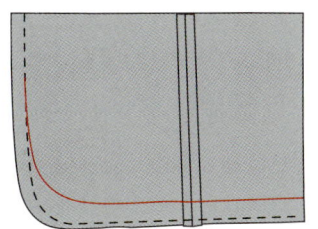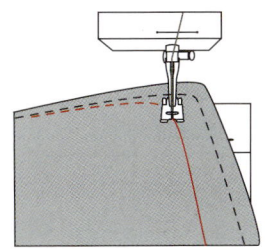

4.5e

6. Clip the fabric between the facing and turned up hem so that it lays flat at the transition and trim the excess fabric (4.5f).

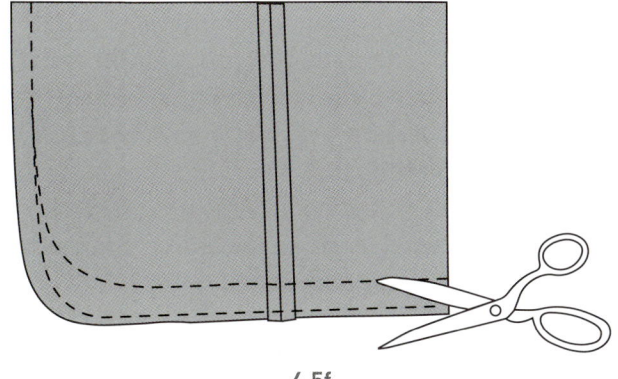

4.5f

7. Stitch the hem up as it was originally. This will often be a blind hem, cross/catch stitch, or can be topstitched (4.5g).

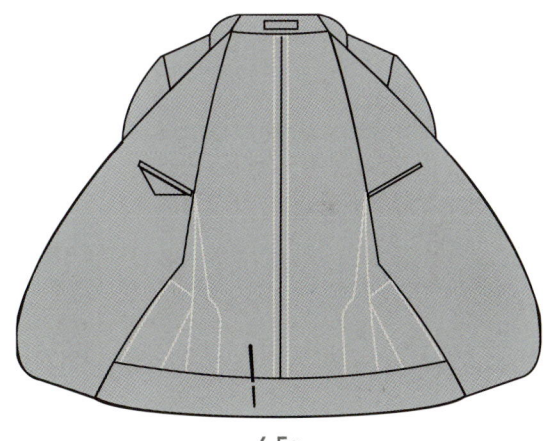

4.5g

8. Press the hem, clip your threads, and check the fit (4.5h).

4.5h

LENGTHENING
MAXING OUT SEAM ALLOWANCE
1+ hours

The example illustrated below is a knit long sleeve shirt. Note that if you are maxing out a suit jacket or woven garment, the order of operations for the alteration may be different. If you don't have enough fabric to max out the garment, you can also add a facing, bias tape, or additional fabric. See pages 69–75 on letting out bottoms for more suggestions.

1. On any top you would like to lengthen, you will need to determine how much longer the hem needs to be. You can do this by having the client put the top on and then have them point to how long they would like it to be at the front, sides, and back. Measure and mark the new desired length at the center front, side seams, and center back (4.6a).

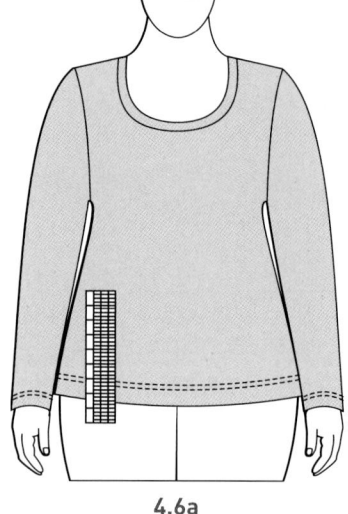

4.6a

2. Measure the seam allowance to see if you have enough to let out. If not, use the bias tape or lace method (see pages 69–75) (4.6b).

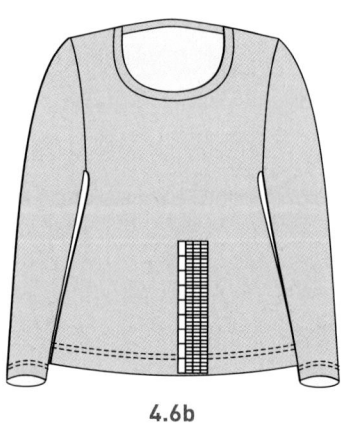

4.6b

3. Remove the stitching and threads and measure and mark down from the crease the new desired hem length (4.6c).

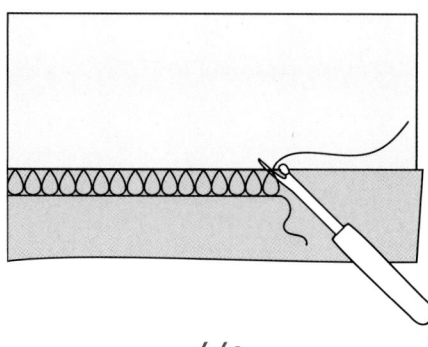

4.6c

4. Press the seam allowance under or use bias tape, extra fabric, lace, or simply serge the raw edge (4.6d).

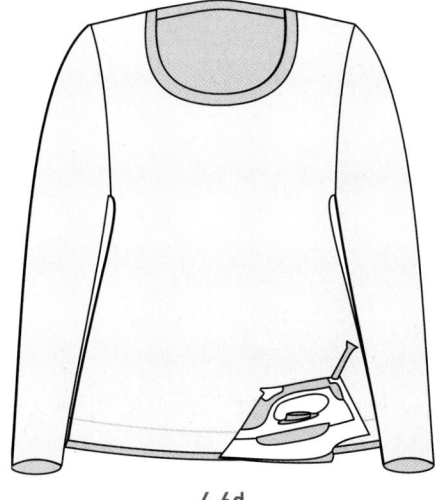

4.6d

5. Turn and press the hem up and replicate the hem stitching if possible. The example below shows a faux coverstitch, but you may use any method you like from chapter 3 (see pages 69–73) (4.6e).

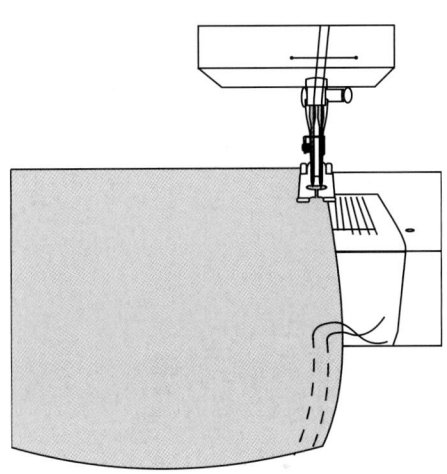

4.6e

6. Press the hem, clip the threads, and check the fit (4.6f).

4.6f

LENGTHENING SUIT JACKET HEM

1+ hours

There are many ways to alter a suit jacket hem and no one way is the perfect solution. Many sewists will completely unpick the hem to alter a jacket and may not even unpick the center back or sleeve seam in order to turn the garment right side out. That method is a great solution and commonly used and I have worked with many people who enjoy this method the most. I prefer to stitch the jacket hem while the lining is still attached to the garment so I can maintain the correct amount of excess lining on the hem as well as keeping the stitching in place and then unpicking the original hem. Do whatever works best for you and try both methods out to see which one you like more. The instructions below outline keeping the original stitching until you have completed your new stitch line.

1. Determine how much longer the hem needs to be on the suit jacket by having the client put the jacket and then have them point to how long they would like it to be at the front, sides, and back. Note the measurements (4.7a).

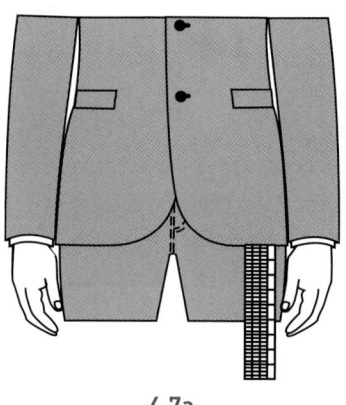

4.7a

2. Unpick the center back seam on the lining and turn the jacket inside out (4.7b).

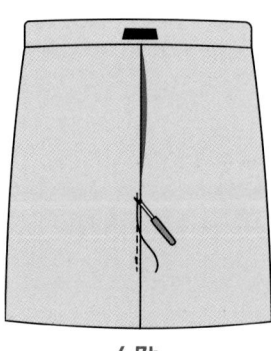

4.7b

3. Unpick the tacks that hold the lining to the main jacket fabric. Press the lining flat up so that the fabric is flat on the stitch line. (The lining will be pressed down ½"–1½" (1.2–3.7 cm) for movement.) (4.7c).

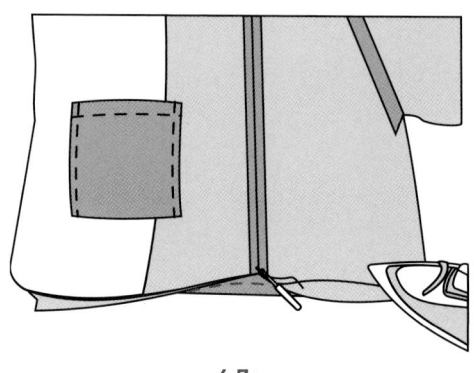

4.7c

4. Mark the new hemline and make sure the front curves on the center front of the jacket look smooth and pleasing to the eye. Dramatic curves may or may not be desirable to your client, so use your judgment to see what looks correct (4.7d).

5. Stitch the new hemline and make sure to begin the stitch directly on the original stitch line and begin and end with a backstitch. If your jacket has a vent, you will need to do the left and right side of the jacket separately (4.7e).

6. Unpick the original stitch line (4.7f).

7. Press the hem fabric up the amount recorded in step 3 and tack the bottom lining seam allowance to the seam allowance in the jacket at the side seam, center back, and/or center back vent (4.7g).

8. Hand or machine sew the side and back seam allowances up so that the outer fabric is pressed under how it was originally and so that the lining does not show (4.7h).

9. Turn the jacket right side out. Press the new hem line noting that the lining will be well above the press line.

10. Close the opening center back seam with a topstitch (4.7i).

11. Press the hem, clip the threads, and check the fit.

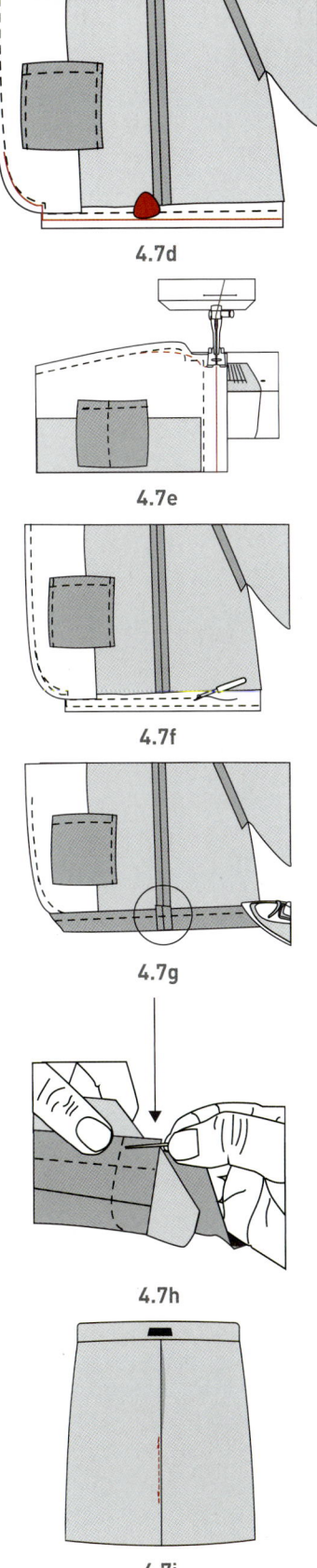

4.7d

4.7e

4.7f

4.7g

4.7h

4.7i

LENGTHENING SUIT JACKET HEM

CHAPTER 5

Taking in Bottoms

For garments that are too large and/or need to be fitted.
- Back gap
- Waistbands
  - Using elastic
- Side seams
- Inseams
- Darts/pleats/tucks
- Ease/gathers
- Zippers

BACK GAP

1+ hours

If you or your client have a smaller waist and fuller hip ratio, this fit problem is very common, and this alteration will make your pants fit much more comfortably!

1. Pinch out the center back of the pant at the waistband, down the seam, and to the vanishing point on the center back. If the vanishing point needs to be in the crotch area, note an approximate distance down visually so that you do not make the client uncomfortable (5.1a).

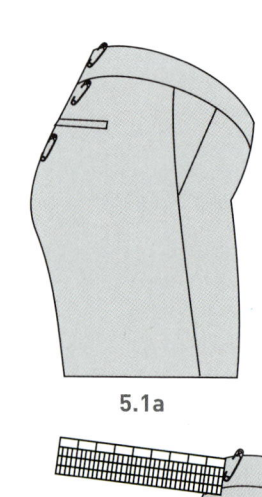

5.1a

2. Remove the pants and write the measurements taken down by noting the total amount needed to be taken in and divide that by two. By doing this you will be able to mark the amount that the pants need to be taken in when the pants are folded in half (5.1b).

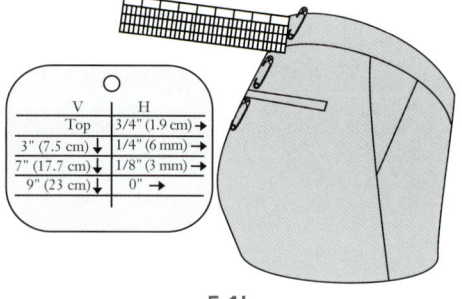

	V		H
Top		3/4" (1.9 cm) →
3" (7.5 cm) ↓		1/4" (6 mm) →
7" (17.7 cm) ↓		1/8" (3 mm) →
9" (23 cm) ↓		0" →

5.1b

3. Mark the amount that needs to be taken in on the inside of the pants with an appropriate marking tool on one half/side of the pant (5.1c).

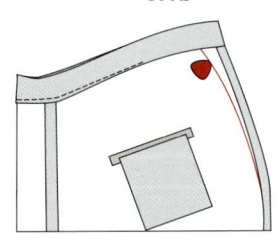

5.1c

4. Remove the waistband stitching 2" (5 cm) past the amount that needs to be taken in on either side of the pant. You may also need to remove any tags that are at the center back of the pant (5.1d).

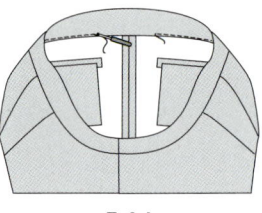

5.1d

5. If there is not a center back seam, cut the waistband in half at the center. Remove any topstitching or understitching from the top of the waistband 2" (5 cm) past the amount needed to be taken in (5.1e).

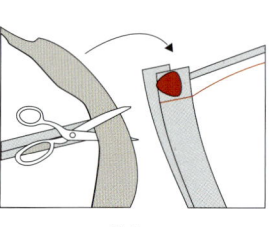

5.1e

6. Stitch the center back seams together on the half and taper to the original stitch line at the vanishing point. Be sure to use a smaller stitch length as this is a seam that can come undone easily (5.1f).

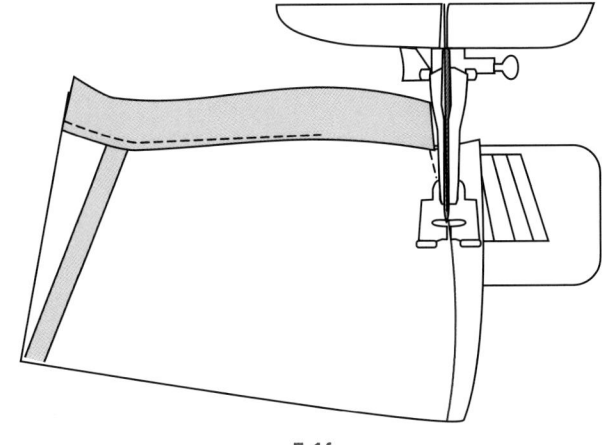

5.1f

7. With right sides together, stitch the waistband pieces at the desired amount (5.1g).

8. Trim and finish the seam allowances on the center back seam as they were with serging separate, serging together, bias bound edges, etc. Use a seam allowance of ½–¾" (1.2–1.9 cm).

9. Restitch topstitching or understitching if needed on the center back seam.

10. Trim the excess seam allowance on the waistband. Press the seam allowance open.

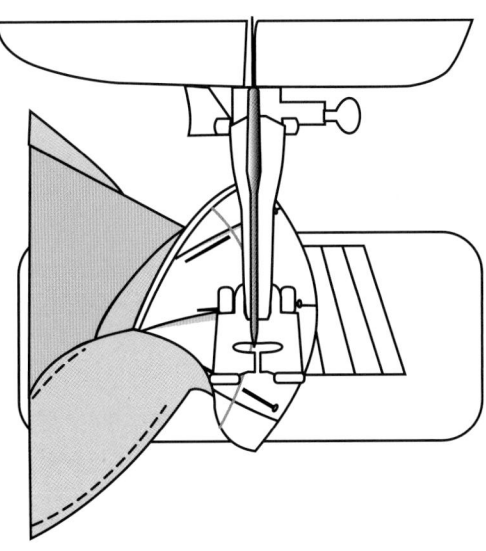

5.1g

11. Attach the waistband back to the pant. This may mean stitching the outer waistband to the outer center back seam and then stitching in the ditch to catch the lining OR it could be topstitching all three layers together. Try to replicate whatever was done originally (5.1h).

12. Press the seams, clip the threads, and check the fit.

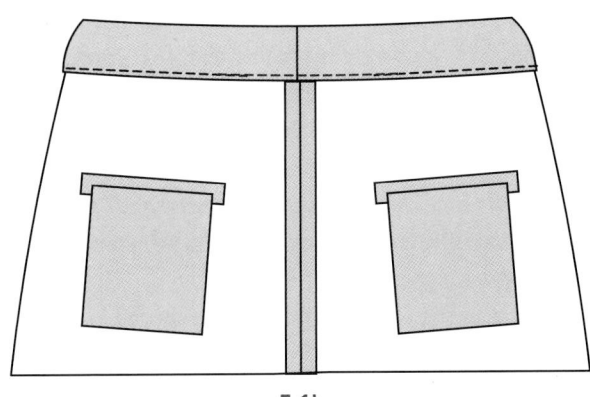

5.1h

WAISTBANDS: USING ELASTIC

1+ hours

If you need to make a waistband smaller and do not want to adjust the center back seam, adding elastic is a fast, simple option, especially in childrenswear.

1. Pinch out the center back of the pant at the waistband and pin the desired amount to be taken in (5.2a).

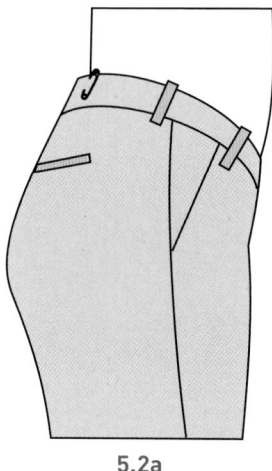

5.2a

2. Note the full measurement amount that needs to be taken out and also note the half measurement (5.2b).

3. Use elastic that is a slightly smaller width than your waistband between the topstitching lines. For example, if you have a 1" (2.5 cm) waistband, purchase ¾" (1.9 cm) wide elastic or smaller.

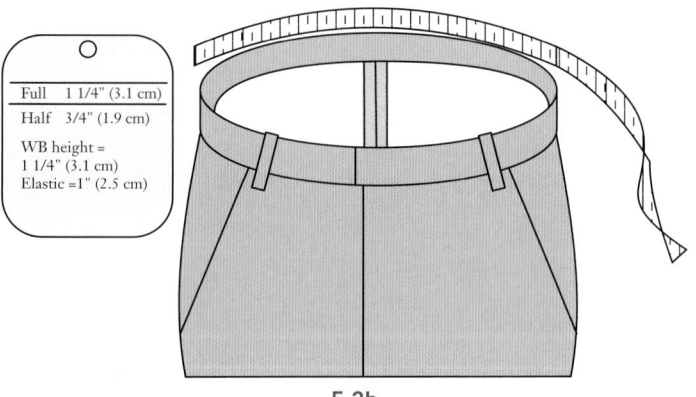

5.2b

4. Next, measure the distance between the side seam belt loops or from the left side seam, center back, to the right side seam. Note that number and subtract the total amount that needs to be taken out minus an additional 4" (10 cm). Once you have determined the amount of elastic that you need, measure and cut the elastic (5.2c).
   a. Example: Belt loop to belt loop = 18" (45.7 cm)
   Total amount to be taken out and amount of elastic to reduce for cinching the waistband
   2" + 4" (5 + 10 cm) = −6" (15 cm)
   18" − 6" (45.7−15 cm) = 12" (30 cm) of elastic.

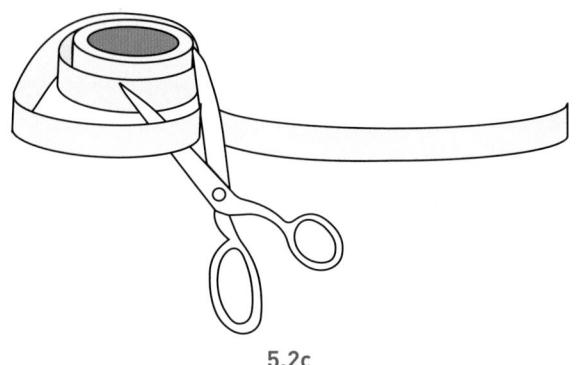

5.2c

5. On the inner waistband only, carefully cut between the topstitching and on the inner edge of the right and left back belt loops or 1" (2.5 cm) in on either side seam (5.2d).

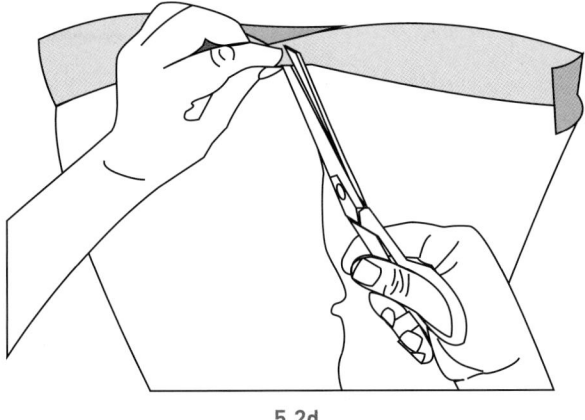

5.2d

6. Using two safety pins, pin one end of the piece of elastic to the inner waistband and attach the other to the loose end of elastic. Pull the elastic through to the other cut using the safety pin as a guide. Pin the elastic in place on the inner waistband ensuring that the elastic is not twisted (5.2e).

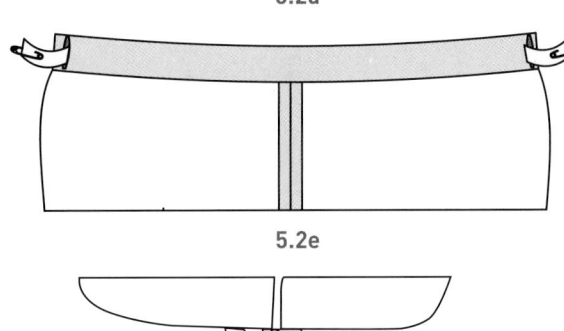

5.2e

7. Stitch the elastic in place from the inside using thread that matches the waistband through the entire waistband. If it is important that you do not see stitching on the outside, you can sew this by hand (5.2f).

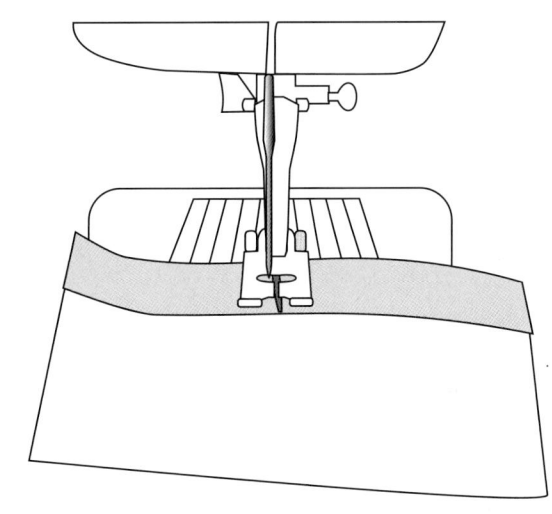

5.2f

8. If the client is available, you can have them try this on and if you need to pull the elastic more, you can do so.

9. After it is in place, stitch the opening shut/the edge of the elastic with a zigzag/bar tack that is wide enough to span the cut.

10. Press the waistband, clip the threads, and check the fit (5.2g).

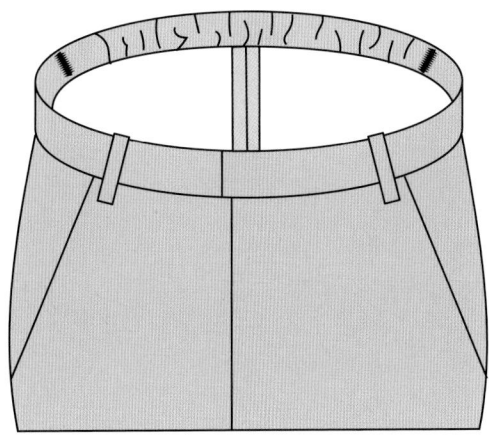

5.2g

WAISTBANDS: USING ELASTIC | 97

SIDE SEAMS/OUTSEAMS AND INSEAM TIPS

It can be challenging to determine whether a pant needs to be taken in at the side seams/outseam, inseam, and/or center back. As a rule of thumb, pinching, pinning, and assessing the look by feel and look is the best way to determine what steps you need to take. The eye naturally can tell when things look in or out of balance, trust your instincts and get a second opinion or set of eyes on your alteration if you need to! If you are needing a little more guidance, follow this guide to see what steps you should take.

If the pant is loose at the waist:

- Pinch out the center back. If the side seams stay put, and the fit looks good, you only need to take in the center back.

If the pant is loose at the hips and legs:

- If you pinch out the center back the side seams pull backwards, you need to take them in at the side seam.
- If you pin out the side seams and the pants are still too large OR the inseam pulls forward or backward, you need to take in the inseams and side seams/outseams.
- If you pin out the side seams and pants look balanced and at the desired fit, you only need to take them in at the side seam
- If you pin out the inseams and there is bunching or the seam swings forward or backward you may need to split the difference of the amount you are taking out to the inseam and outseam.
- If you pin the inseam and the fit is desirable, you only need to do that alteration.

Below I have included a sample chart of how to determine how much seam allowance to take in/let out when you have measured each side of the body. Often these measurements are slightly different. If the client seems to be somewhat symmetrical, average the measurements so they are equal and balanced on each side. If the client has a notable difference on either side of the body, alter the garment differently on each side based on the measurements. Notable differences can be common in people with scoliosis, athletes who might favor one side of their body, or if the person has had an injury. I like to note alterations by first noting how far up or down the body/y-axis/vertical measurement, and then measure the full distance of how far in towards or away from the right and left side of the body/x-axis/horizontal measurement. If I want to even the measurements, I will average the two numbers and then divide that by two so I know how much to take out with the seam is folded in half.

Sample Measurement Table

VERTICAL MEASUREMENT	HORIZONTAL MEASUREMENT RIGHT SIDE	HORIZONTAL MEASUREMENT LEFT SIDE	AVERAGE MEASUREMENTS	HALF MEASUREMENTS
Top Waist	2" (5 cm)	1½" (3.8 cm)	2 + 1½ = 3½/2 = 1¾" (4.5 cm)	⅞" (2.2 cm)
2" (5 cm) ↓	1½" (3.8 cm)	2" (5 cm)	1½ + 2 = 3½/2 = ¾" (1.9 cm)	⅜" (1 cm)
6" (15.2 cm) ↓	1" (2.5 cm)	¾" (1.9 cm)	1 + ¾ = 1¾/2 = ⅜" (1 cm)	3⁄16" (5 mm)
Crotch point	½" (1.2 cm)	½" (1.2 cm)	Same	¼" (6 mm)
6" (15.2 cm) ↑	1" (2.5 cm)	¾" (1.9 cm)	1 + ¾ = 1¾/2 = ⅜" (1 cm)	3⁄16" (5 mm)
2" (5 cm) ↑	1" (2.5 cm)	½" (1.2 cm)	1 + 1½ = 1½/2 = ¾" (1.9 cm)	⅜" (1 cm)
Bottom Hem	½" (1.2 cm)	½" (1.2 cm)	Same	¼" (6 mm)

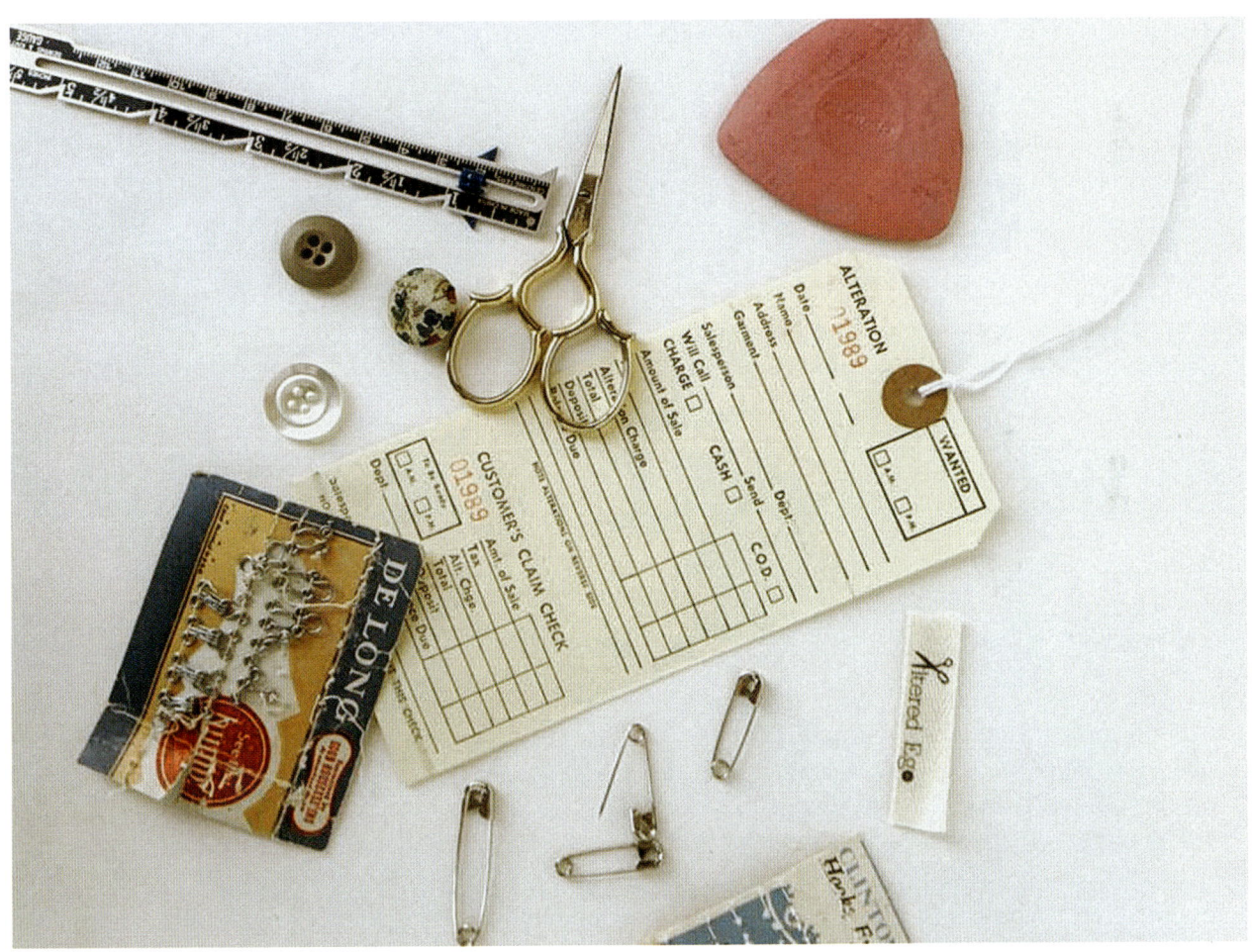

SIDE SEAMS/OUTSEAMS AND INSEAM TIPS

SIDE SEAMS/OUTSEAMS

1+ hours

1. Pinch out and pin the side seams on either side of the waistband. Try to pinch out the same amount, but don't worry too much about it, you will be splitting the difference after you add the two sides together and divide them in half. Continue to pin and pinch out the side seams on either side of the body past the hips. Once you get to the thigh, you can either pin one side or both. Ask the client if they notice having one leg that is smaller than the other. If so, do both legs. If not, one leg is sufficient. Pin to the hem of the pant or as far down as desired by the client (5.3a). If taking in the pants at the side seams is sufficient, go to the next step. If more needs to be taken out, see pages 102–3 for inseam alterations.

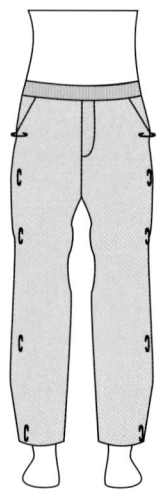

5.3a

2. Once the client has removed the pants, get out your calculator, pencil, and paper—it's time to do some math! Use the measurement chart on page 99 to mark how far the garment needs to be taken in and how far up or down from your marker points the pant will be taken in (5.3b).

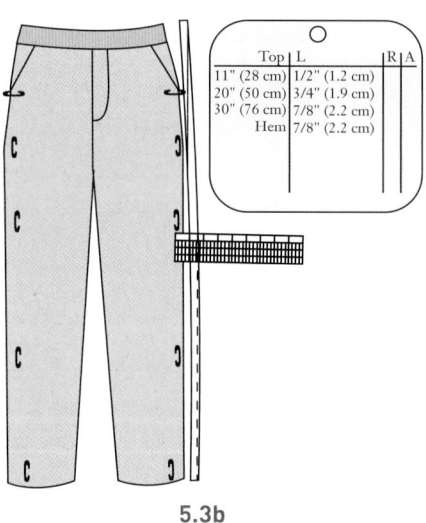

5.3b

3. Unpick topstitching on the side seams if present on the pant. If you are taking in the waistband, you will need to remove/unpick it to the distance it needs to be taken out plus 2" (5 cm) on either side (5.3c).

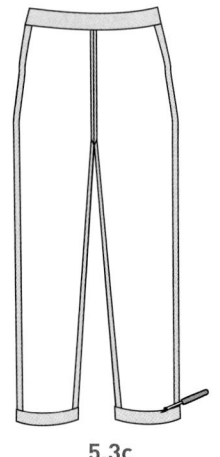

5.3c

4. Press the seam flat and mark the new measurements on the inside of the garment (5.3d).

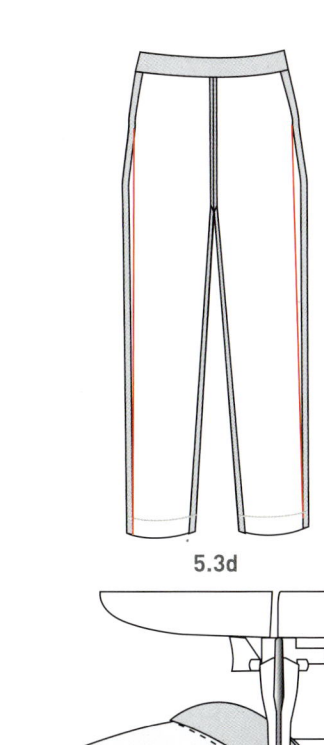

5.3d

5. Stitch the new seam lines beginning and ending with a backstitch (5.3e).

6. Unpick the old stitch line and press the seams open.

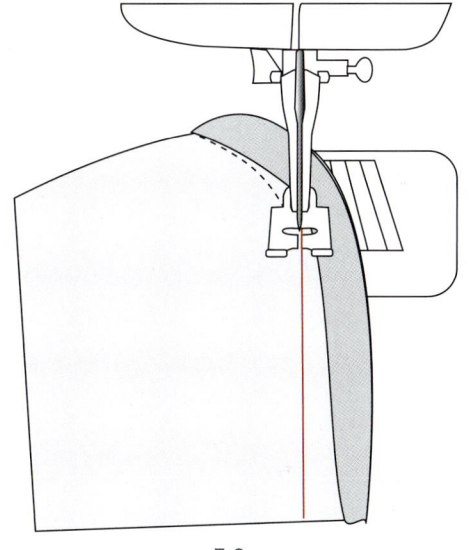

5.3e

7. Trim the excess seam allowance if it is more than ¾" (1.9 cm) with a serge or seam finish of your choice. You may also keep all the seam allowance if you would like to have the option to let the side seams out again at some point (5.3f).

8. Stitch and reattach the waistband if needed (see pages 94–5).

9. Restitch topstitching and hems if necessary.

10. Press the seams, clip the threads, and check the fit.

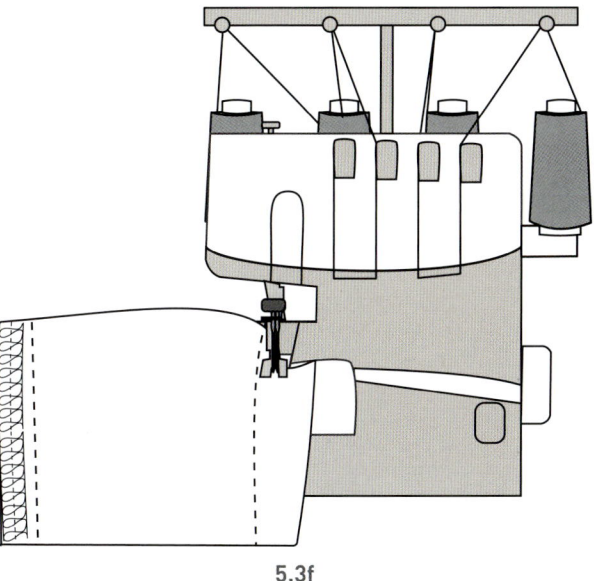

5.3f

SIDE SEAMS/OUTSEAMS | 101

INSEAMS

30 minutes–1 hour

1. Pinch out and pin the inseams from the hem up to the knee. If the inseams need to be taken in past the knee, ask the client to pin the amount out for you to maintain comfort and professionalism (5.4a).

2. If taking in the pants at the inseams is sufficient, go to the next step. If more needs to be taken out, go to the side seams instructions on pages 100–1.

3. Once the client has removed the pants, take out your calculator, pencil, and paper—it's time to do some math! Use the measurement chart on page 99 to mark how far the garment needs to be taken in and how far up or down from your marker points the pant will be taken in (5.4b).

4. Unpick topstitching on the inseams if present on the pant (5.4c).

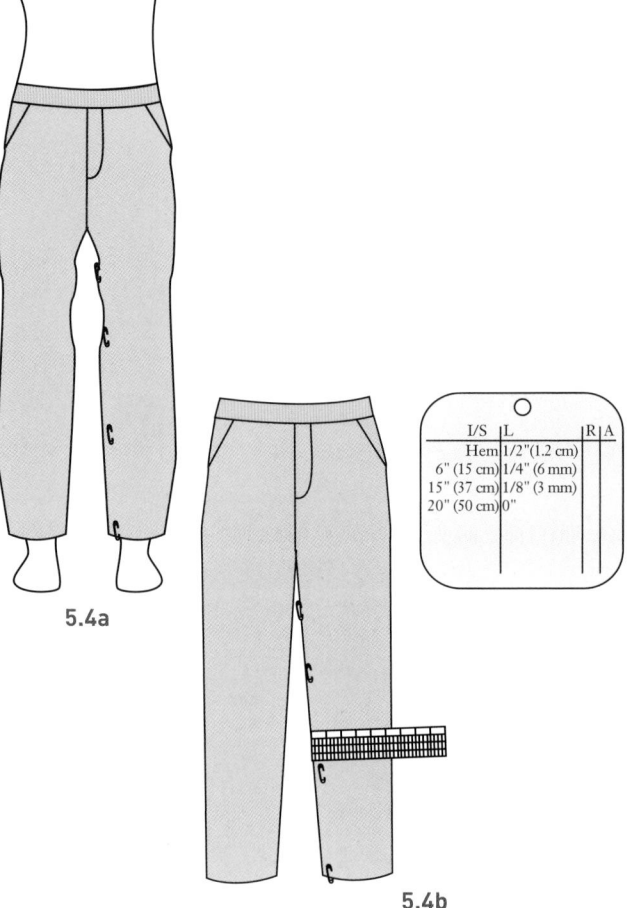

5.4a

5.4b

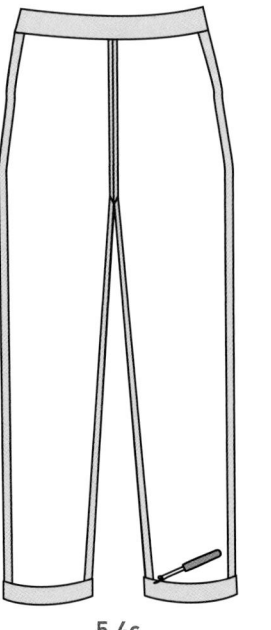

5.4c

CHAPTER 5 TAKING IN BOTTOMS

5. Press the seam flat and mark the new measurements on the inside of the garment (5.4d).

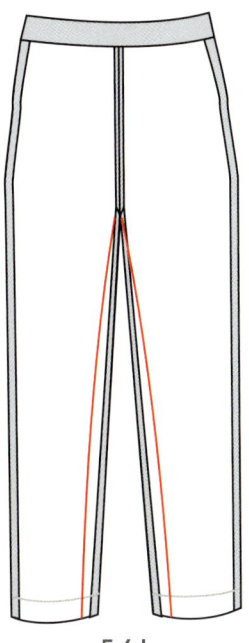

5.4d

6. Stitch the new seam lines (5.4e).

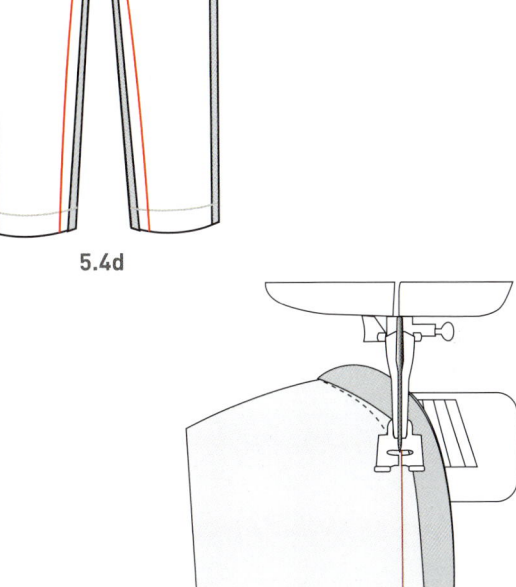

5.4e

7. Unpick the old stitch line and press the seams open.

8. Trim the excess seam allowance if it is more than ¾" (1.9 cm) with a serge or seam finish of your choice (5.4f).

9. Restitch topstitching if necessary.

10. Press the seams, clip the threads, and check the fit.

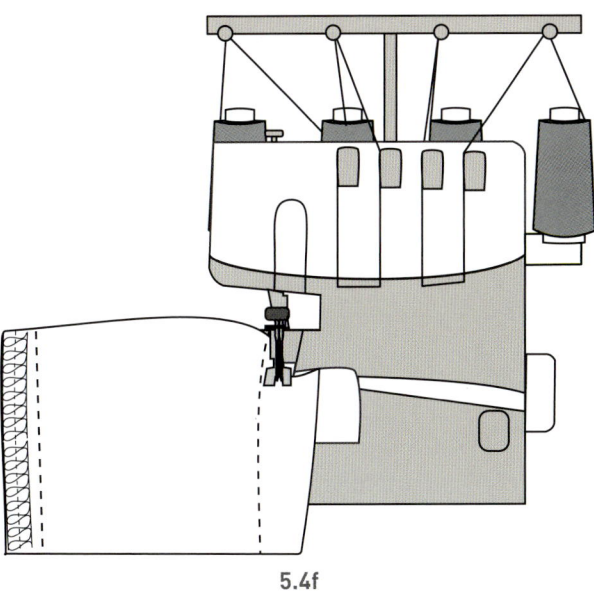

5.4f

INSEAMS

104 | CHAPTER 5 TAKING IN BOTTOMS

DARTS/PLEATS/TUCKS

30 minutes–1+ hours

Darts are a method of taking in and adding shape to a garment. They are often triangular or fisheye shaped and can really be sewn anywhere on a garment. The most common placement of darts in bottoms are in the princess seams at the waist, but can also be taken in in places like the knee (5.5a).

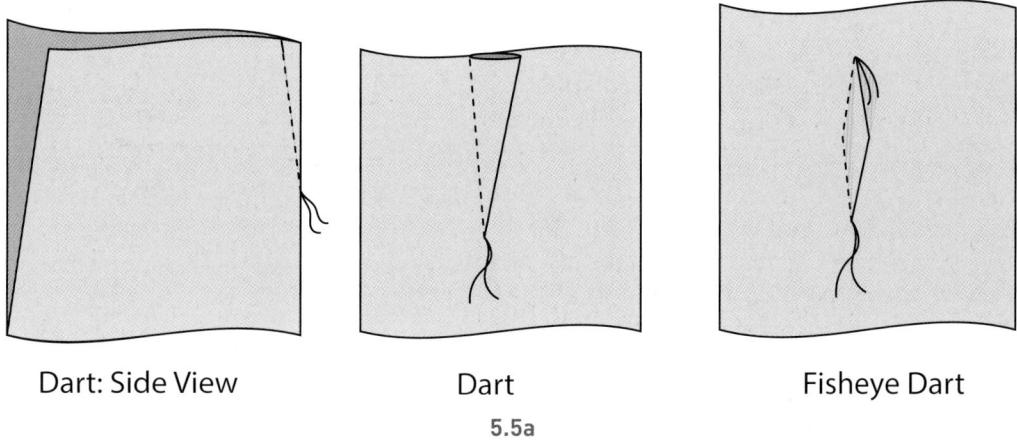

Dart: Side View | Dart | Fisheye Dart

5.5a

Pleats and tucks are a method of taking in a garment by folding the fabric on top of itself and stitching it in place. You can create box pleats, inverted pleats, knife pleats (5.5b), tucks, and pin tucks (5.5c).

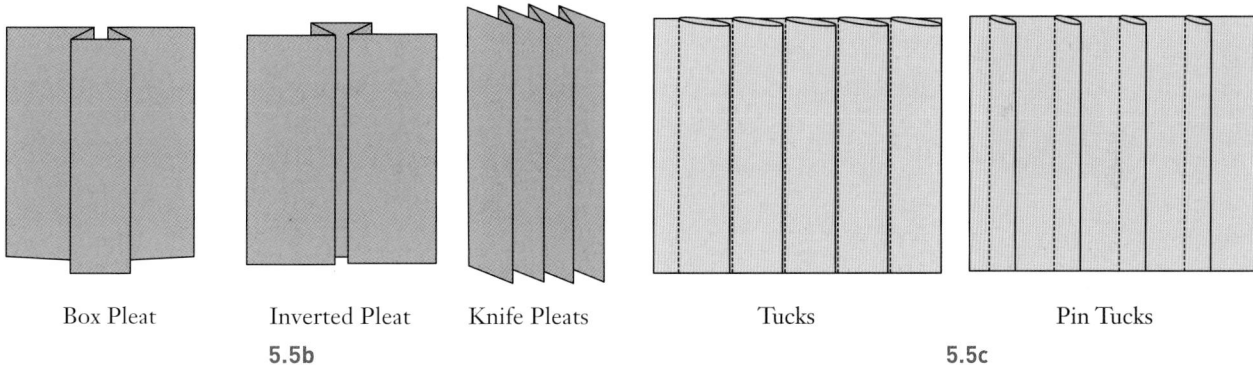

Box Pleat | Inverted Pleat | Knife Pleats | Tucks | Pin Tucks

5.5b 5.5c

For the next alteration, you can use darts, pleats, or tucks to take in the skirt at the waist. This illustration will demonstrate how to take in the waist using front waist darts. To see an example of using pleats/tucks for an alteration, see page 152.

1. Pinch and pin out the fabric as desired. Note the amount that needs to be taken in on each side (5.5d).

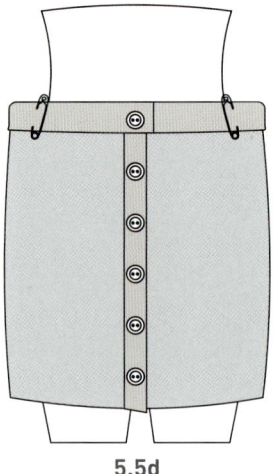

5.5d

2. If necessary, remove the waistband or topstitching (5.5e).

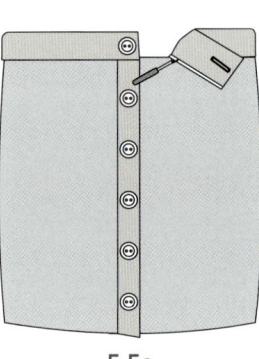

5.5e

3. Even out the placement of the darts/pleats/tucks on either side of the body and mark on the inside of the garment (5.5f).

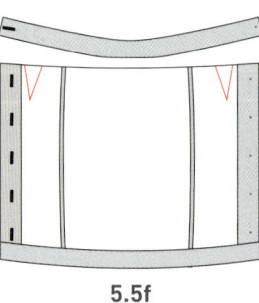

5.5f

4. Stitch the dart/pleat/tuck. Note that the ends of darts should not be backstitched, but tied off with a knot and with a ½" (1.2 cm) tail left at the end (5.5g).

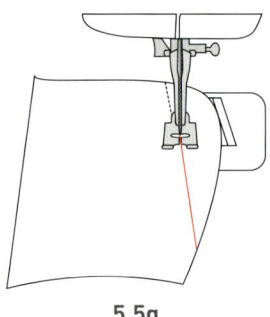

5.5g

5. Press the darts towards the side seams of the body (5.5h).

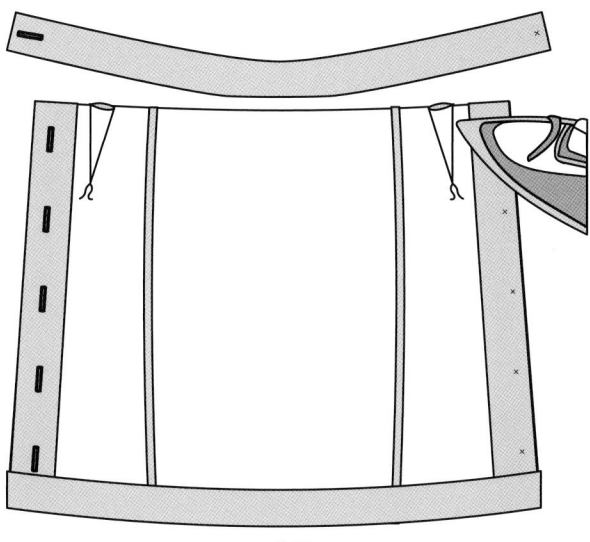

5.5h

6. Adjust the waistband if needed by taking in the center back, side, or center front seam or by creating a new seam. If there is a buttonhole or jean tack, you will not be able to take in the waistband at the center front and must use a side seam, center back seam, or create a new seam by cutting the waistband and stitching a new seam (5.5i).

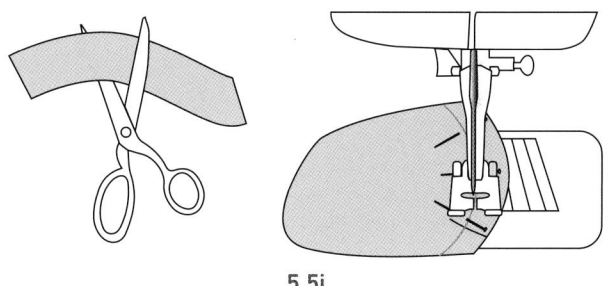

5.5i

7. Reattach the waistband.

8. Press the seams, clip the threads and check the fit (5.5j).

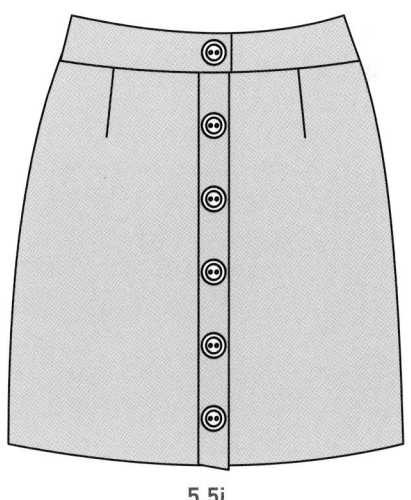

5.5j

DARTS/PLEATS/TUCKS | 107

EASE/GATHERS

30 minutes–1+ hour

Ease and gathers are created by running one to two rows of basting stitches (the longest stitch length on your sewing machine), pulling the thread to cinch in the fabric to fit the body, and then attaching the gathered fabric to a band (see 5.6e and 5.6f).

1. Pinch out the fabric on the garment so it takes in the desired amount at the side seam or center back. Note the measurement (5.6a).

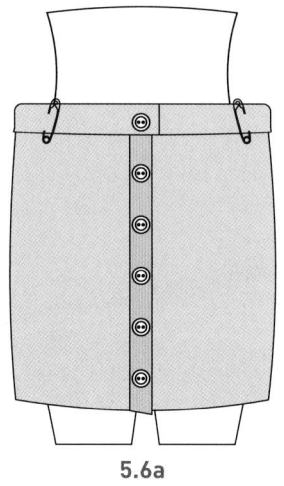

5.6a

2. Remove the waistband from the area that needs to be taken in (5.6b).

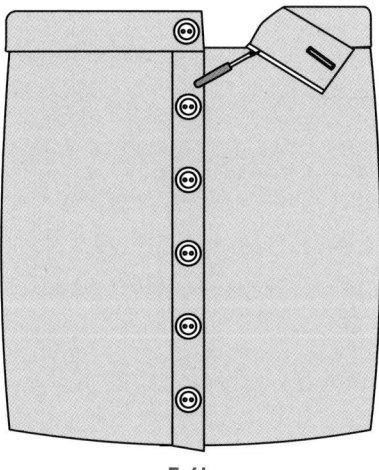

5.6b

3. Take in the waistband to the desired amount. Adjust the waistband if needed by taking in the center back, side, or center front seam or by creating a new seam. If there is a buttonhole or jean tack, you will not be able to take in the waistband at the center front and must use a side seam, center back seam, or create a new seam by cutting the waistband and stitching a new seam (5.6c).

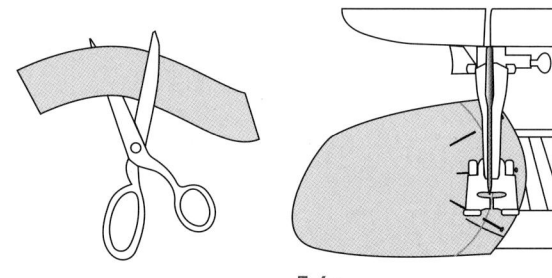

5.6c

108 | CHAPTER 5 TAKING IN BOTTOMS

4. Run two rows of basting stitches on the top of the waist on the skirt (5.6d).

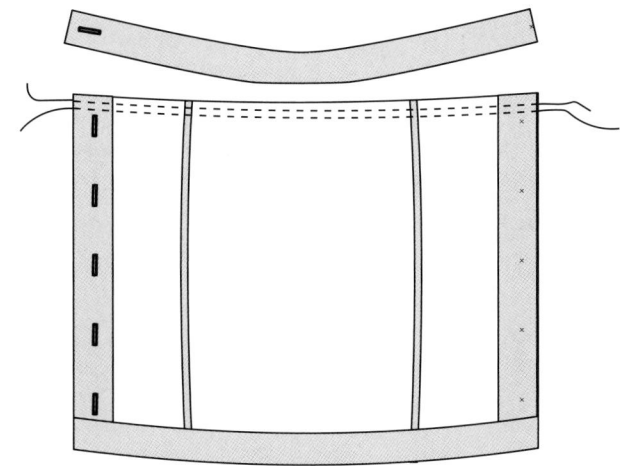

5.6d

5. Portion the waistband and waist fabric in half, thirds, or quarters. Pin in place.

6. Pull the gathering stitches (top threads only) until they match the waistband taking care to evenly distribute the fabric (5.6e).

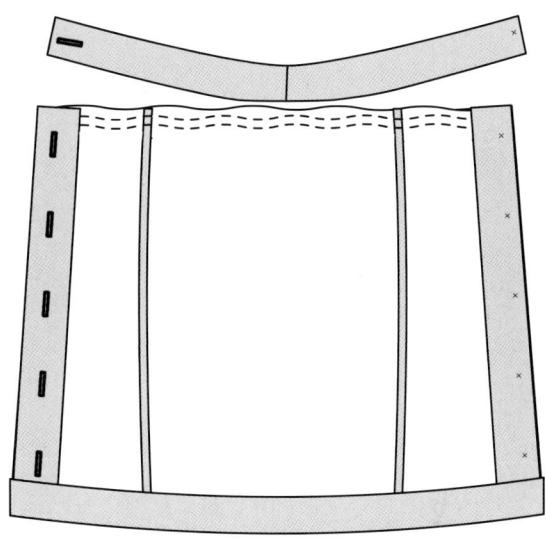

5.6e

7. Stitch the waistband onto the waist fabric.

8. Restitch topstitching if necessary.

9. Press the seams, clip the threads, and check the fit (5.6f).

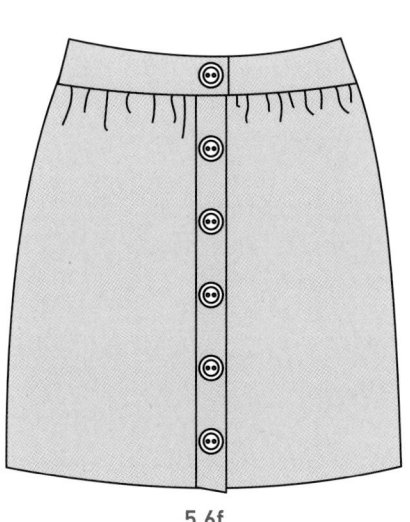

5.6f

EASE/GATHERS | 109

TAKING IN A SKIRT OR PANT WITH A SIDE ZIPPER

1+ hours

If a garment needs to be taken in at the location of a zipper, a left side zipper on a skirt for example, it is important to take in the side seams equally on the left and right sides of the body to maintain balance. Please note that there are many different types of zipper application including invisible, lapped, centered, and exposed zippers.

1. Pinch out and pin the side seams on either side of the waistband. Try to pinch out the same amount, but don't worry too much about it, you will be splitting the difference after you add the two sides together and divide them in half. Re-pin each side of the zipper side with safety pins so the garment can be taken off (5.7a).

5.7a

2. Note the measurements and unpin the garment.

3. Remove the waistband entirely (5.7b).

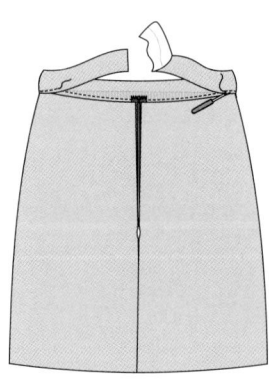

5.7b

4. Note the zipper application method.

5. Remove the zipper (5.7c).

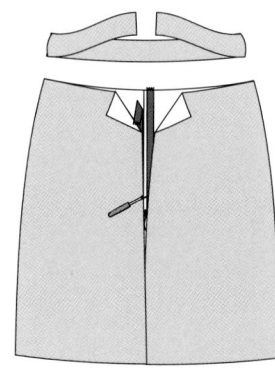

5.7c

6. Take in the side seams on the right side. Restitch the zipper at the new side seam lines, trim excess seam allowance (5.7d).

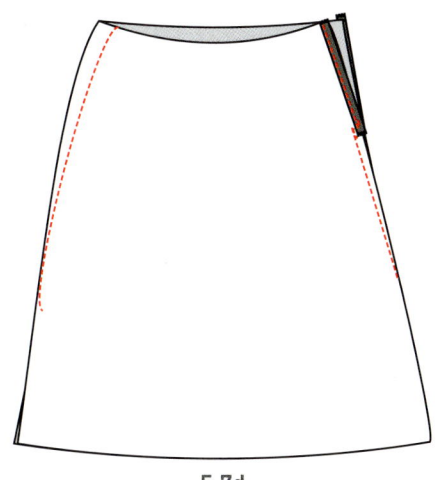

5.7d

7. Take in the waistband to the desired amount. Adjust the waistband if needed by taking in the center back, side, or center front seam or by creating a new seam. Reattach the waistband (5.7e).

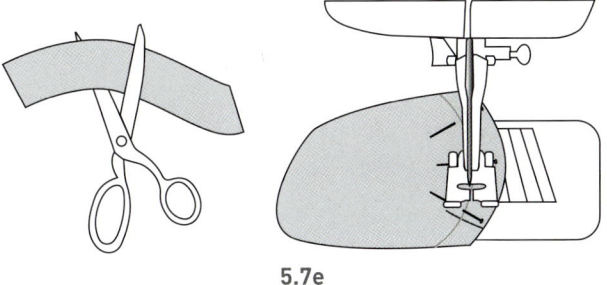

5.7e

8. Press the seams, clip the threads, and check the fit (5.7f).

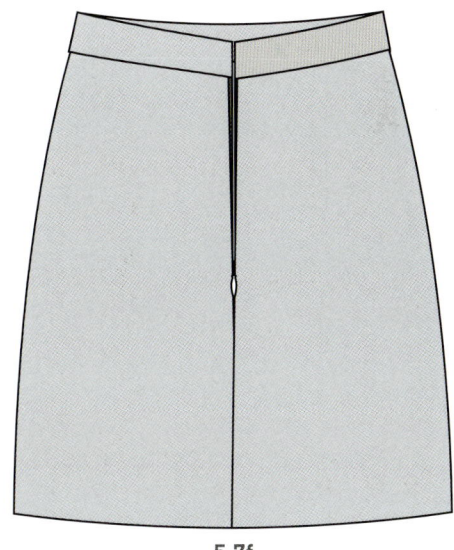

5.7f

TAKING IN A SKIRT OR PANT WITH A SIDE ZIPPER

CHAPTER 6

Letting Out Bottoms

For garments that are too small.
- Side seams
- Inseams
- Waistbands/side seams/center back seams
    - Using seam allowance
    - Using elastic
    - Using gussets/fabric panels

SIDE SEAMS

30 minutes–1 hour

1. Check to ensure that there is seam allowance on the side seams and note how much is on each seam to determine if there is enough to alter the garment. If there is some seam allowance, have the client try on the garment and use safety pins to mark where the pants are too tight (6.1a).

2. Before or after the client has removed the garment, measure their waist, and note the measurement. Next, measure the waist of the pants with the waistband closed. Note the difference to determine how much to let out. Remember that if you are letting out the pants over four seams, you will need to divide your total that needs to be let out by four (6.1b).

3. Remove the waistband if necessary.

4. Press the side seams flat and mark the new side seam stitch lines (6.1c).

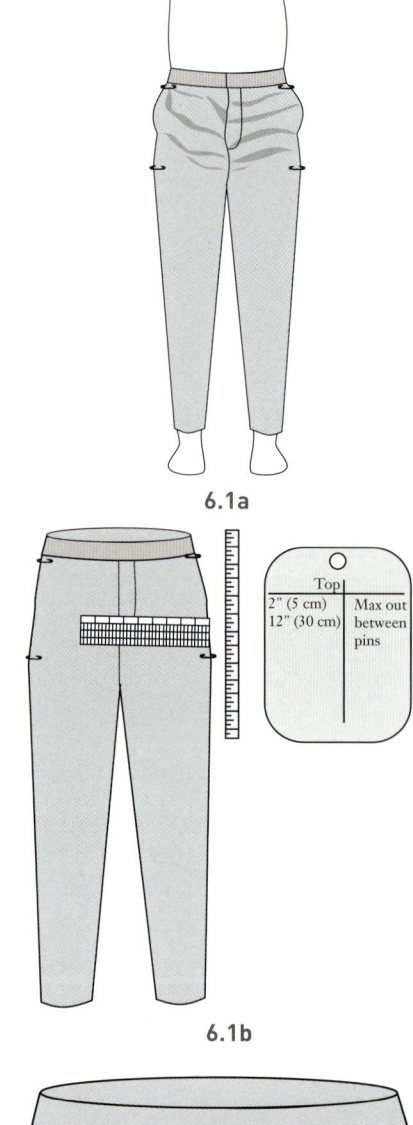

6.1a

6.1b

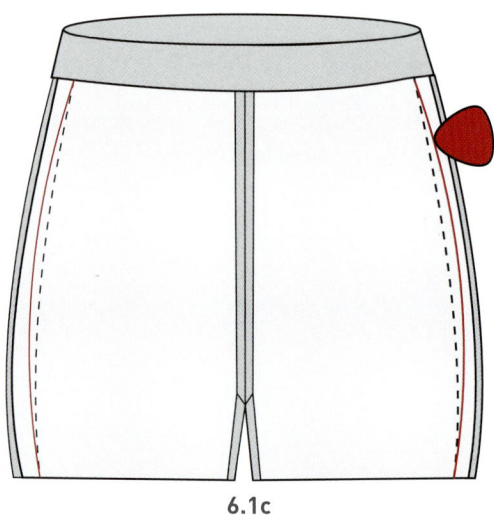

6.1c

CHAPTER 6   LETTING OUT BOTTOMS

5. Stitch the new line and backstitch directly over the vanishing point (6.1d).

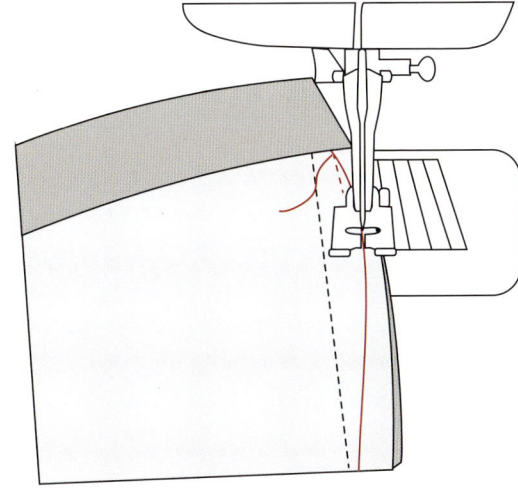

6.1d

6. Unpick the original seam stitching (6.1e).

7. Press the side seams open.

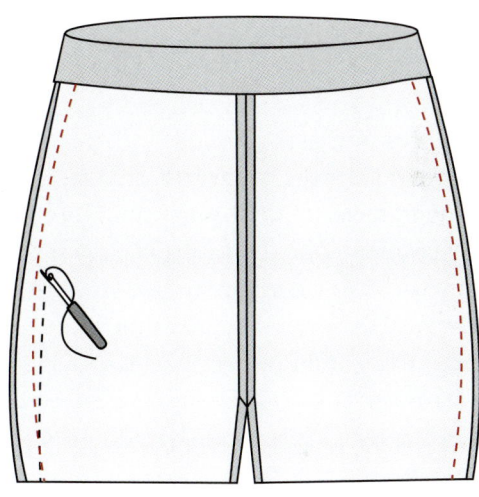

6.1e

8. If you removed the waistband, let it out if needed and then reattach it to the pants. If you need more seam allowance at the waistband, follow the instructions on pages 123–4.

9. Press the seams, clip the threads, and check the fit (6.1f).

6.1f

INSEAMS

30 minutes–1 hour

1. Check to ensure that there is seam allowance on the side seams and note how much is on each seam to determine if there is enough to alter the garment. If there is some seam allowance, have the client try on the garment and use safety pins to mark where the pants are too tight (6.2a).

2. Note that you may let out the garment with the inseams and side seams and/or more or less of the front or back pant leg.

3. Before or after the client has removed the garment, measure their ankles, calf, knee, and/or thigh and note the measurements where the garment is too tight. Next, measure the circumference of the pants with the waistband closed. Note the difference to determine how much to let out. Remember that if you are letting out the pants over four seams, you will need to divide your total that needs to be let out by four (6.2b).

4. If the seam allowance needs to be taken out through the hem, unpick the hem (6.2c).

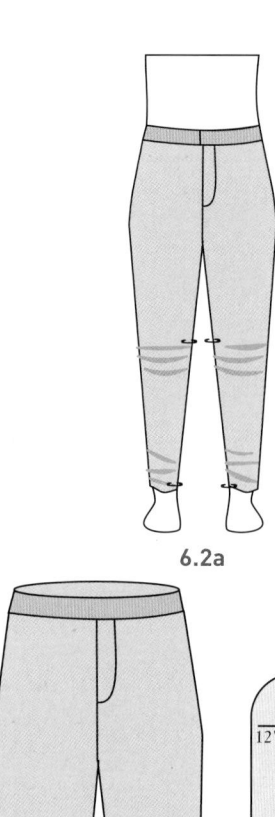

6.2a

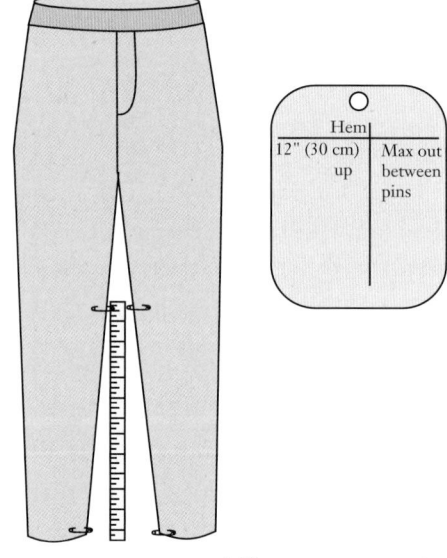

6.2b

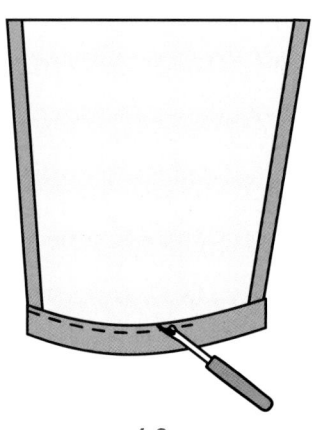

6.2c

116 | CHAPTER 6 LETTING OUT BOTTOMS

5. Press the inseams flat. Mark the new inseam stitch lines (6.2d).

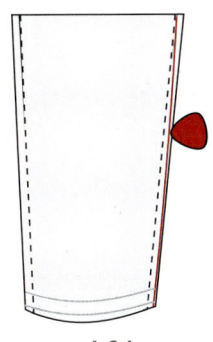
6.2d

6. Stitch the new line and backstitch directly over the vanishing point (6.2e).

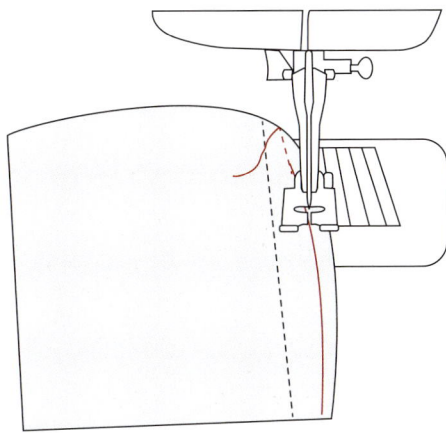
6.2e

7. Unpick the original inseam stitching (6.2f).

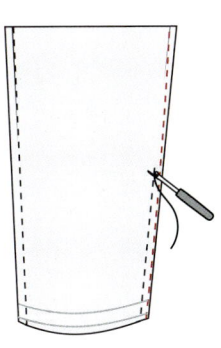
6.2f

8. Press the inseams as they originally were stitched. Restitch topstitching if it was originally on the inseam.

9. Restitch the hem if needed.

10. Press the seams, clip the threads, and check the fit (6.2g).

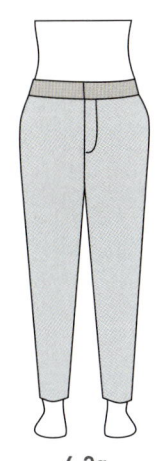
6.2g

WAISTBANDS: USING SEAM ALLOWANCE, ELASTIC, OR GUSSETS

30 minutes–1 hour

Follow steps 1–2 for all waistband alterations and then determine which method is best for your garment.

1. Check that the client has washed and dried the garment. If they have not washed it and it is already too small, recommend that they use a cold wash cycle and air dry or use a dry-cleaning service so that the garment does not shrink when washing.

2. There are two ways you can determine how much larger a garment needs to be.
   a. Option 1: Ask the client to put the bottoms on as far as they can. Measure the distance between the far edge of the buttonhole/bar and the center of the button/hook at the waistband. If the bottoms do not zip up, note at what point the zipper or closure can zip up to. Note the measurements (6.3a).

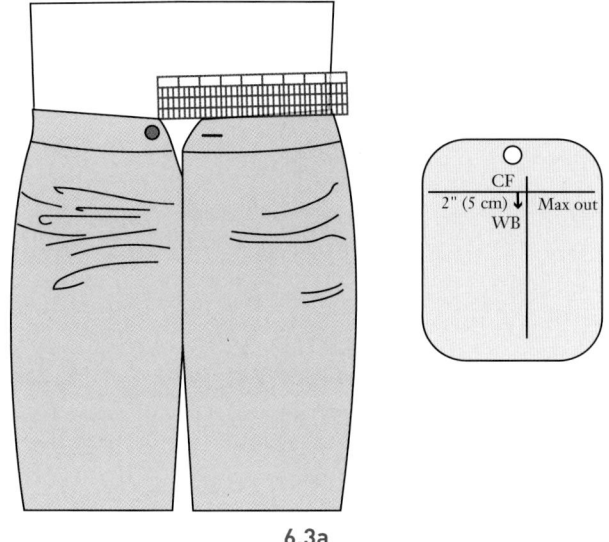

6.3a

   b. Option 2: Measure the client's waist at the point where the top of the bottoms will rest and then measure the circumference of the bottoms when they are closed/buttoned. Note the difference (6.3b).

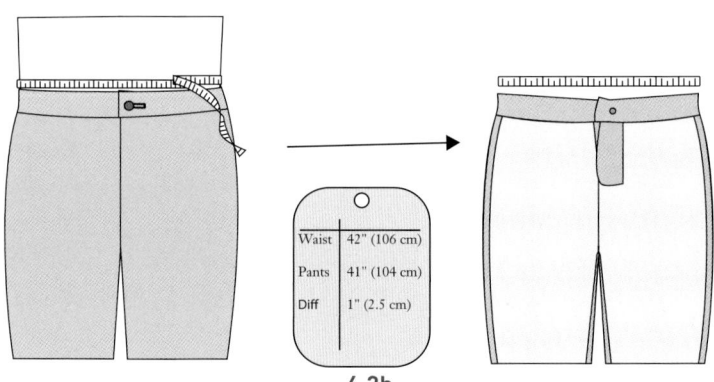

6.3b

WAISTBANDS: USING SEAM ALLOWANCE

30 minutes–1 hour

Using the seam allowance to let out a waistband is best in garments that have, you guessed it, excess seam allowance! This occurs often in men's dress pants, formalwear, and many woven garments. Check to see if there is seam allowance at the center back and side seams. If so, note how much extra room the client needs in their garment and compare it to how much seam allowance you have over the span of the center back and/or side seams while allowing an absolute minimum of ⅛" (3 mm) seam allowance on all seams. If there is enough seam allowance, this is the simplest option to let out a waistband.

1. Remove the waistband at the center back to the side seams if there is a front closure OR remove the entire waistband if there is a side closure (6.4a).

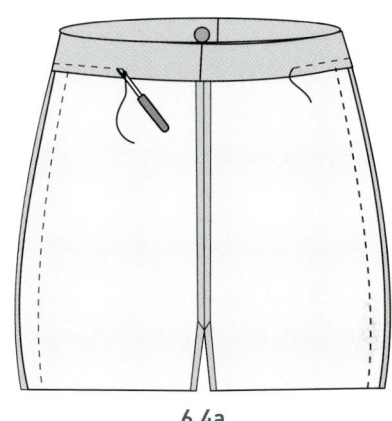

6.4a

2. Press the center back and/or side seams flat.

3. Mark the desired stitch line(s) to let out the bottoms the correct amount. This can be done by letting out the side seams and/or center back (6.4b).

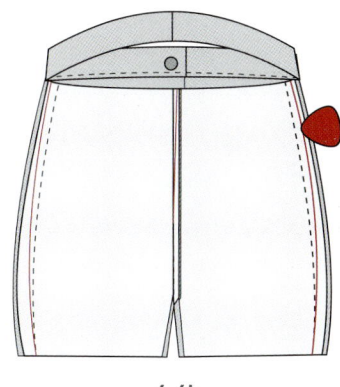

6.4b

4. Stitch the new line from the waistband down to the vanishing point (6.4c). Backstitch directly over the original stitching.

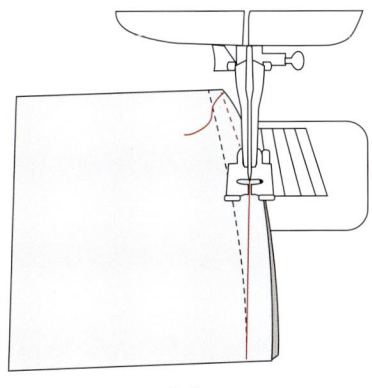

6.4c

5. Unpick the original stitch to the vanishing point (6.4d).

6. Press the seams open.

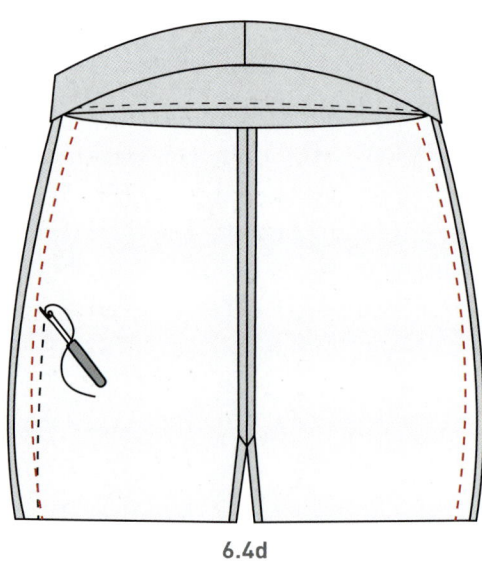

6.4d

7. If needed, let out the waistband at the center back and/or side seams if there is seam allowance (6.4e).

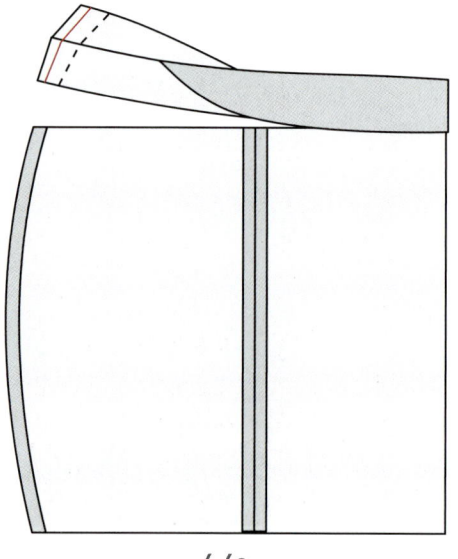

6.4e

8. Reattach the waistband (6.4f).

9. Press the seams, clip the threads, and check the fit.

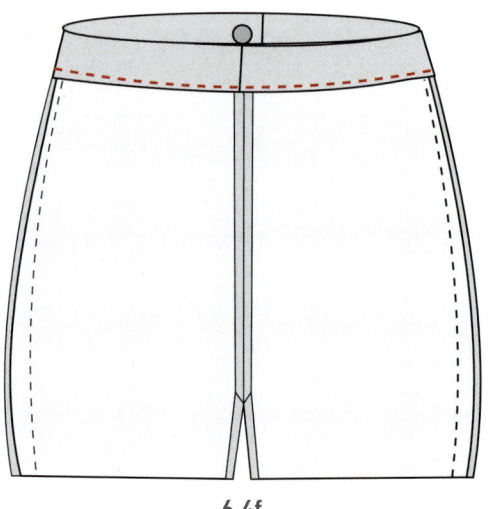

6.4f

WAISTBANDS: USING ELASTIC

30 minutes–1+ hours

Using elastic is a great option if the client fluctuates in their weight. Note that you can do this at the side seams or the center back. I have included instructions for side seams because the balance tends to look more aesthetically sound, but doing this at the center back only is a great option if you like how it looks!

1. Cut the side seam waistband and unpick the side seams to the vanishing point (6.5a).

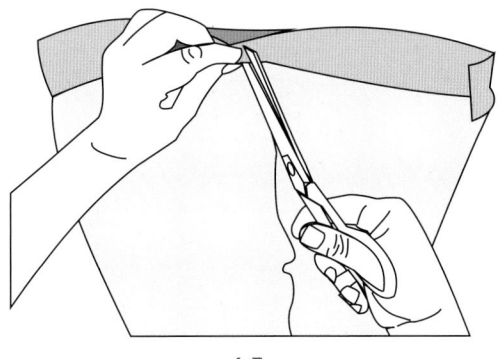

6.5a

2. Stitch the side seam at the vanishing point to secure it and press the seams flat (6.5b).

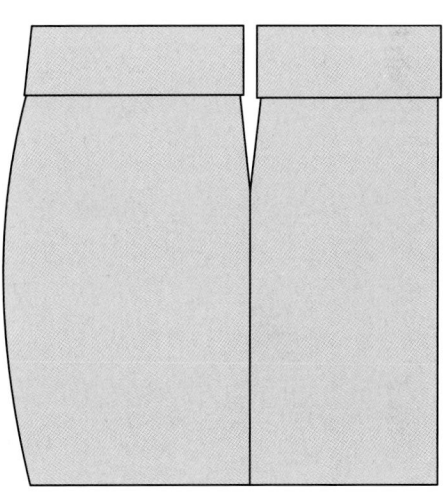

6.5b

3. Select elastic that is slightly wider than the space between seams, to allow for proper coverage (6.5c).

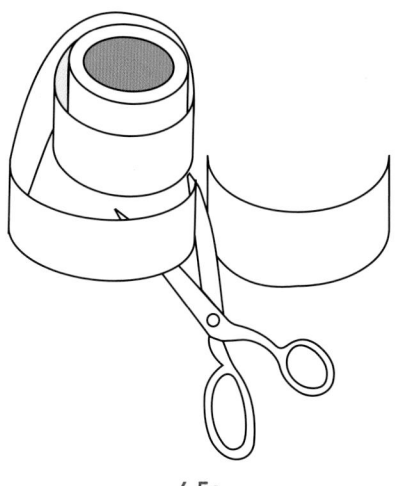

6.5c

WAISTBANDS: USING ELASTIC | 121

4. Mark out the elastic with the amount you need for the alteration at the top and taper down at the bottom of the elastic. Mark out ¼" (6 mm) to ½" (12 mm) seam allowance on the side and cut the elastic (6.5d).

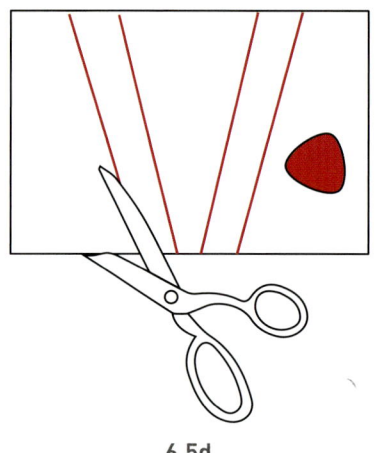

6.5d

5. Pin the elastic on the inside of the garment to the front side seams and serge or zigzag the raw edges together so the edges don't fray. Repeat the process on the back side seams (6.5e).

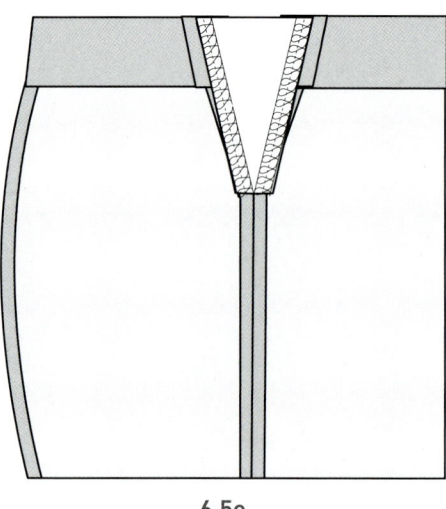

6.5e

6. Press the seams away from the elastic and topstitch the seam allowance down (6.5f).

7. Press the seams, clip the threads, and check the fit.

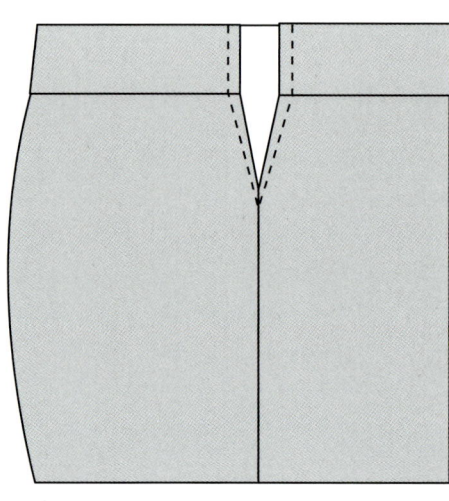

6.5f

WAISTBANDS: USING GUSSETS/FABRIC PANELS

1+ hours

A gusset is a piece of fabric that has been cut to a specific shape and size, often a football, triangle, or diamond shape, that is then sewn to a garment to allow for extra movement in a garment. Gussets are most common in the armpit and crotch seams. Using a gusset is similar to using elastic, except there will be less stretch. This is a great option if you have extra fabric that matches the original garment in fiber type and structure. You can use this method in the center back only or both side seams.

1. Cut the side seam waistband and unpick the side seams to the vanishing point (6.6a).

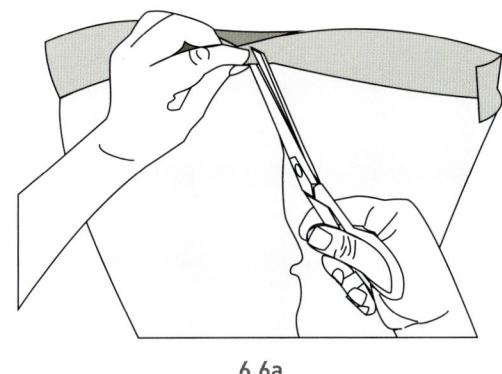

6.6a

2. Stitch the side seam at the vanishing point to secure it (6.6b).

3. Select fabric that is the same, or very similar, to the structure and fiber content of the original garment. For example, if you have a pant that is 100% polyester twill weave, look for a fabric that matches those credentials so that it will perform and wear the same as the rest of the garment.

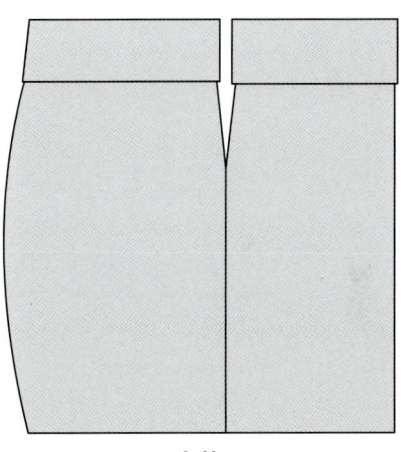

6.6b

4. Cut two (for center back alterations) or four (for side seams) triangle or gusset shapes that are the correct width and length plus ½" (1.2 cm) seam allowance on all sides (6.6c).

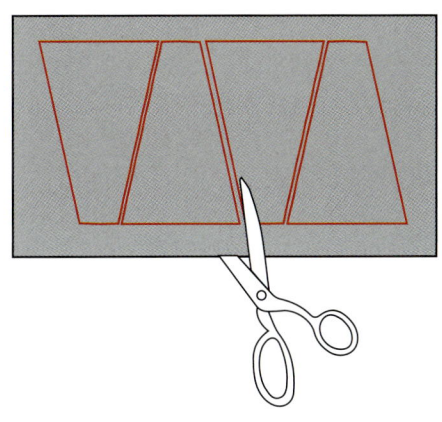

6.6c

5. With the right sides together, stitch two of the sides of the gusset at the top edge. Press the seam open and then press the seam flat so the top edge is finished. Serge or zigzag the remaining edges (6.6d).

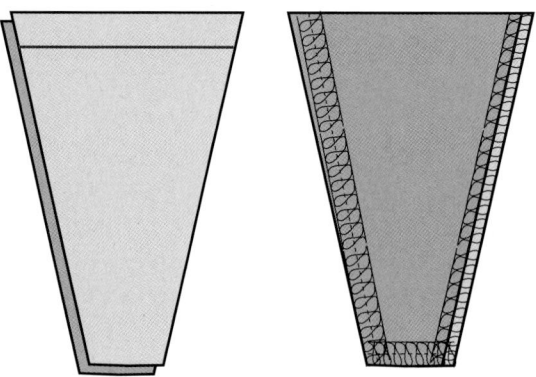

6.6d

6. Press the seams away from the gusset and topstitch the seam allowance down (6.6e).

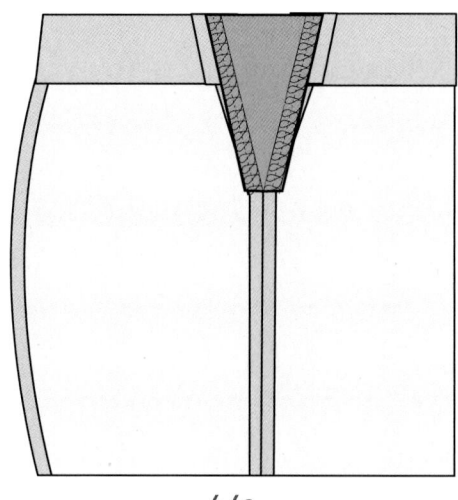

6.6e

7. Press the seams, clip the threads, and check the fit (6.6f).

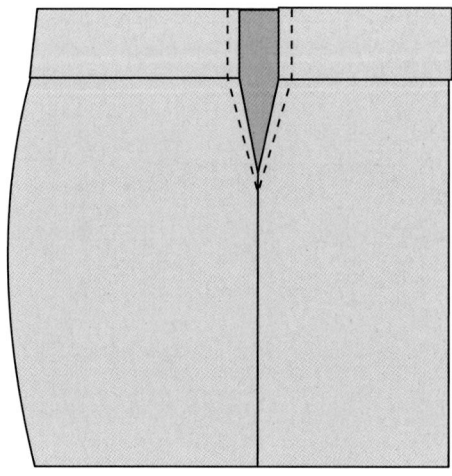

6.6f

CHAPTER 7

Jeans

Alterations specific to jeans or garments with construction similar to jeans.

- Taking in the center back/back gap: jeans
- Jeans hem with option to distress
- Original jeans hem
- Taking in the outseams/inseams

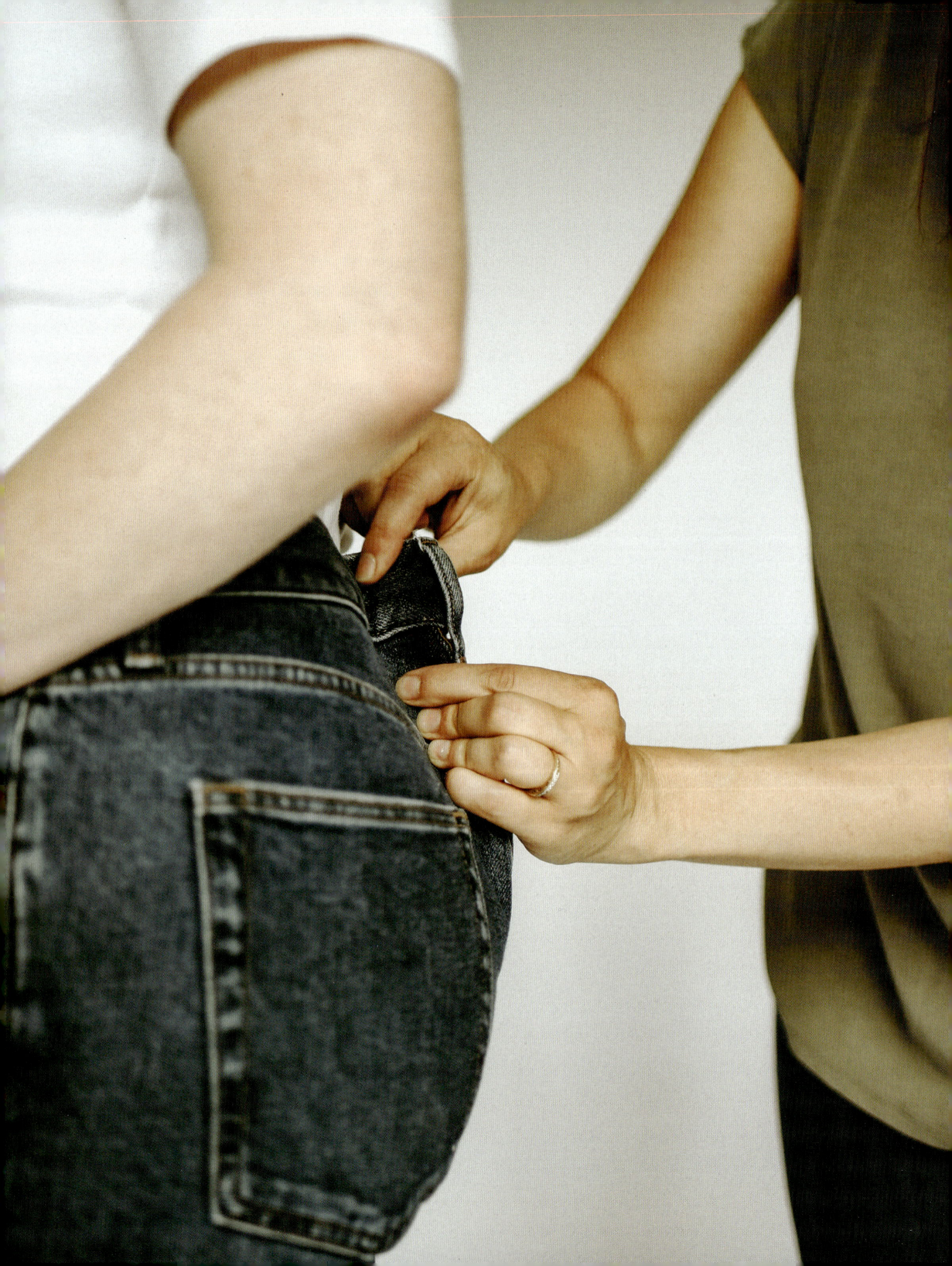

TAKING IN THE CENTER BACK/BACK GAP

1+ hours

I am not sure who coined the term "back gap," but I give full credit to my friend Emily who used to have this problem with every pair of pants she owned. People with a smaller waist to hip ratio may find this fit problem to be common.

1. Pinch out the center back of the jeans at the waistband, down the seam and to the vanishing point on the center back. If the vanishing point needs to be in the crotch area, note an approximate distance down so that you do not make the client uncomfortable (7.1a).

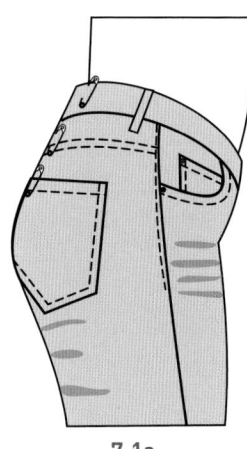

7.1a

2. Once the client has removed the pants, note the total amount needed to be taken in and divide that number by two (7.1b).

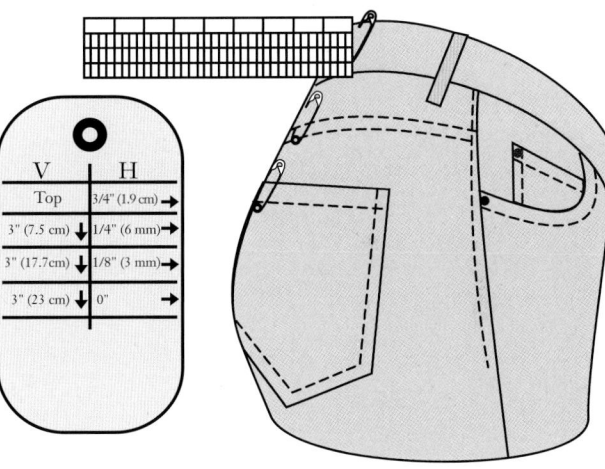

7.1b

3. Remove the waistband 2" (5 cm) past the amount that needs to be taken in on either side of the pant. Remove the center belt loop(s). I use a razor blade to the stitch line to remove the bar tack, or you can use a seam ripper (7.1c).

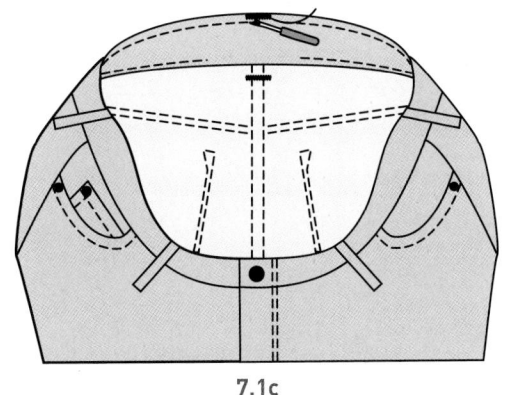

7.1c

4. Cut the waist band in half at the center. Remove the topstitching from the top and bottom of the waistband 2" (5 cm) past the amount that needs to be taken in on either side of the cut (7.1d).

5. Remove the two rows of topstitching 1" (2.5 cm) below the vanishing point. This is often stitched with a chain stitch, so unpick 1" (2.5 cm) below your vanishing point on the back crotch/rise seam and see if either end will unchain to avoid more seam ripping!

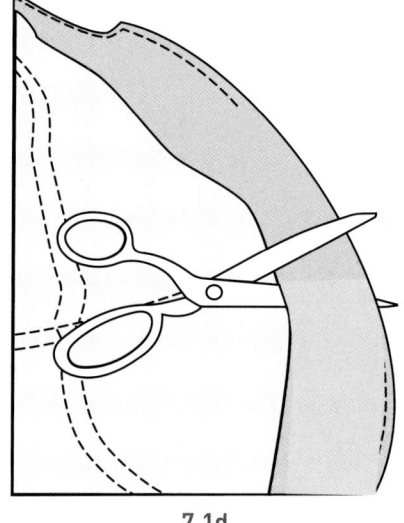

7.1d

6. Depending on how your jeans were constructed, serged, or flat felled, you will want to try to replicate it. It can be confusing to determine which stitch line to mark from since there are often two stitch lines on a flat fell seam. Use the line that is further away from the seam allowance as your "center" to mark from. After you have marked the seam, unpick the stitching, press the seam allowance flat taking care to not erase your chalk mark (7.1e).

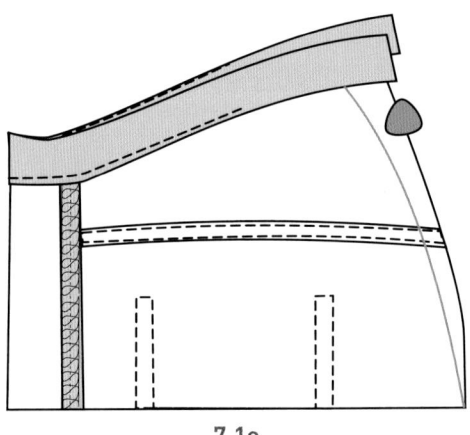

7.1e

7. Stitch the center back seams together on the half and taper to the original stitch line at the vanishing point. Be sure to use a smaller stitch length (2–2.5 SPI/SPC) as this is a seam that can easily come undone (7.1f).

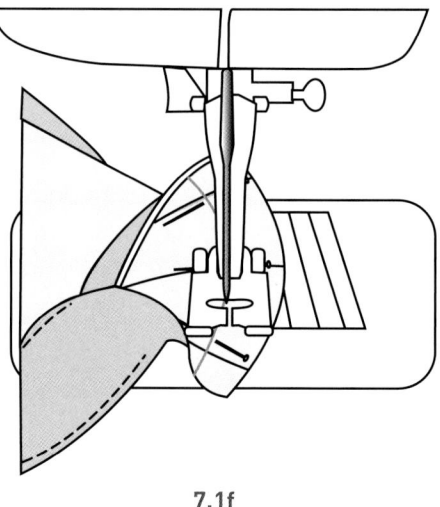

7.1f

130 | CHAPTER 7 JEANS

8. With right sides together, stitch the center back waistband at the desired amount to be taken in. Press the seams open and hammer them flat (7.1g).

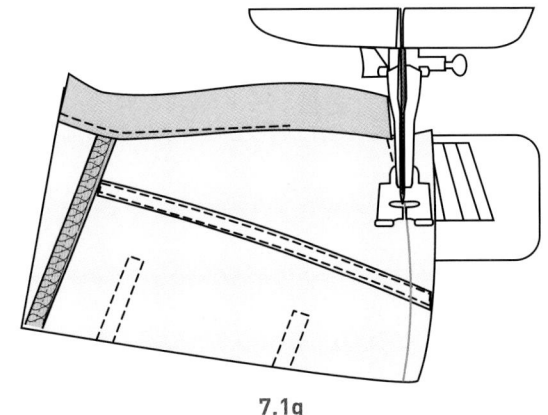

7.1g

9. Trim excess seam allowance on the center back and replicate the original seam finish if possible. Most likely this will be a faux flat fell seam (7.1h).

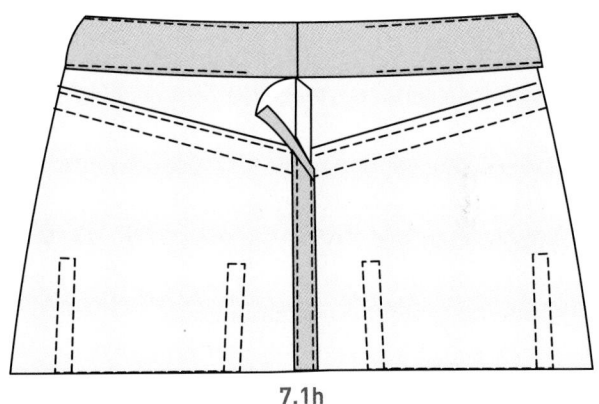

7.1h

10. Attach the waistband back to the pant to replicate what was done originally. Reattach the belt loops with a straight stitch. I have rarely succeeded in doing a bar tack with a home sewing machine on the multiple layers involved in a belt loop and waistband no matter the needle type and size. If you have a heavy duty bar tack or zigzag machine, use that machine and more power to you! If not, use a home machine, use the height compensation tool if you have it, and stitch back and forth over the top and bottom edges of the belt loops 3–4 times (7.1i).

11. Press the seams, clip the threads, and check the fit.

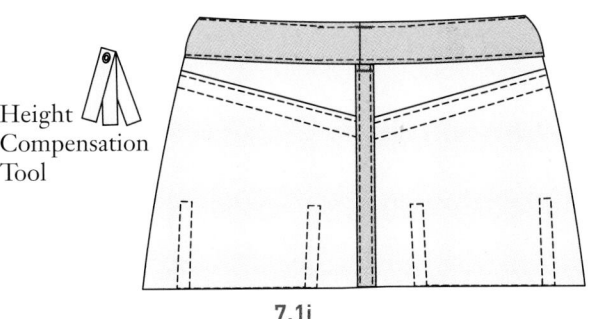

Height Compensation Tool

7.1i

JEANS HEM WITH OPTION TO DISTRESS

30 minutes–1 hour

1. Have the client put on the shoes, belt, and/or suspenders that they will most typically wear with the jeans. Determine the desired length of jeans and place a safety pin at the center back of the pant at that point (7.2a) (see pages 44–5 for pinning instructions).

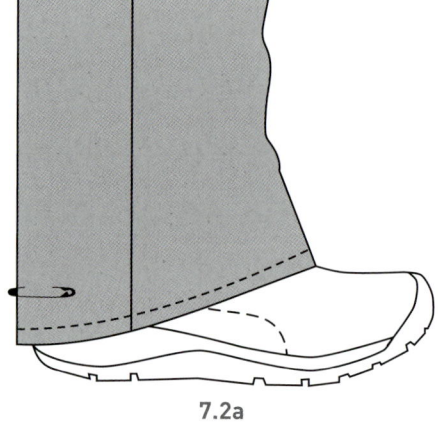

7.2a

2. Remove jeans and measure how far up from the original hem the safety pin is. Note this measurement (7.2b).

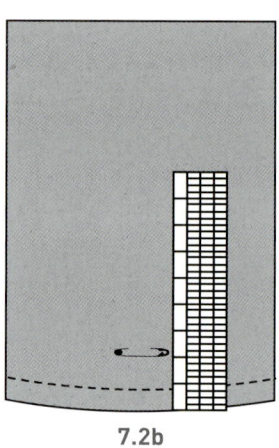

7.2b

3. Remove the safety pin and mark a straight line from the center back to each side seam. Flip the jeans over and mark side seam to side seam. Turn the jeans so that the side seams are touching to be sure your line is straight. Because it is common for jeans hems to be uneven from the manufacturer, it is important to measure from this line rather than measuring the same distance all the way around the hem (7.2c).

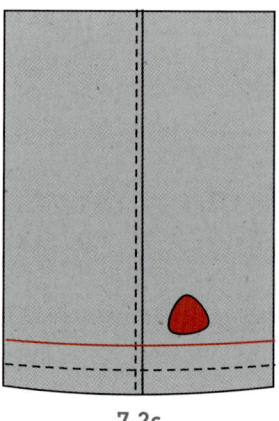

7.2c

132 | CHAPTER 7 JEANS

4. Measure the hem depth and add ⅜" (1 cm) to ½" (1.2 cm) of seam allowance to that measurement (if the original hem was ½" (1.2 cm) you would add ⅜" (1 cm) for a total of ⅞" / 2.2 cm). Draw a line below your original chalk line at this distance. This is your cut line. Note that you may have to unpick the hem if the cut line goes through the stitch line.
5. Be sure you are cutting the bottom line and remove the excess fabric. Pinch the fabric at the center front and clip it to keep the jeans hem in a complete circle in case of an error (7.2d).

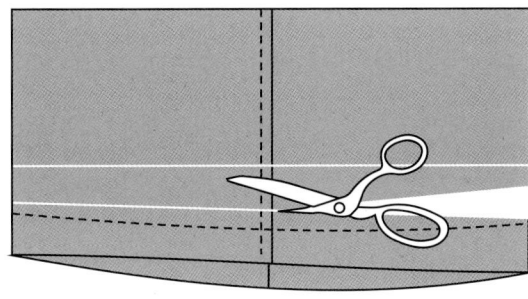

7.2d

6. Press at the top line and then mark, turn, pin, and press the seam allowance under at the ⅜" (1 cm) or ½" (1.2 cm) point. To speed up the process, I like to press at the center front, center back, side seams which causes the seam allowance in-between to naturally fall in place. Hammer the side and inseam to flatten the seam allowance on the inside of the hem.

***Go to step 10 if you would like to distress the hem.

7. Insert the correct needle into your machine: denim needle for wovens OR ball point needle for jeans with stretch. Set your stitch length to something longer than you would use for seams and shorter than a basting stitch, usually 4 to 4.5 SPI. Thread the bottom of your machine with jeans thread and the top in all-purpose thread (a). OR use all-purpose on the top and bottom (b). OR use jeans thread in the top and bobbin (c). Each option has a different aesthetic, and some options will work better than others depending on your machine.

8. If you have a blind hem/edge foot, sew on the inside fold of the jeans with jeans thread in the bobbin (7.2e). If you do not have this foot, keep your hem consistent by sewing as close to the turn of the cloth on the seam allowance as possible (1/16" (2.6 cm)). Begin and end your stitch on the back of the inseam to conceal the backstitch.

9. Clip your threads and press the hem. Try the pants on with the shoes to check the length.

***If you would like to replicate the distressing at the bottom of your jean hem there are several options to imitate the discoloration. If you are happy with the look of the jeans after step 8, do not continue on to the next step.

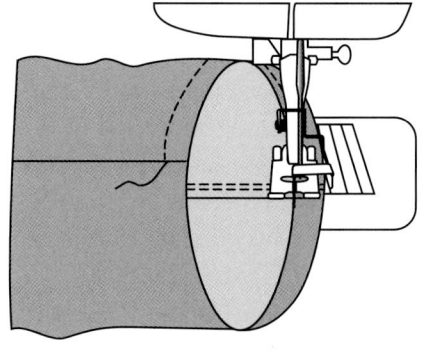

7.2e

To Distress

10. Take a piece of sandpaper and wrap/staple it to a small piece of wood OR use a hand sander. Use sandpaper with a #220 grit or coarser. Using a downward motion, sand on the outside of the jeans where the seam allowance has been folded down to the turned edge. Be careful not to rip holes in the hem and do as much or as little distressing as you like. You may also distress the jeans after you stitch them, but you run the risk of damaging the stitching that is holding the jean hem in place (7.2f).

11. Go back to step 6 and complete sewing the hem.

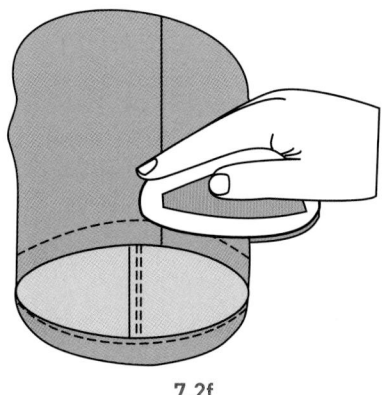

7.2f

TIPS:

This method of shortening jeans is permanent. If you are looking for something that is adjustable, especially for children and teenagers, consider the next hemming method—the original jean hem.

Test a sample of your topstitching on the scrap of hem that you cut off. If the hem mark is within ⅞" (2.2 cm) of the hem topstitching line you will have to seam rip the original hem, press the fabric, and then mark your turn, seam allowance, and cut lines.

ORIGINAL JEANS HEM

30 minutes–1 hour

1. Have the client put on the shoes, belt, and/or suspenders that they will most typically wear with the jeans. Determine the desired length of jeans and place a safety pin at the center back of the pant at that point (7.3a) (see pages 44–5 for pinning instructions).

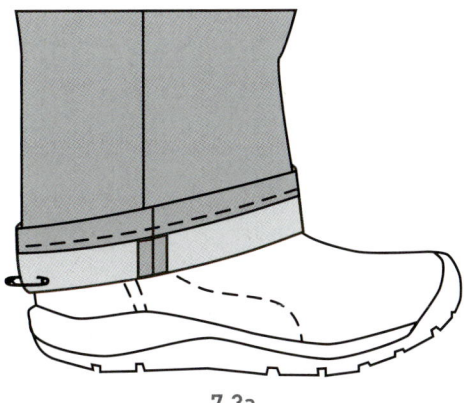

7.3a

2. Remove jeans and measure how far up from the original hem the safety pin is. Note this measurement. Remove the safety pin and mark a straight, horizontal line from the center back to each side seam. Flip the jeans over and mark side seam to side seam. Turn the jeans so that the side seams are touching to be sure your line is straight. Because it is common for jeans hems to be uneven from the manufacturer it is important to measure from this line rather than measuring the same distance all the way around the hem (7.3b).

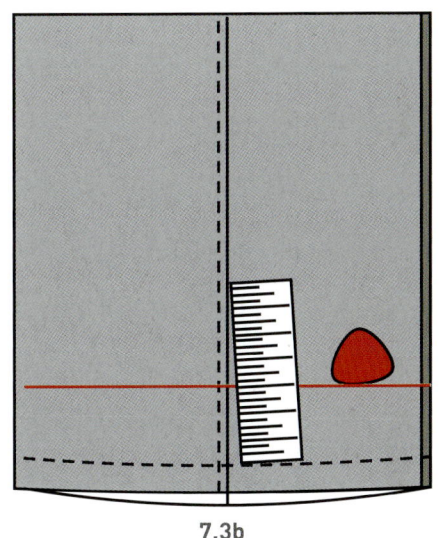

7.3b

3. Measure the distance from the topstitching on the hem to the bottom hem and note that measurement. Draw a line ABOVE your original chalk line at this distance. Line up the original hem up to this top line and pin at the center front, center back, and pin in the ditch on both side seams (7.3c).

***Alternatively, you can measure the distance from the original hem to the new hem line and add the hem depth to that measurement and mark one line.

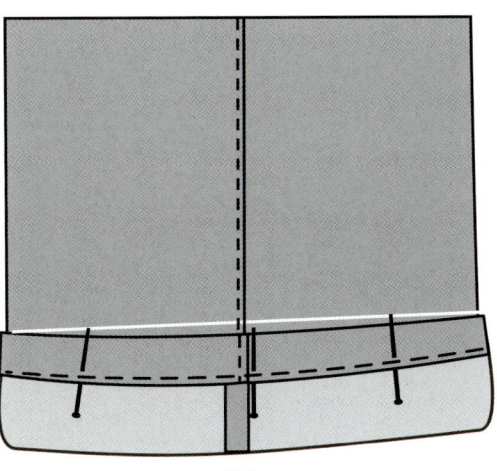

7.3c

ORIGINAL JEANS HEM | 137

4. Using thread that matches the color of the outside of the pant, stitch as close as you can to the original turn of the seam allowance just to the side of the topstitching thread. Begin your stitching just before the inseam and end with a backstitch in the same spot. It is difficult to go over the bulk of the seams, so you may need to hand crank your sewing machine wheel over those sections or use the jeans gauge to level the front and back of the presser foot (7.3d).

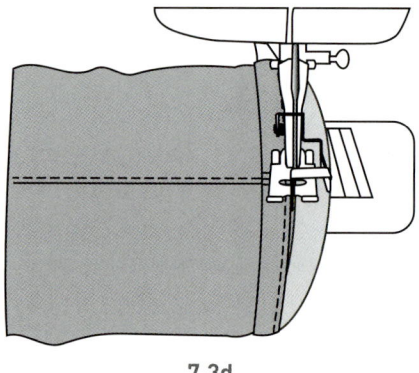

7.3d

5. Turn the hem down and check your accuracy on the other side. If the seams are too far off, unpick, re-pin, and try again (7.3e).

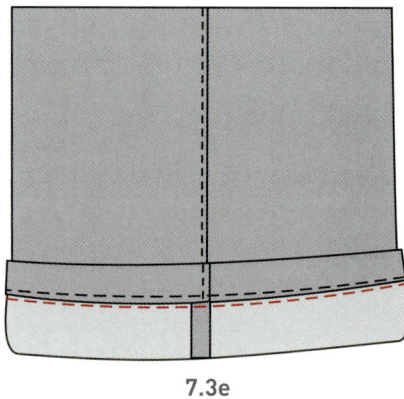

7.3e

6. If you are pleased with your stitch, press the excess fabric up and away from the hem and use a thread that matches the fabric to stitch in the ditch to keep the new hem in place (7.3f).

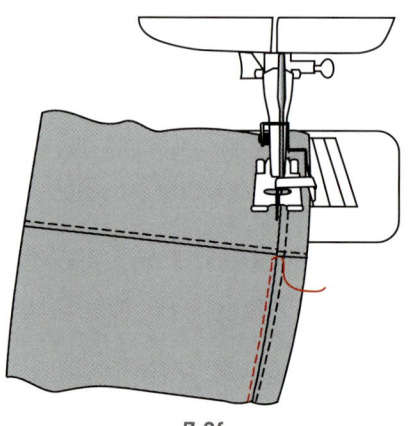

7.3f

7. There are a few options to finish the excess fabric on the inside of the jeans. Read through each option to determine which method will best suit your alteration needs.

   a. Hand stitch with a cross-stitch, around the excess fabric if you would like to keep the length (7.3g). This option is great for children's and teens' clothing so you can let the hem out as they grow.

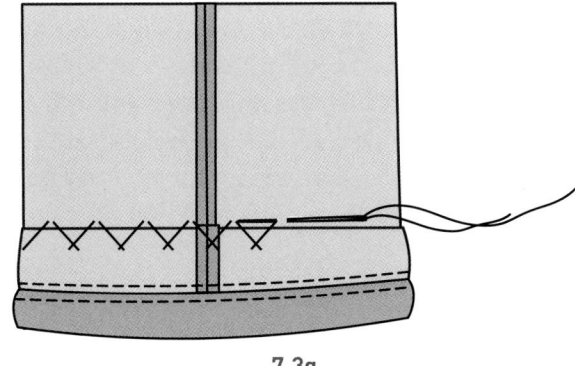

7.3g

   b. Stitch in the ditch up the edges of the side and outseams if there is less than ¾" (1.9 cm) excess fold to secure seam allowance (7.3h).

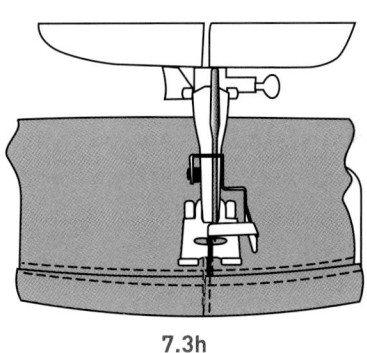

7.3h

   c. Serge or cut and zigzag the excess seam allowance down to ½" (1.2 cm) if there is more than ¾" (1.9 cm). Stitch in the ditch at the inseam and outseam to secure seam allowance (7.3i).

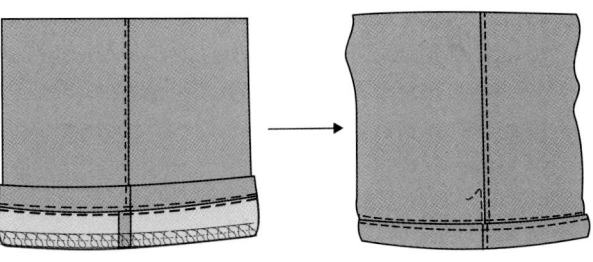

7.3i

TAKING IN THE OUTSEAMS/INSEAMS

1+ hour

Occasionally you will have a pair of pants that only need the outseam or inseam taken in. More commonly, both need to be taken in for the pants to feel balanced. Usually, the pants can be taken in evenly from the inseams and outseams, but sometimes you will need to take more fullness from the front pant or the back pant so that the side seam/inseam are perpendicular to the ground. If the seams are not perpendicular, you may notice that the seam swings forward and backward and feels uncomfortable or twisted for the wearer.

1. Pinch out the outseam on one leg unless the client has noticeably different leg sizes from the hem up (7.4a).

2. Pinch out and pin the inseams from the hem up to the knee. If the inseams need to be taken in past the knee, ask the client to pin the amount out for you to maintain comfort and professionalism.

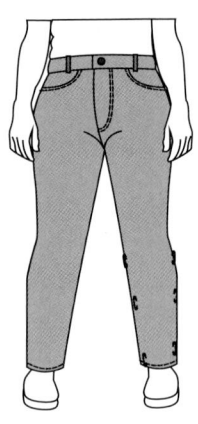

7.4a

3. Once the client has removed the jeans, take out your calculator, pencil, and paper—it's time to do some math! Use the measurement chart on page 99 to mark the alteration measurements (7.4b).

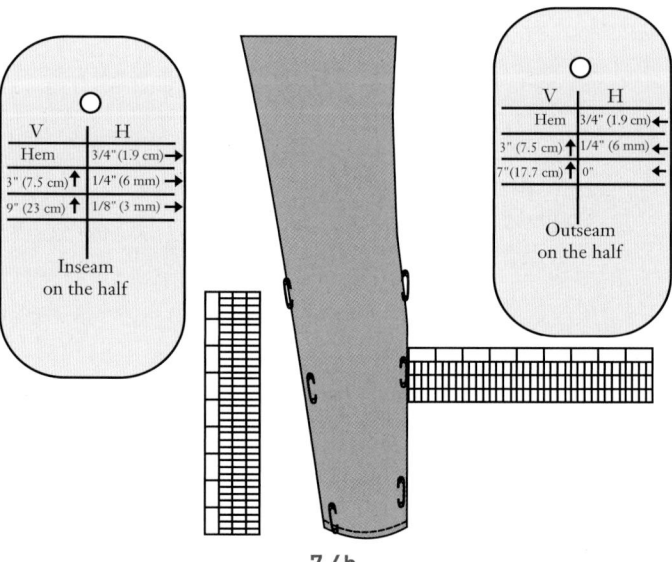

7.4b

140 | CHAPTER 7 JEANS

4. Unpick the hem and topstitching on the inseams on the jeans (7.4c).

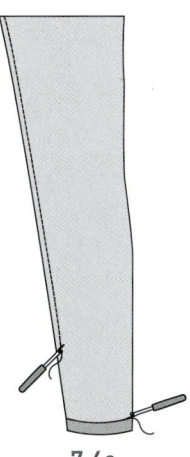

7.4c

5. Press the seam flat and mark the new measurements on the inside of the garment (7.4d).

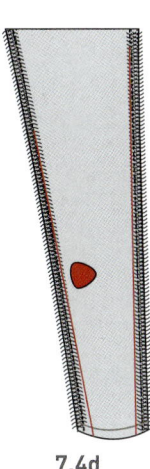

7.4d

6. Stitch the new seam lines making sure to backstitch and stitch directly over the original stitching to secure the seam at the top vanishing point (7.4e).

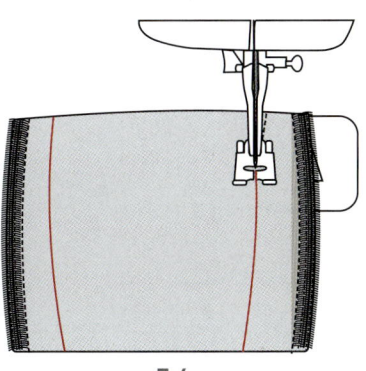

7.4e

7. Unpick the old stitch lines on the inseams and outseams and press them to their original position.

8. Trim the excess seam allowance if it is more than ¾" (1.9 cm) with a serge or seam finish of your choice (7.4f).

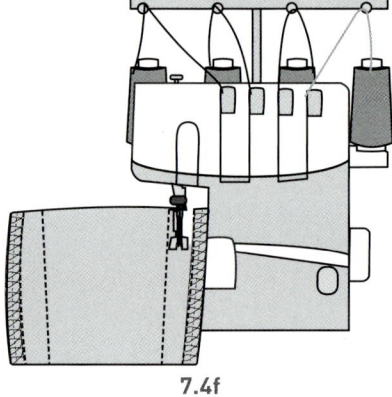

7.4f

9. Restitch topstitching and the hem (7.4g).

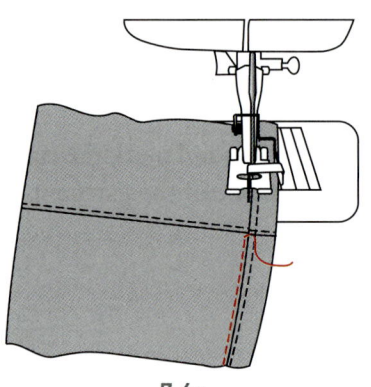

7.4g

10. Press the seams, clip the threads, and check the fit.

CHAPTER 8

Taking in Tops

For tops that are too large and/or need to be fitted.

Note that the fabric type (knit or woven) and seam styles (serged, flat fell, French seam, etc.) will affect how you take in the garment. The illustrations in this section may or may not reflect your project.

- Side seams
- Princess seams/darts on front top
- Princess seams/darts on back top
- Pleats/tucks
- Boned bodices in formalwear

SIDE SEAMS

30 minutes–1+ hours 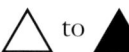 to

1. Pinch out and use safety pins to pin the side seams of the shirt from the top to the bottom establishing a vanishing point OR pinning through the sleeve (8.1a).

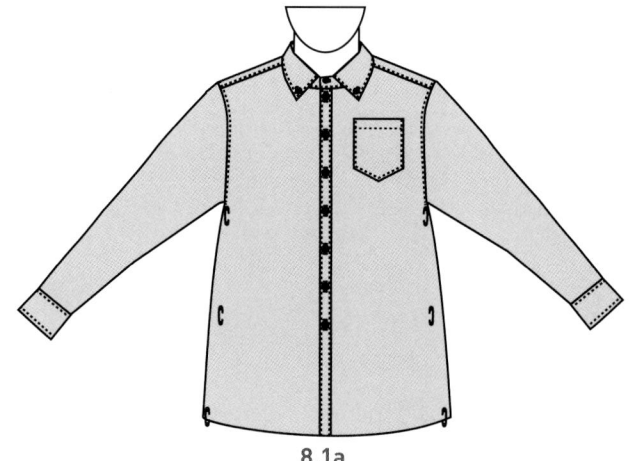

8.1a

2. Have the client remove the shirt. Make or use the measurement chart (page 99) to note and even out the measurements on either side of the body (8.1b).

3. Once you have the measurements noted, remove the pins, turn the garment inside out, and determine how to replicate the seam finish.

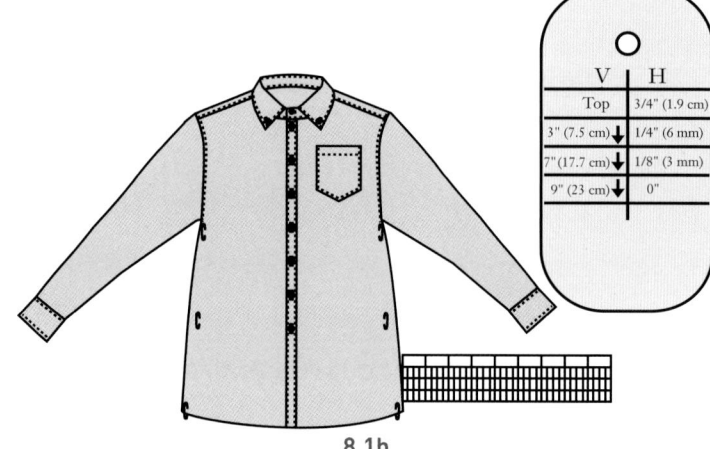

8.1b

4. If the side seams need to be taken in through the bottom hem or sleeve hem, unpick the hem 1" (2.5 cm) past the amount that needs to be taken in on either side (8.1c).

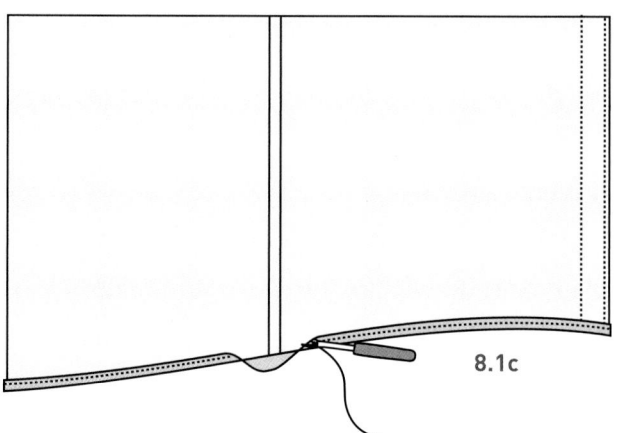

8.1c

5. Mark and sew the new side seams (8.1d). See the guide below to determine how to restitch your side seams (8.1e).

   a. Serge

   b. Flat fell: if the shirt is opaque, you can get away with a mock flat fell/serge and stitch. If it is transparent at all (white shirts), you must recreate the flat fell seam. Charge more for this alteration as it will take you much longer than other seam finish types.

   c. French seam

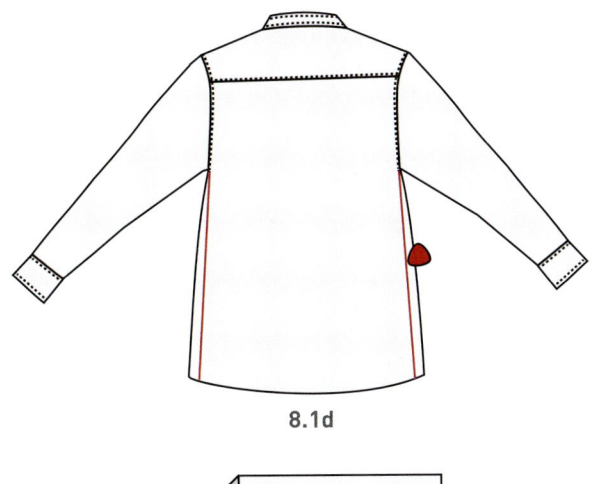

8.1d

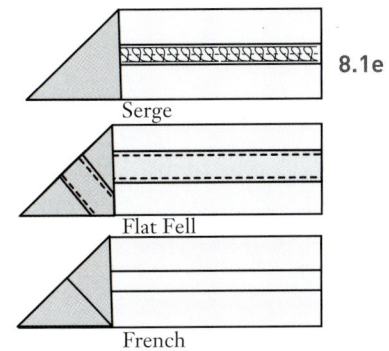

8.1e

6. Stitch the new side seams (8.1f).

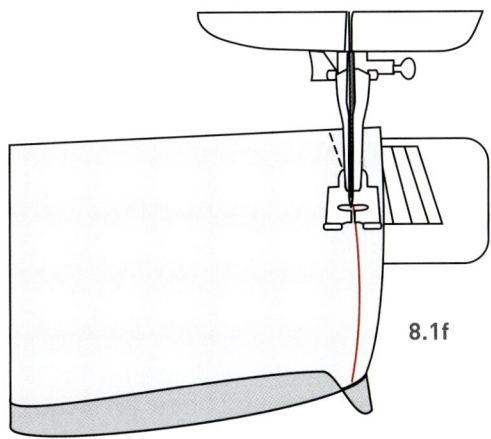

8.1f

7. Restitch the hem if needed (8.1g).

8. Press the seams, clip the threads, and check the fit.

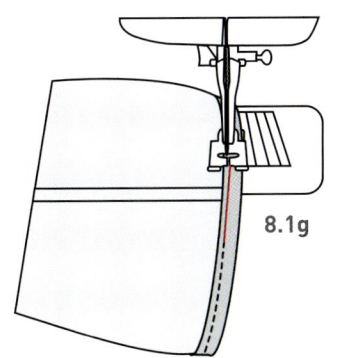

8.1g

PRINCESS SEAMS/DARTS ON FRONT TOP

30 minutes–1+ hours

1. Pinch out and use safety pins to pin the existing seam or to create princess seams in the front and/or back of the garment (8.2a).

2. Have the client remove the shirt. Make or use the measurement chart (page 99) to note and even out the measurements on either side of the body (8.2b).

3. Once you have the measurements noted, remove the pins, turn the garment inside out, and mark the princess seams evenly from the center front and sides of the garment. Determine how to replicate or create the seam finish (8.2c).

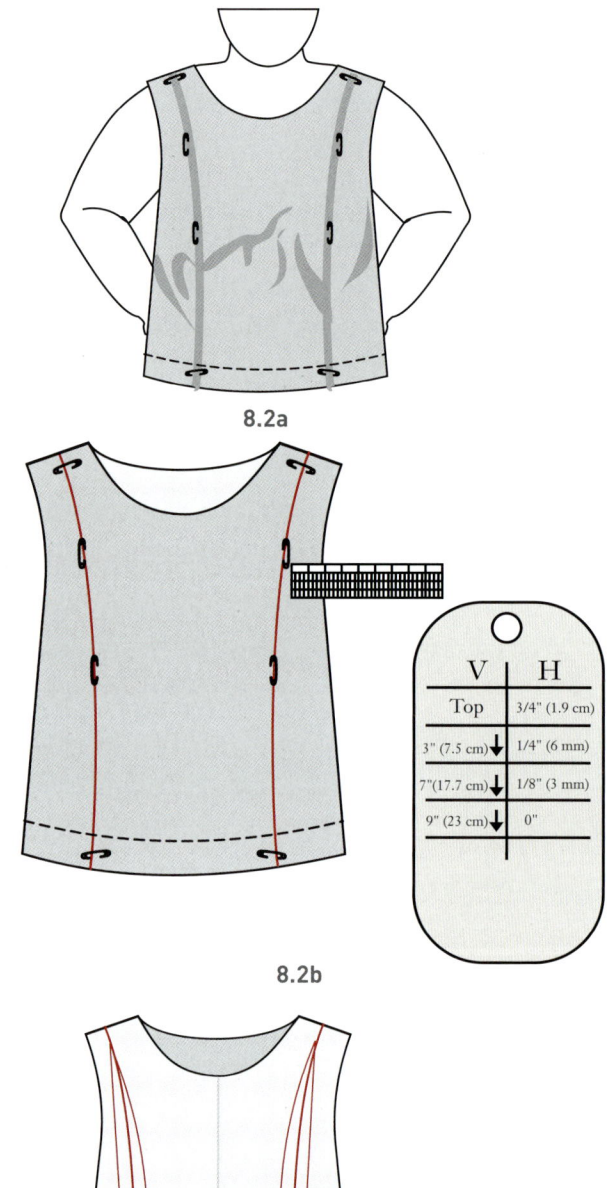

8.2a

8.2b

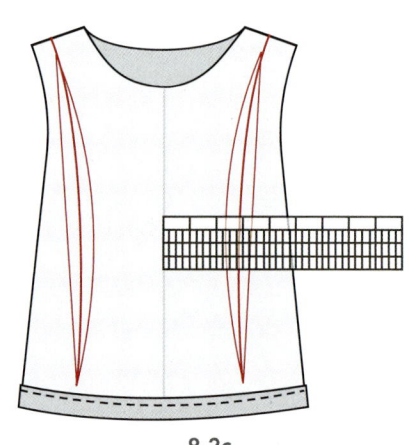

8.2c

4. If the princess seams need to be taken in through the bottom hem, unpick the hem 1" (2.5 cm) past the amount that needs to be taken in on either side (8.2d).

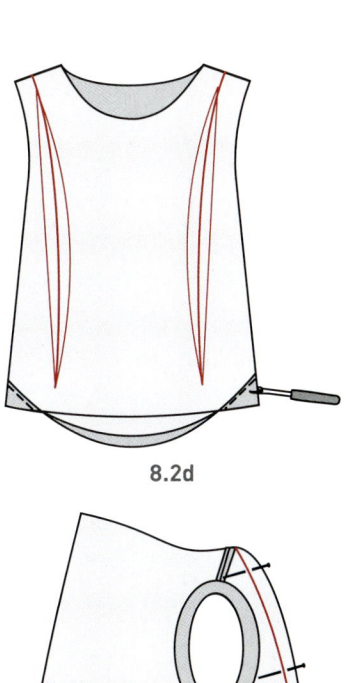

8.2d

5. Stitch the princess seams/darts. If the excess seam allowance causes puckering, you can trim and finish the raw edge of the new seam (8.2e).

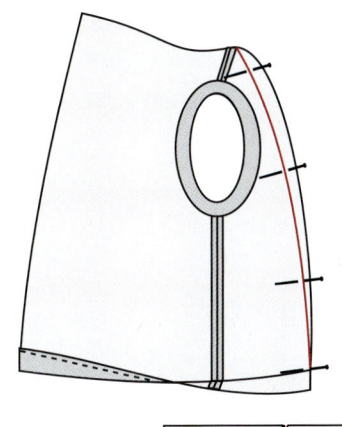

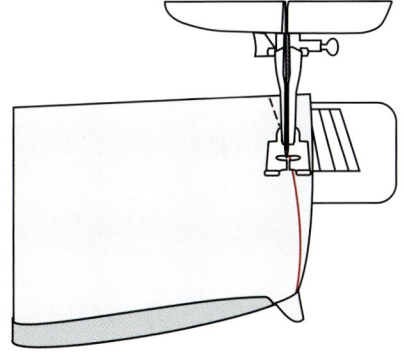

8.2e

6. Restitch the hem if needed.

7. Press the seams, clip the threads, and check the fit (8.2f).

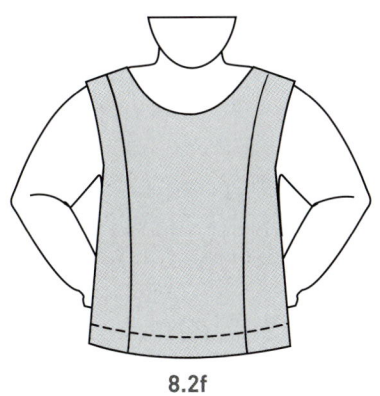

8.2f

PRINCESS SEAMS/DARTS ON FRONT TOP

PRINCESS SEAMS/DARTS ON BACK TOP

30 minutes–1 hour

Adding darts is an excellent way to take in a top and to provide shaping to the garment. Darts can be added just about anywhere, especially to the front or back at the princess seams, at the front or back waist, at the shoulders, or at the bust. Darts can be shaped like a triangle, a fisheye, or a diamond. Whatever way you pin/pinch out the darts on the garment will help you determine what shape and size is needed for the correct fit. The following illustrations show a fisheye dart that does not extend into the hem.

1. Pinch out and use safety pins to pin out the desired dart(s) and pin out the darts as evenly as you can on either side of the body without agonizing over it. You will be able to easily adjust this when you mark the garment later (8.3a).

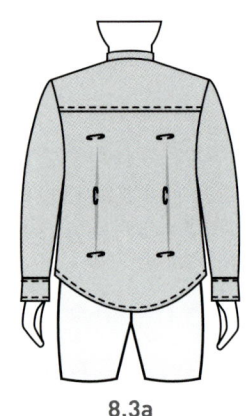
8.3a

2. Have the client remove the shirt. Make or use the measurement chart (page 99) to note the amounts to be taken in (8.3b).

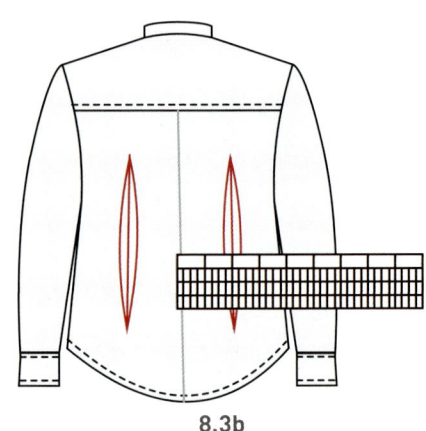
8.3b

3. Once you have the measurements noted, remove the pins, turn the garment inside out, and mark the center of the dart lines evenly spaced from the center line or side seams of the garment. Press the garment on that line and measure and mark the amount to be taken in on the darts. Note that the desired shape will happen naturally whether it be a straight triangle dart, curved/fisheye dart, or diamond shape (8.3c).

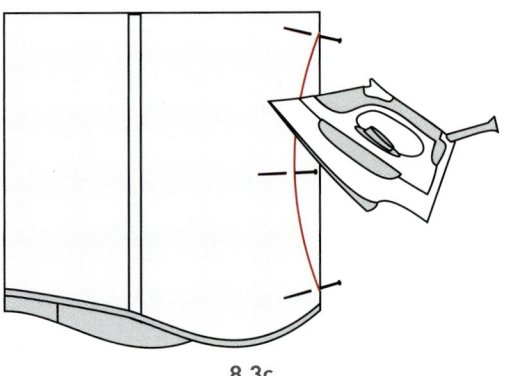
8.3c

4. If the dart needs to be taken in through a seam or hem, unpick the stitching 1" (2.5 cm) past the point that the alteration will be taken out to. In some cases, you can simply fold the hem and carefully stitch the two ends together. This, however, does not look quite as nice as refinishing the hems, but is a great fix for childrenswear and garments that are not being worn professionally.

5. Begin at the tip of your darts right at the edge of the fabric and leave a long tail. Do not backstitch at the tip of the darts. Stitch down the length of the darts and only end with a backstitch if the dart goes through the hem. If the dart does not go through the hem, end without a backstitch and leave a long tail (8.3d).

6. Tie off the ends of the dart with a double knot. Doing this allows for a smooth point that can be pressed easily to curve with the body. Backstitching at the tip of a dart will make the fabric point out and is undesirable unless you are going for a Madonna/Jean Paul Gaultier cone bra look! (8.3e).

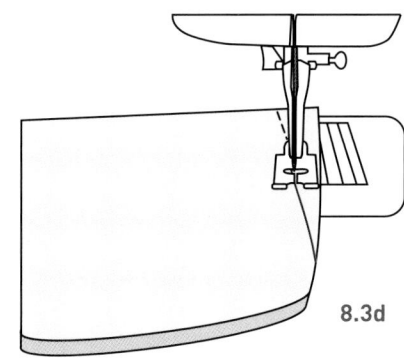

8.3d

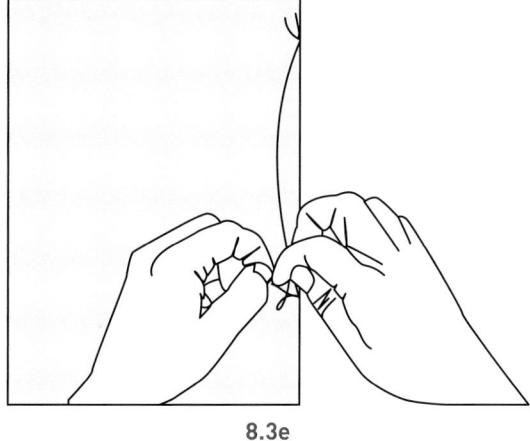

8.3e

7. Press the darts using a ham or sausage roll if available. You may either press them away from the body towards the side seams or in towards the center front/center back of the body. Whatever you choose, do so consistently.

8. Restitch the hem or seams if needed.

9. Press the seams, clip the threads, and check the fit (8.3f).

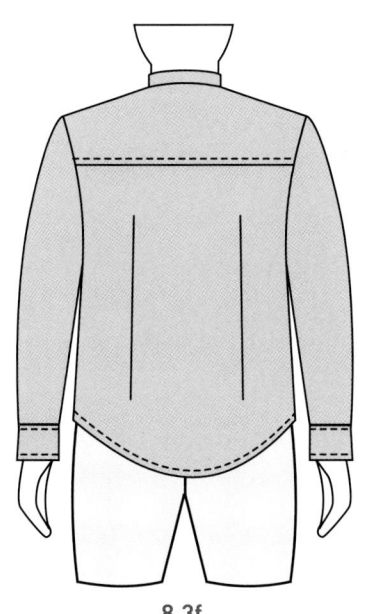

8.3f

PRINCESS SEAMS/DARTS ON BACK TOP

PLEATS/TUCKS

30 minutes–1 hour

Pleats and tucks were used historically to allow childrenswear to be worn for many years. For example, a shirt would have a series of tucks at the hem or in the bodice of a top that could be removed as the child grew taller and wider. This is a great way to easily alter a garment for our continually changing bodies. Pleat and tuck options are as follows (8.4a):

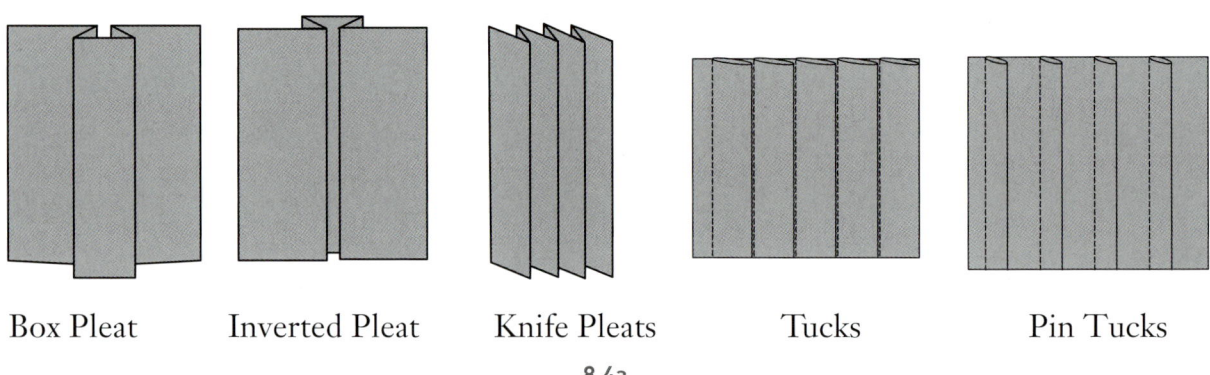

8.4a

1. Pinch out and use safety pins to create a pleat(s) or tuck(s) (8.4b).

8.4b

2. Have the client remove the shirt. Note the amount to be taken in and whether that amount will be taken in with one or more pleats/tucks (8.4c).

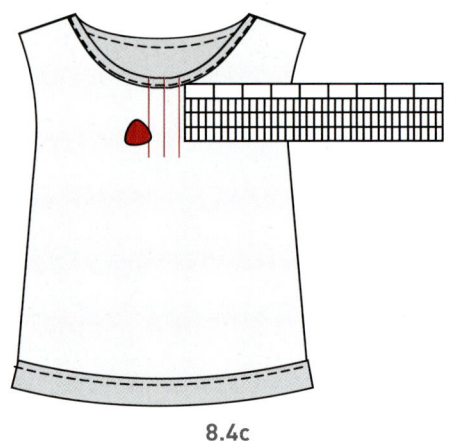

8.4c

152 | CHAPTER 8 TAKING IN TOPS

3. Once you have the measurements noted, remove the pins, turn the garment inside out, and mark the pleats or tucks. If the pleat/tuck needs to be taken in through the neckline or hem, unpick them 1" (2.5 cm) past the point that the alteration will be taken out to (8.4d). In some cases, you can simply fold the neckline or hem and carefully stitch them together. This, however, does not look quite as nice as refinishing the hems/necklines but is a great fix for childrenswear and garments that are not being worn professionally. Press the garment on that line and measure and mark the amount to be taken in on one side of the garment (8.4e).

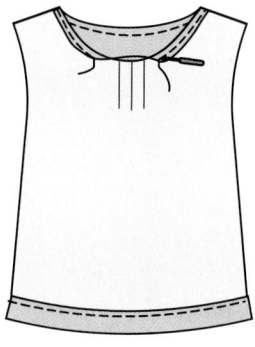

8.4d

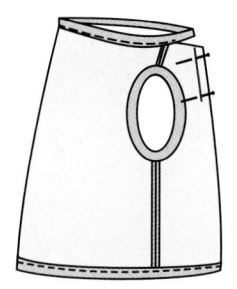

8.4e

4. Sew the pleats or tucks (8.4f). Pleats can be sewn just at the top or they can be sewn down an inch or more from the top. Tucks are sewn all the way down. The edge foot or a pintuck presser foot can be used for this alteration if available. Any of these options work and are up to the client and the aesthetic they are looking for!

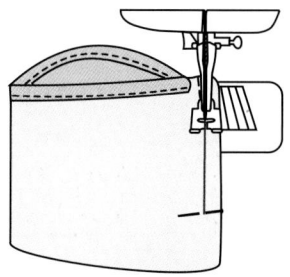

8.4f

5. Restitch the neckline finish and hem if needed (8.4g).

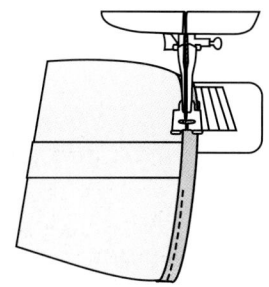

8.4g

6. Press the seams, clip the threads, and check the fit (8.4h).

8.4h

BONED BODICES IN FORMALWEAR

1+ hours

Boning in formalwear provides structure to a garment. When altering a top with boning, you will often have to remove the boning and its casing, make the alteration on the seams, and reattach the casing and boning. Most boning in modern apparel is made of plastic that can be sewn through or it may have a fabric tape casing that you can stitch. You may, however, encounter boning in costumes and high-quality garments that is made of steel or spiral boning. In these circumstances, you may need access to specialty tools to shorten the boning. For the following instructions I will give an example using plastic boning. Search online for steel and spiral boning corset resources and supplies.

1. Pinch out and use safety pins to pin out the desired amount to be taken in on the garment. If the fabric is delicate or scars easily, use silk pins or bridal clamps (8.5a).

8.5a

2. Have the client remove the top. Make or use the measurement chart (page 99) to note the amount to be taken in (8.5b).

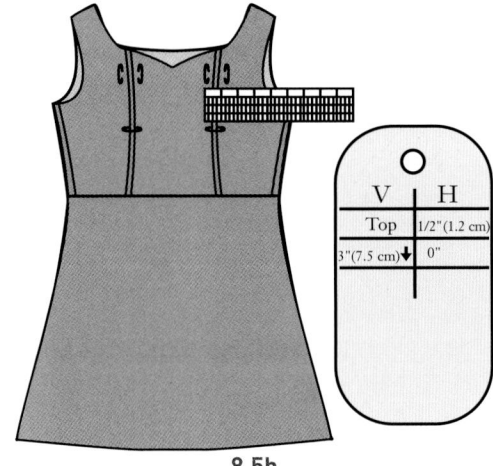

8.5b

3. Once you have the measurements noted, remove the pins or clamps, turn the garment inside out, and unpick any attachments that hold the front of the garment to the lining. If the garment needs to be taken in through the neckline or top bodice, you will need to unpick the seam for 1" (2.5 cm) beyond the desired alteration measurement. If you are new to formalwear construction, take reference photographs to help you navigate your way in and out of the alteration (8.5c).

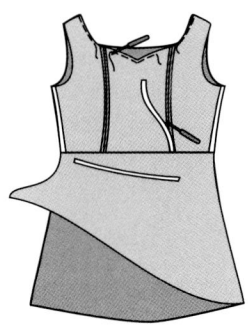

8.5c

4. Remove boning and casing if necessary. Label what bones go where (center front (CF), side front (SF), side seams (SS), side back (SB), center back (CB) with masking tape or paper and safety pins (8.5d).

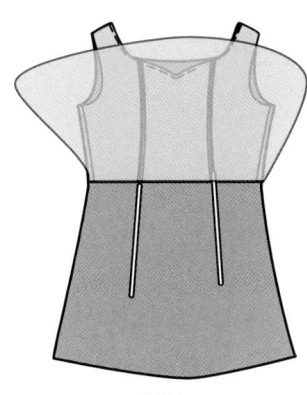

8.5d

5. Press the garment so the seams are flat and measure and mark the amount to be taken in on one side of the garment. Stitch the new seam line and then unpick the original seam and press it open (8.5e).

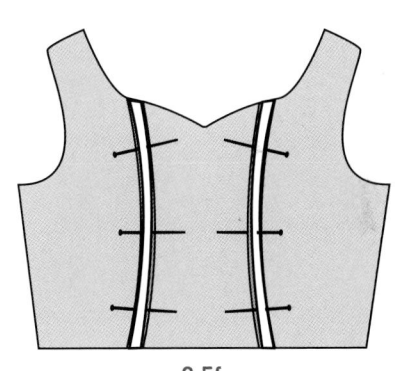

8.5e

6. Reattach the casing to the seams if necessary. Be sure to stitch the casing as close to either side of the long edges as possible 1/16" (1.5–3 mm)–1/8" (8.5f).

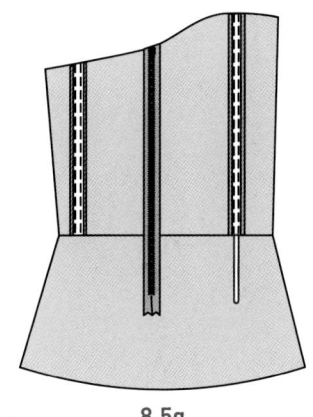

8.5f

7. Restitch the top of the bodice/neckline. You may also need to restitch the understitching.

8. Insert the boning into the casing (8.5g).

9. Secure seam allowance anchor points if necessary and restitch the hem if needed.

10. Press the seams, clip the threads, and check the fit.

8.5g

BONED BODICES IN FORMALWEAR

CHAPTER 9

Letting Out Tops

For tops that are too small.

Note that the illustrations in this chapter may or may not reflect the garment type, seam/hem finishes, or fabric structure. Be sure to check if your fabric is knit or woven and try to replicate the original seam and hem finishes.

- Side seams
- Panels
- Boned bodices in formalwear

SIDE SEAMS

30 minutes–1 hour

1. Check to ensure that there is seam allowance available in the garment. If not, you will need to use an alternative alteration method. Most contemporary garments have small seam allowances, so this alteration will be more common in vintage and handmade garments.

2. Have the client put on the garment if possible and measure the distance that needs to be let out marking areas with pins as a guide OR measure the client and then the garment at the over bust, bust, under bust, natural waist, low waist, and/or hips. Remember—drag lines will point to the problem, use them as your guide! (9.1a).

3. Have the client remove the top if worn and note the desired vertical points and horizontal measurements.

4. Once you have the measurements noted, turn the garment inside out and determine how to replicate the seam finish (9.1b).

5. Unpick the hem 1" (2.5 cm) past the stitch line on either side of the seam if the garment is too tight through the bottom of the shirt (9.1c).

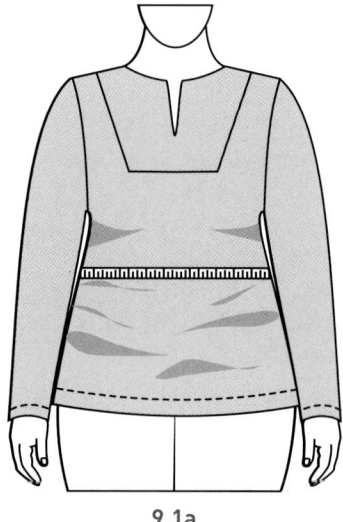

9.1a

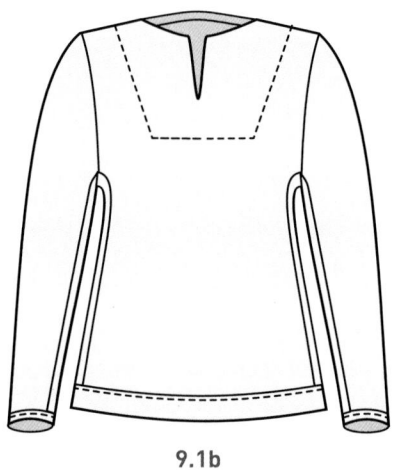

9.1b

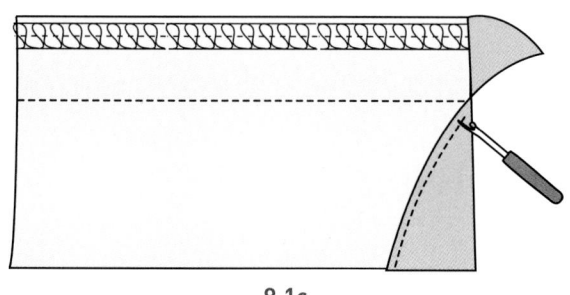

9.1c

6. Stitch at the new seam line (9.1d).

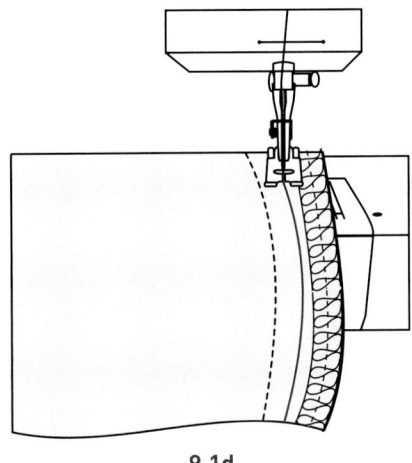

9.1d

7. Unpick the old stitching (9.1e).

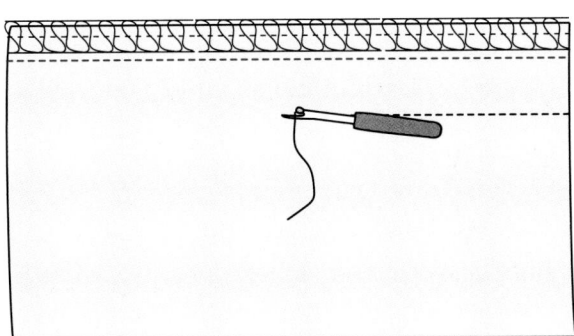

9.1e

8. Press the seams, clip the threads, and check the fit (9.1f).

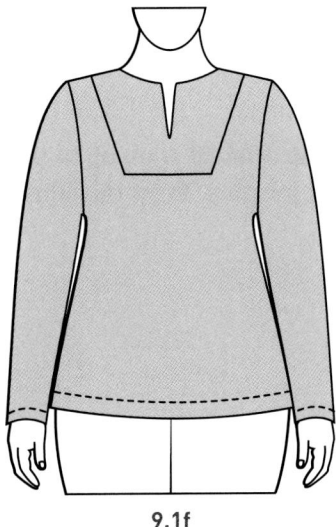

9.1f

PANELS

1+ hours

You can use this method if there is not excess seam allowance and if you have a fabric that is similar to your original fabric in weight, knit/weave type, and fiber type.

1. Have the client put on the garment if possible and measure the distance that needs to be let out marking areas with pins as a guide OR measure the client and then the garment at the over bust, bust, under bust, natural waist, low waist, and/or hips. Remember—drag lines will point to the problem, use them as your guide! (9.2a).

9.2a

2. Have the client remove the top if worn and note the desired vertical points and horizontal measurements.

3. Once you have the measurements noted, turn the garment inside out and determine where to add the panels. You can do this anywhere, and for this book I will show how to insert panels on the side seams.

4. Unpick the hem 1"–2" (2.5–5 cm) past either side of the side seam if the top is too tight at the hem (9.2b).

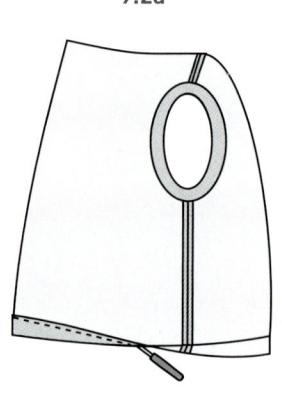

9.2b

5. Unpick the original seam up to the desired alteration location. Press the fabric flat (9.2c).

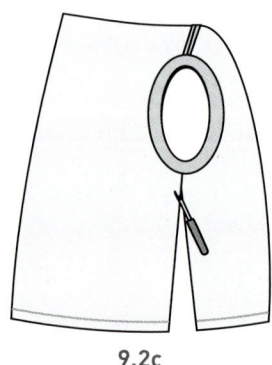

9.2c

6. Measure mark and add seam allowance to your panel fabric. Be sure your fabric is cut on the grain (9.2d).

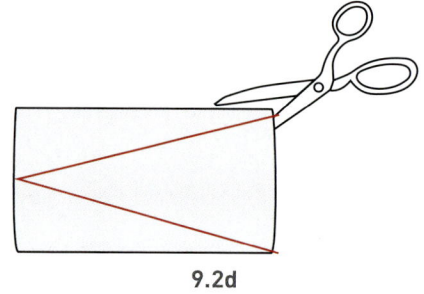

9.2d

7. Lay the fabric panel underneath the side seams to make sure the length and width are correct (9.2e).

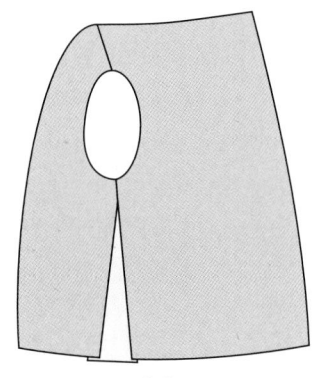

9.2e

8. Pin and stitch the front side seam to the panel first, and then stitch the back side seam to the panel. Repeat this step on the second side seam (9.2f).

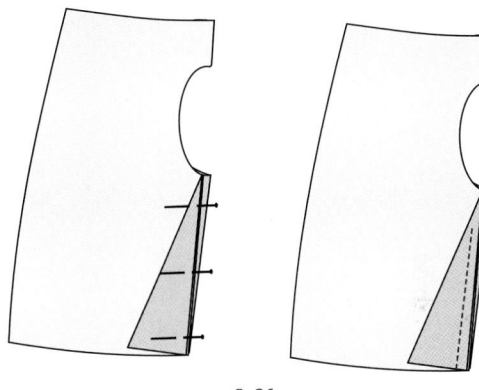

9.2f

9. Finish the raw edges using an appropriate seam finish (see page 147 for seam finishing options) (9.2g).

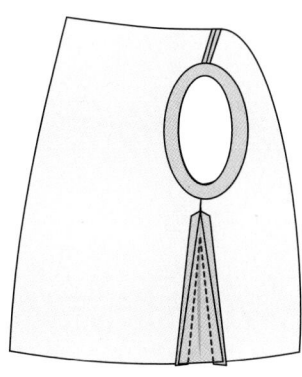

9.2g

10. Press the seams, clip the threads, and check the fit (9.2h).

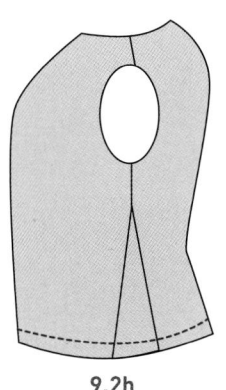

9.2h

BONED BODICES IN FORMALWEAR

1+ hours

Boning in formalwear provides structure to a garment. When altering a top with boning, you will often have to remove the boning and its casing, make the alteration on the seams, and reattach the casing and boning. Most boning in modern apparel is made of plastic that can be sewn through or it may have a fabric tape casing that you can stitch. You may, however, encounter boning in costumes and high-quality garments that is made of steel or spiral boning. In these circumstances, you may need access to specialty tools to shorten the boning. For the following instructions I will give an example using plastic boning. Search online for steel and spiral corset boning resources and supplies.

1. Check to ensure that there is seam allowance in the garment at the seams and note how much is available.
2. Have the client put on the garment if possible and measure the distance that needs to be let out marking areas with pins as a guide OR measure the client and then the garment at the over bust, bust, under bust, natural waist, low waist, and/or hips. Remember—drag lines will point to the problem, use them as your guide! (9.3a).

9.3a

3. Have the client remove the garment. Make or use the measurement chart (see page 99) to note the amount to be let out. Letting out the garment may span over one or many seams. Once you have the measurements noted, turn the garment inside out and unpick any attachments that hold the front of the garment to the lining. If the garment needs to be let out through the neckline or top bodice, you will need to unpick the seam for 1" (2.5 cm) beyond the desired alteration measurement (9.3b).

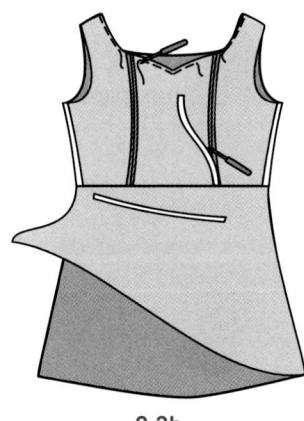

9.3b

4. Remove boning and casing if necessary. Label which bones go where (center front (CF), side front (SF), side seams (SS), side back (SB), center back (CB) with masking tape or paper and safety pins (9.3c).

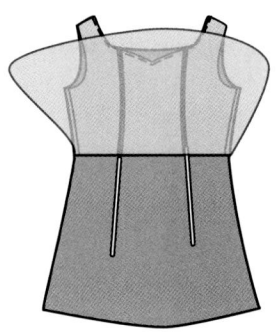

9.3c

5. Press the garment flat on the seam allowance you are letting out and measure and mark the amount to be taken in on one side of the garment. Stitch the new seam line and then unpick the original seam and press it open (9.3d).

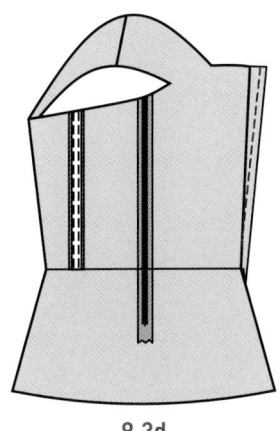

9.3d

6. Unpick the original stitch line and press the seam (9.3e).

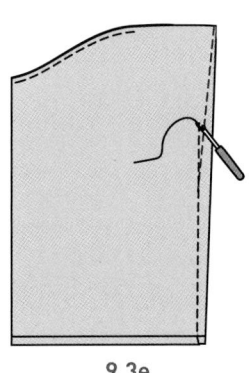

9.3e

7. Reattach the casing to the seams if necessary. Be sure to stitch the casing as close to either side of the long edges as possible ¹⁄₁₆"–⅛" (1.5–3 mm) (9.3f).

8. Restitch the top of the bodice/neckline if needed. You may also need to restitch the understitching.

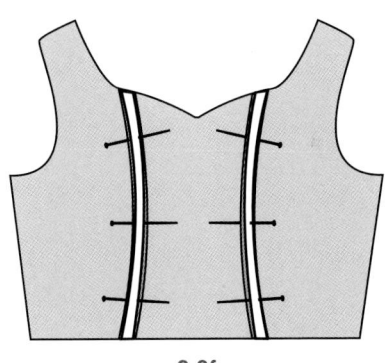

9.3f

9. Insert the boning into the casing (9.3g).

10. Secure seam allowance anchor points if necessary

11. Press the seams, clip the threads, and check the fit.

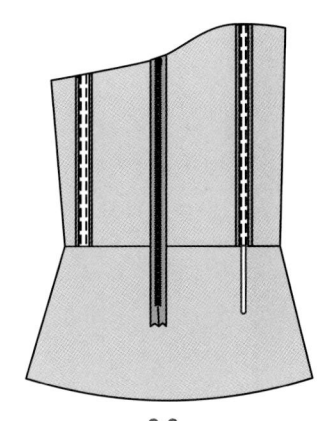

9.3g

CHAPTER 10

Sleeves, Shoulders, and Armscyes

For garments with sleeves, shoulders, and armscyes that are too small, too large, too short, or too long.

- When to say "No!"
- Taking up shoulders
- Taking in sleeves or sleeves and side seams
- Lined suit jacket sleeve hems
- Button down shirt cuffs and plackets

WHEN TO SAY "NO!"

One of my greatest teachers, who also worked with me in my clothing alterations shop, gave some of the best advice I have ever received when it comes to altering suit jackets and I will forever be grateful to her. If someone comes in with a structured suit jacket and the shoulders are too small or too big, urge them to get a new jacket! The sleeves have to be taken out entirely because the sleeve seams usually don't match with the side panels of the bodice. The padding in the shoulder can also make it very challenging to alter the shoulder. Unless you are a skilled tailor, altering suit jacket shoulders for fit is an alteration I recommend saying "no" to! (10.1)

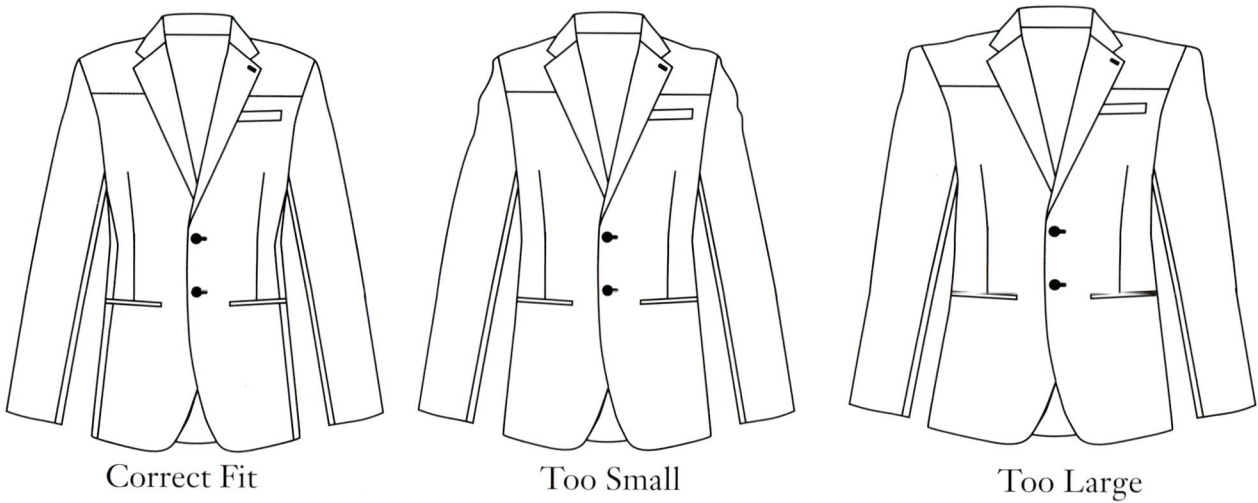

Correct Fit Too Small Too Large

10.1

TAKING UP SHOULDERS

30 minutes–1+ hours △ to ▲

Whether you are taking up shoulder seams to raise the neckline or to prevent straps from falling off the shoulder, you must remember that taking up shoulder seams will shorten the length of your garment. Also note that if your garment is lined or if the shaping of the shoulder has a rapid increase or decrease into the bodice, this step can be more complicated!

1. Pinch out and use safety pins to pin the shoulder seams of the top. Ensure that the hem length is desirable to the client with the shoulder seam alteration (10.2a).

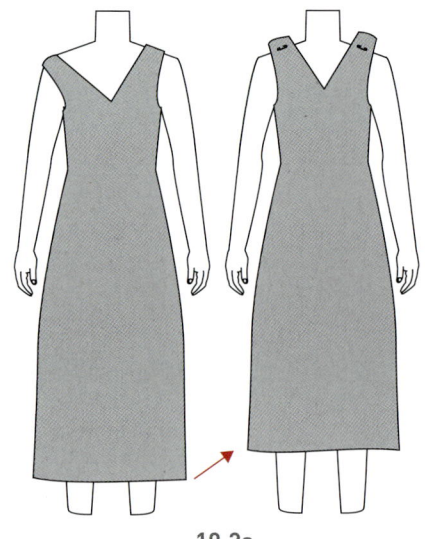

10.2a

2. Have the client remove the top. Make or use the measurement chart (see page 99) to note and even out the measurements on either side of the body (10.2b).

3. If the top has a collar or sleeves the alteration will either need to taper to nothing at the collar/sleeve OR you will need to alter the collar or sleeve. This can be done by removing the sleeve/collar and making or using a seam to make it smaller OR by extending the seam into the sleeve or collar.

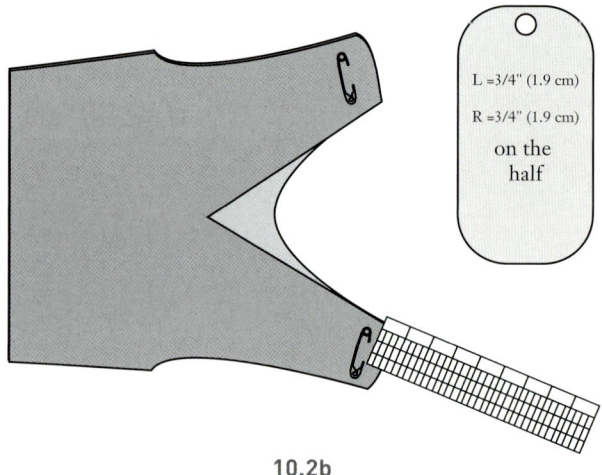

10.2b

4. Once you have the measurements noted, remove the pins, turn the garment inside out and determine how to replicate the seam finish. Note that if your sleeve seams to not line up, you may need to adjust the shaping of the back and front necklines. The left side of the image with the X shows uneven necklines, and the right side shows an appropriate slope on the shoulder seam and neckline (10.2c). Also note that shoulder seams on lined garments are a slight challenge because you may need to rip a seam in the lining in order to get to the shoulder seam.

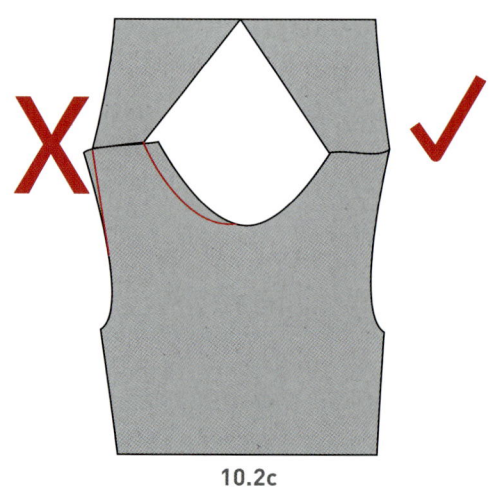

10.2c

5. Mark the new shoulder seam line (10.2d).

10.2d

6. Restitch the shoulder seam (10.2e).

7. Finish the raw edge of the shoulder seam if necessary.

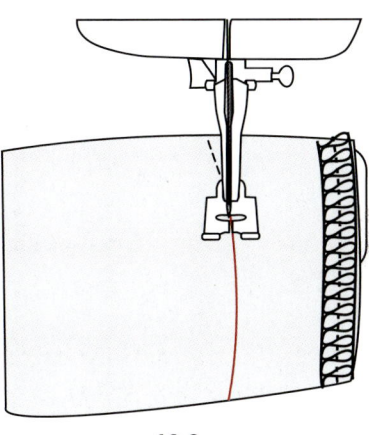

10.2e

8. Press the seams, clip the threads, and check the fit (10.2f).

10.2f

TAKING IN SLEEVES OR SLEEVES AND SIDE SEAMS

30 minutes–1+ hour △ to ▲

If you are planning to take in a knit or simple t-shirt where you do not have to remove any hems or cuffs, this alteration can be fast and easy. If you are taking in a shirt with flat felled seams and cuffs, the alteration can take a bit longer. The illustration for this alteration shows how to take in a button-down shirt but you can follow the same order of instructions for garments with a simple construction.

1. Pinch out and use safety pins to pin the sleeves seams of the top (10.3a).

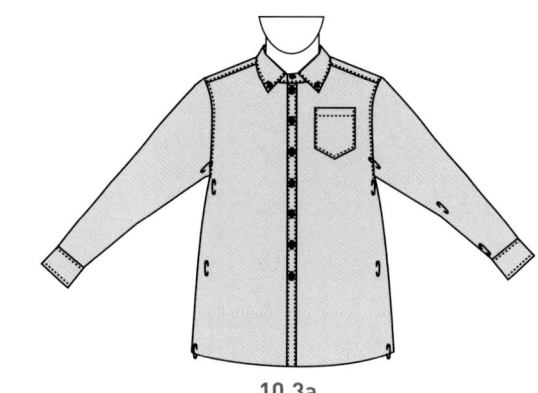

10.3a

2. Have the client remove the top. Make or use the measurement chart (page 99) to note and even out the measurements on either side of the body (10.3b).

3. Once you have the measurements noted, remove the pins, turn the garment inside out, and determine how to replicate the seam finish.

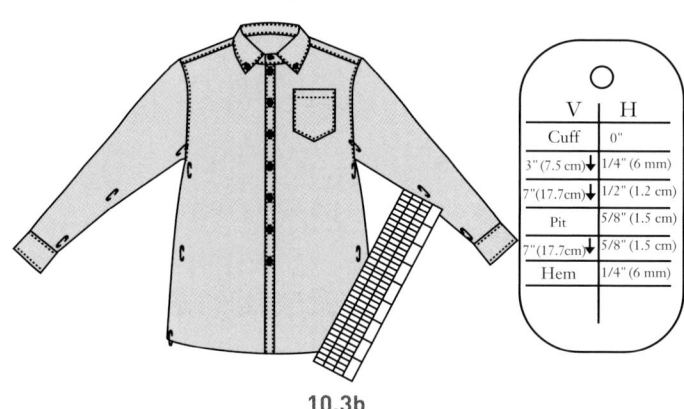

10.3b

4. If the alteration goes through the hem or cuff, do not be tempted to force the hems together or to taper to the cuff if there is a flat fell seam. Unpick the hem and/or the section of the cuff where the pleat and side seam are and continue with the alteration (10.3c).

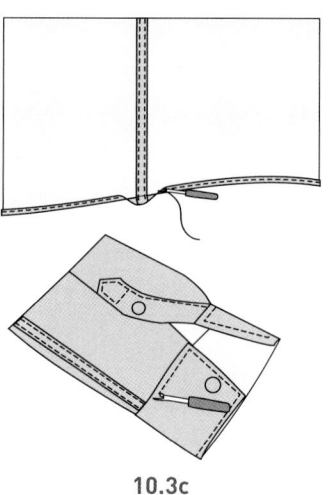

10.3c

5. Mark the new sleeve measurements on the inside of the garment (10.3d).

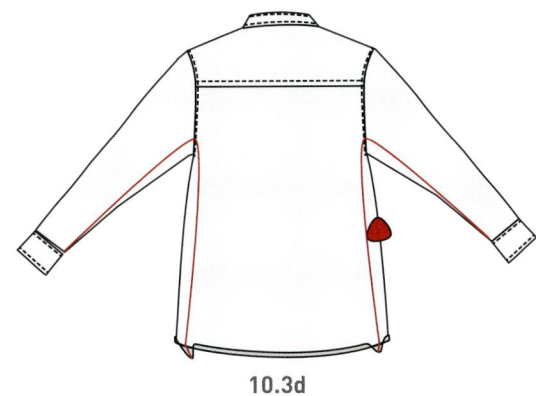

10.3d

6. Stitch the new seam (10.3e).

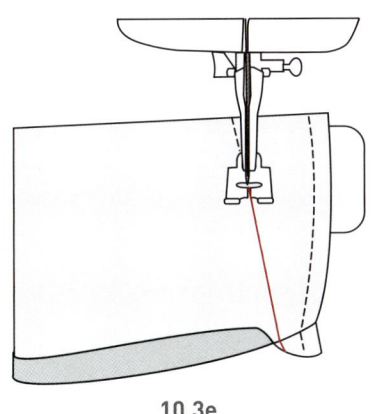

10.3e

7. Trim the excess seam allowance and finish the raw edge if necessary (10.3f).

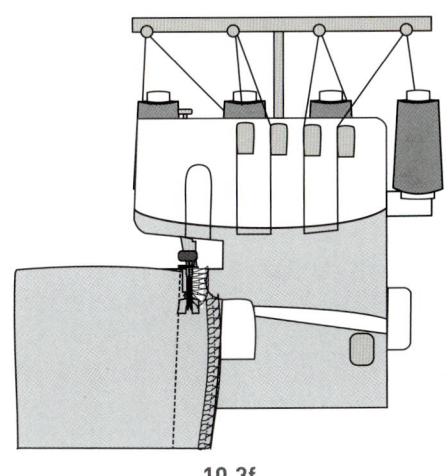

10.3f

8. Restitch the hem and cuff if necessary. If the cuff is larger than the sleeve, you can remove the cuff pleat or make the pleat smaller to fit the sleeve (10.3g).

9. Press the seams, clip the threads, and check the fit.

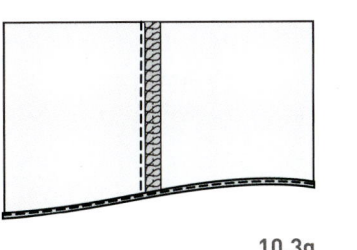 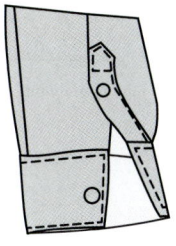

10.3g

TAKING IN SLEEVES OR SLEEVES AND SIDE SEAMS

LINED SUIT JACKET SLEEVE HEMS

1+ hours

Please note that if the buttonholes have been cut out, this alteration may not be possible while maintaining an attractive distance between the hem and the buttons. Some people will attempt to fix this issue from the shoulder—I am not one of them! Most of the faux/uncut buttonholes you encounter will be sewn with a chain stitch and can easily be unstitched.

1. Have the client put on the jacket and rest their arms by their sides and instruct them to look straight ahead. Pinch the sleeve and lining up above the wrist equally around the sleeve to leave the desired amount above the wrist. Do this on both sides and note if one arm is longer than the other (10.4a).

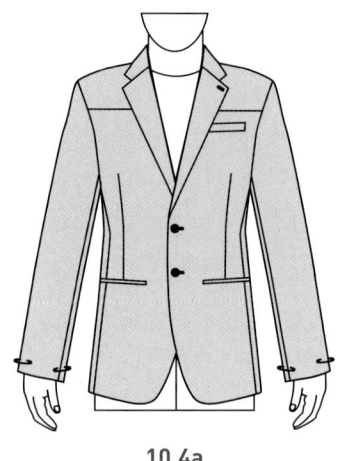

10.4a

2. The ratio of shirt cuff to suit jacket sleeve is a personal preference based on the client's wants and needs. If they are uncertain of what they want, reference figure 10.4b for a general guide.

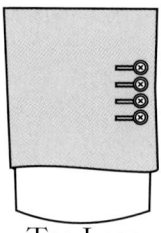 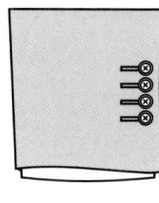 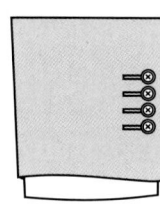

Too Long   Too Short   Just Right
¼"– ½" (6 mm–1.2 cm)
Shirt Cuff Showing

10.4b

3. Have the client remove the jacket. Average the amount that needs to be taken up from the pinned points. If the client has one arm that is noticeably longer, you may choose to have the sleeves altered with different measurements so long as the distance between the sleeve and the thumb to wrist joint are even (10.4c).

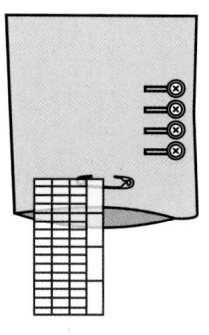 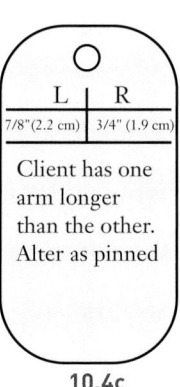 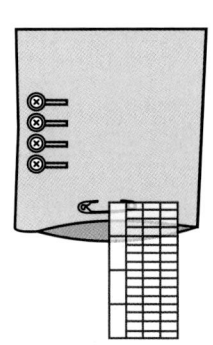

L | R
7/8" (2.2 cm) | 3/4" (1.9 cm)

Client has one arm longer than the other. Alter as pinned

10.4c

4. Remove the buttons at the bottom of the sleeves and store them in a container or bag. Only unpick the false buttonholes if the alteration is greater than ¾" (1.9 cm). Generally, the buttons and buttonholes will still look fine if the alteration is ¾" (1.9 cm) or less. If it is greater than ¾" (1.9 cm) it will look disproportional. Even if the right and left arm alterations are different, stay consistent with what you do with the buttons and buttonholes (10.4d).

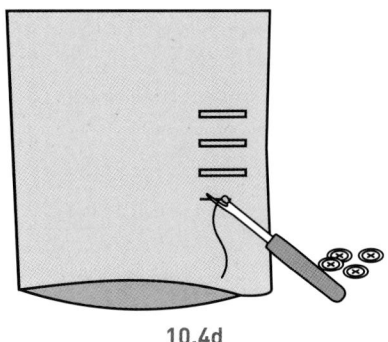

10.4d

5. Find the opening in the suit jacket on the sleeve seam, back hem OR center back and unpick it enough so that you can pull the jacket or sleeve inside out. Jackets can be constructed in a variety of ways so you may have to do some detective work to determine the best method for your alteration. For example, some jackets have the sleeves sewn into the armscye in which case you wouldn't be able to access the sleeve through the center back and would need to unpick the sleeve seam to get to the cuff and cuff lining (10.4e).

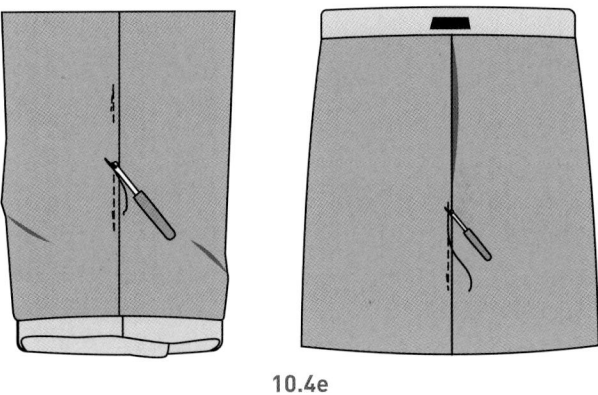

10.4e

6. Unpick the stitches that hold the lining to the sleeve. Sometimes there will be small rectangular pieces of fabric that attach the lining to the sleeve. Unpick the corner seam. If the sleeve has a mitered corner, you can restitch the corner if you have enough seam allowance. If you do not have enough seam allowance, you can change the mitered corner to a straight line. Note that there is usually interfacing on this part of the cuff. If the interfacing is too worn you can remove it by gently peeling it back, then cut a new piece of fusible interfacing and press it to the inside of the sleeve for structure (10.4f).

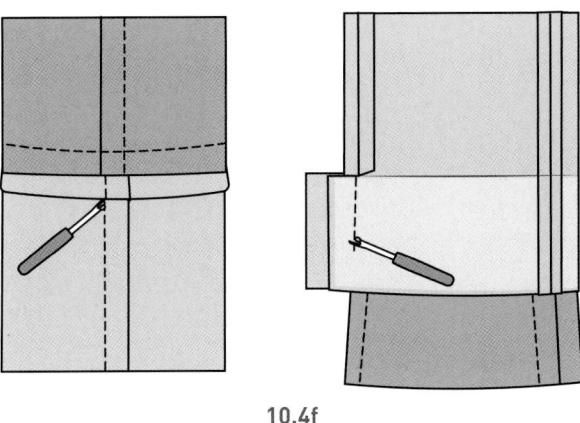

10.4f

LINED SUIT JACKET SLEEVE HEMS

7. Mark the new sleeve length and hand stitch the new desired measurement above the current stitch line catching the lining and the outer fabric. Some sewists like to unpick the sleeve seam because the side seam/overlap/mitered corner can be challenging to work around. I like to sew the lining and outer fabric together prior to unpicking it to avoid twisting in the sleeve lining. Make sure to keep the corner seam out of the way as you do this (10.4g).

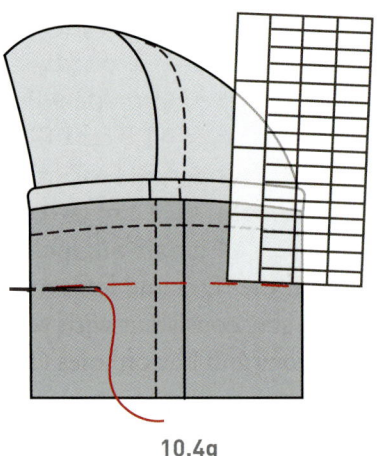

10.4g

8. Trim the excess seam allowance down to the amount of seam allowance originally in the sleeve (typically 1"–1½" / 2.5–3.7 cm)) (10.4h).

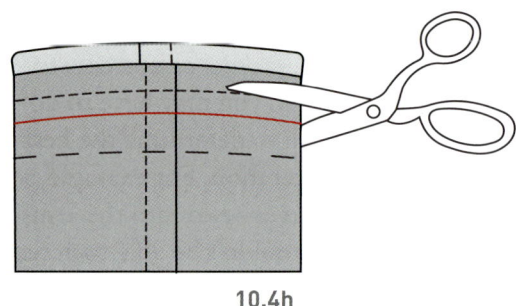

10.4h

9. Mark and stitch the mitered corner or seamline and machine stitch the hem that you sewed by hand. Stitch any seam tacks back in place. Turn the sleeve right side out. You will notice that the lining sits above the outer fabric and also folds over itself, and this is what you want! If the lining does not fold back over itself, it will tug on and twist the sleeve in an undesirable way (10.4i).

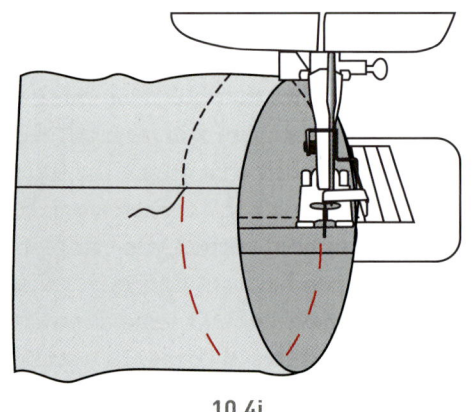

10.4i

10. Unless you feel very comfortable, I recommend leaving the buttonholes off the garment. If you want them and can confidently sew them, do so now.

11. Reattach the buttons—you can do this all the way through the lining or just through the garment. A button gauge is very helpful! (10.4j).

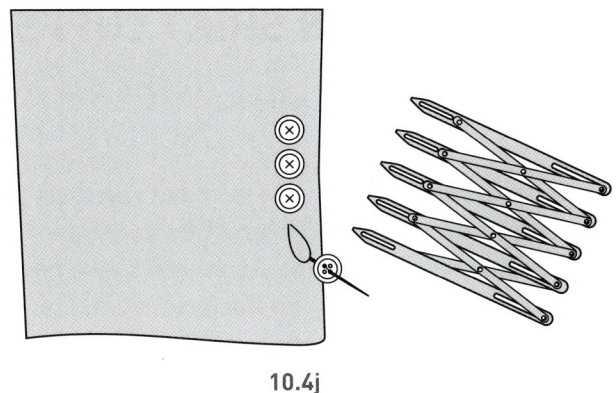

10.4j

12. Stitch the sleeve seam or center back seam that you opened in step 5 closed (10.4k).

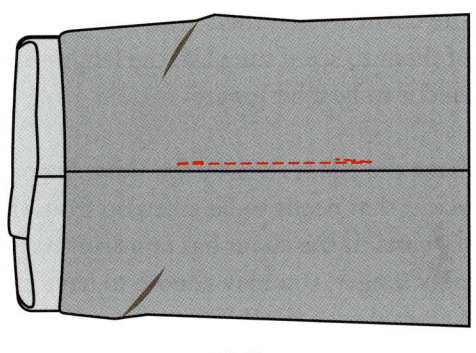

10.4k

13. Press the seams, clip the threads, and check the fit (10.4l).

10.4l

BUTTON DOWN SHIRT CUFFS AND PLACKETS

1+ hours

1. Have the client put on the shirt and rest their arms by their sides and instruct them to look straight ahead. Pinch the sleeve well above the placket, about midway up the forearm, and pin equally around the sleeve to take up the desired amount. Do this on both sides and note if one arm is longer than the other (10.5a).

2. Have the client stretch their arms straight in front of them to see if they like the length or if they need it to be a bit longer.

3. Next, have the client remove the shirt. Average the amount that needs to be taken up from the pinned points. If the client has one arm that is noticeably longer, you may choose to have the sleeves altered with the different measurements so long as the distance between the sleeve and the thumb to wrist joint are even. Make sure you measure the full amount/double the pin amount.

4. Determine whether or not you will need to remove the placket. If the sleeve needs to be shortened ½" (1.2 cm) or less, you can get away with just moving the cuff up. If it is greater than ½" (1.2 cm), the placket may become too small so you will need to remove it and reattach it.

5. Seam rip to remove the cuff and the placket button and placket if necessary. Measure and note the seam allowance that was in the cuff on the bottom of the sleeve for reference (usually ¼"–½" (6 mm–1.2 cm)) (10.5b).

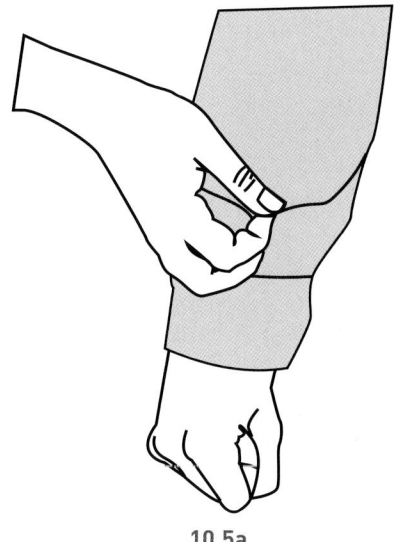

10.5a

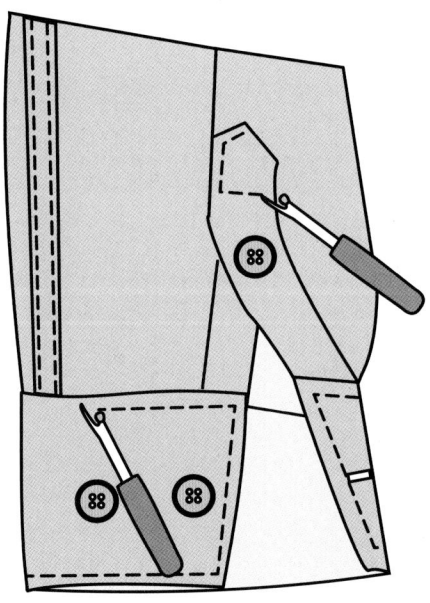

10.5b

6. Once the cuff and placket(s) are separate from the sleeve, measure the desired alteration amount that the sleeve needs to be shortened from the raw edge of the fabric and mark it around the sleeve. This will be your new cut line and you will stitch above that line using the seam allowance amount noted in step 7. Measure and note where the pleats are located in the sleeve cuff and mark the information on your notes. Also measure the placket cut length not including the V cut (10.5c).

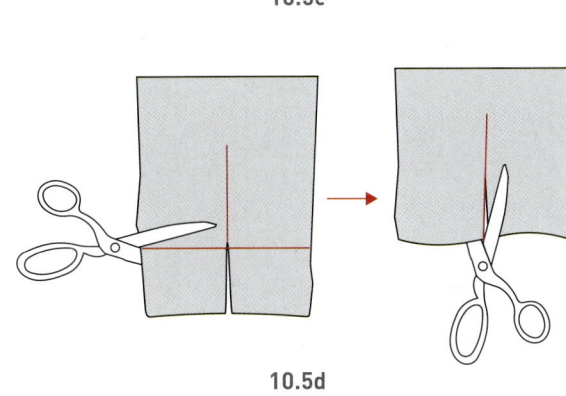

10.5c

7. Cut the sleeve at the new cut line and cut the placket line straight up to the original placket length. If you mess this up and cut too far, you can always get another piece of similar fabric to recover the placket (10.5d).

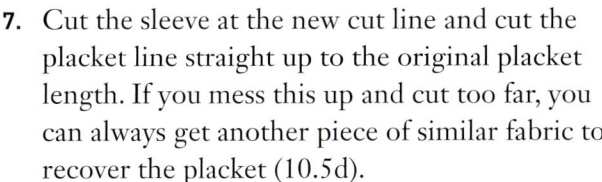

10.5d

8. Reattach the placket(s). Measure and pin the pleat marks and stitch them flat on the seam allowance with a staystitch (10.5e).

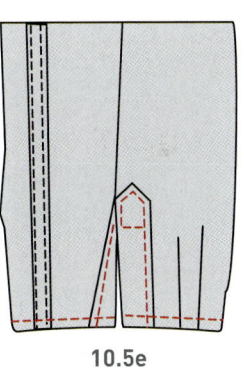

10.5e

9. Reattach the cuff. Press the seam allowance at either end of the sleeve into a small triangular corner so that you can butt up the sleeve with the cuff as close as possible (10.5f).

10. Resew the placket buttonhole and button if present and needed.

11. Press the seams and pleats, clip the threads, and check the fit.

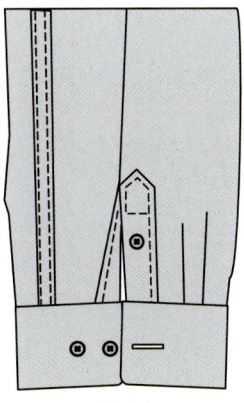

10.5f

BUTTON DOWN SHIRT CUFFS AND PLACKETS

CHAPTER 11

Crotch Seams

Adjusting the crotch seam/rise of a pair of pants.

- How to measure crotch seams
- Taking in crotch seams
- Letting out crotch seams
- Adding gussets

HOW TO MEASURE CROTCH SEAMS

There really isn't a stranger place to do an alteration than the crotch seam. But fear not, you can do this professionally and with relative ease!

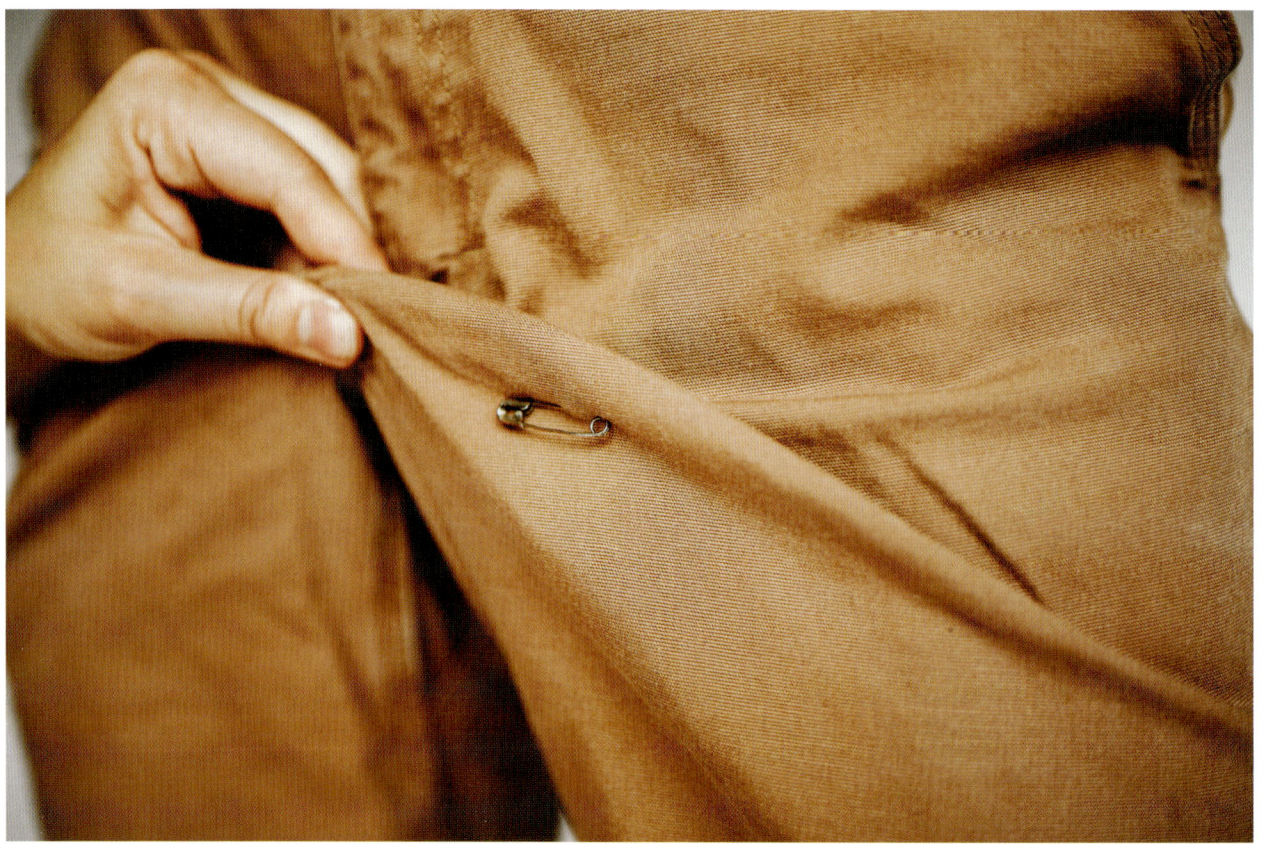

Measuring To Take In

1. Have the client put on the pants they need altered. Ask them to pinch out the front of the crotch seam the desired amount (11.1a).

2. At this point you can ask if they are comfortable with you putting a safety pin in that location or if they would prefer to.

3. Be sure the client does not pin their underwear to the pants. If they do, start the process over and take extra care not to catch both layers.

4. Have the client remove the pants.

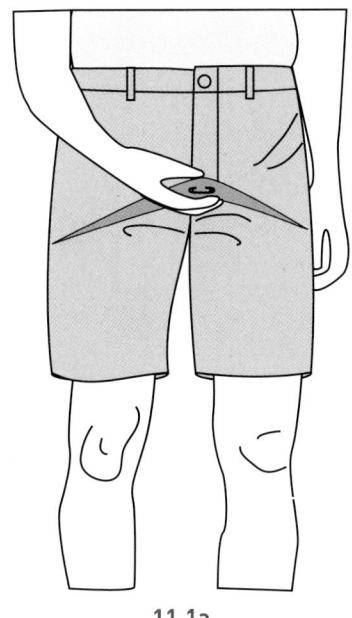

11.1a

5. For here, you will be doing the alteration in the lowest part of the crotch seam, but you will use the measurement that was pinched out to determine how much of the crotch seam to take out (11.1b).

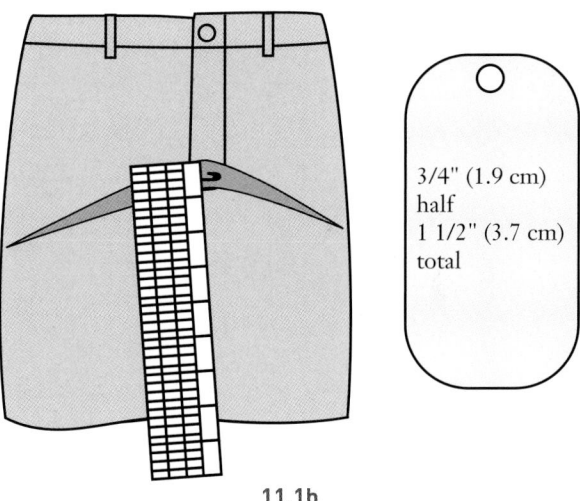

3/4" (1.9 cm) half
1 1/2" (3.7 cm) total

11.1b

HOW TO MEASURE CROTCH SEAMS

Measuring To Let Out

1. The client does not need to try on the pants to check how much to let out. You will simply need to measure the client's full rise and the pants they would like to let out or make larger.

2. Ask the client where they would like the pants to sit on their center front, by the belly button, and center back.

3. Have them hold a tape measure at the center front location and let them know that you will be pulling the tape between their legs to their back (11.1c).

4. If the crotch seam needs to sit lower, let the tape have some slack. If it should be close fitting, pull the tape taut.

5. Note the measurement (11.1d).

6. Next, measure the crotch seam/full rise of the pants including the waist band (11.1e).

7. Note the difference to determine how much length you need to add or let out of the crotch seam.

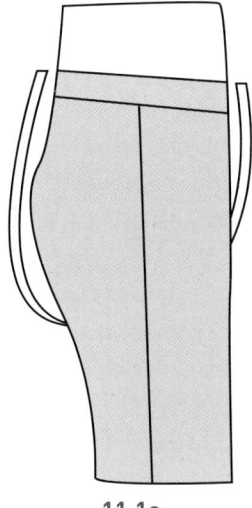

11.1c

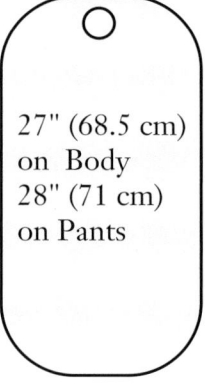

27" (68.5 cm) on Body
28" (71 cm) on Pants

11.1d

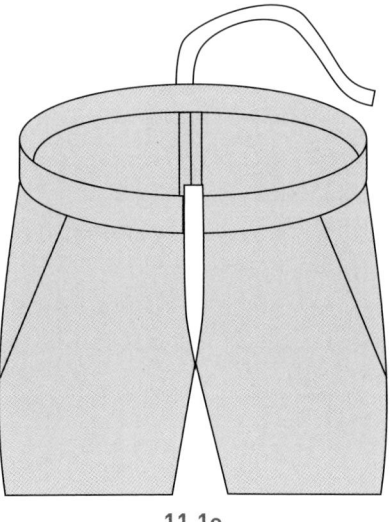

11.1e

TAKING IN CROTCH SEAMS

30 minutes–1 hour

1. Follow the instructions on measuring how much to take in the crotch seam (see page 181) (11.2a). Note that taking up the crotch may also shorten the pants on the inseam, so confirm that the client will be okay with that outcome.

11.2a

2. Turn the pants inside out. Remove any topstitching about 4" (10 cm) on either side of the crotch seam if needed (11.2b).

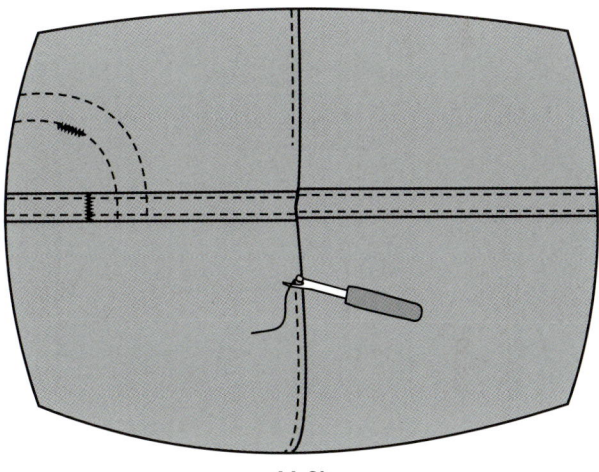

11.2b

3. Mark the amount that needs to be taken in at the intersection of the front and back crotch/rise/inseams. Use a ruler to taper the crotch out to nothing approximately 4" on either side of the intersection. If the pants need to be taken in more at the inseam, you can extend this length and vice versa (11.2c).

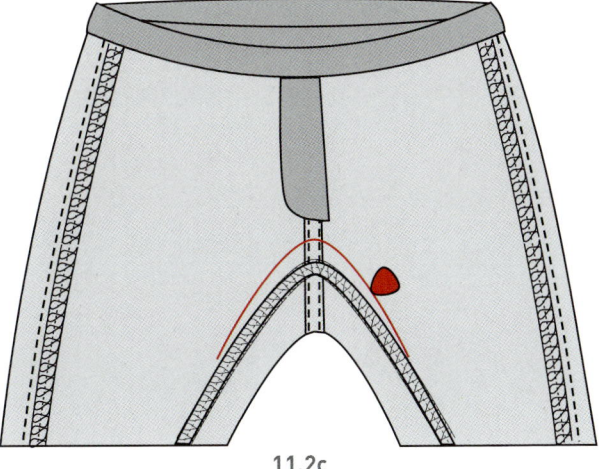

11.2c

TAKING IN CROTCH SEAMS

4. Pin the crotch seams in the ditch at the new stitch line so the seams match up after you sew them. Stitch the new line (11.2d).

5. At this point, you may have the client try the pants on to check the fit. If you feel confident or have checked the fit, move to the next step. If not, adjust the alteration amount and re-sew the new line.

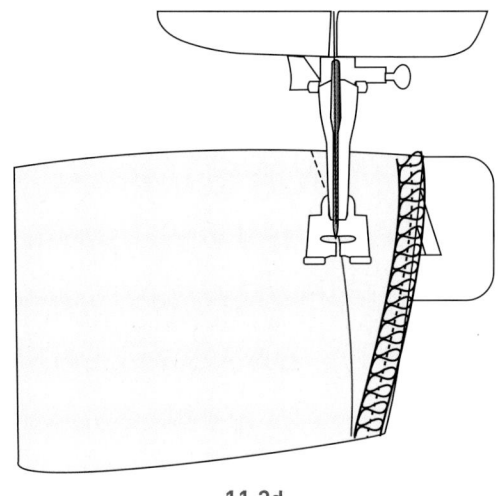

11.2d

6. Serge, cut, or restitch the seam allowance if needed (11.2e).

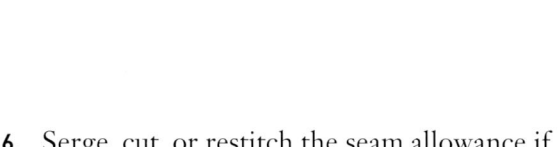

11.2e

7. Press the seam allowance and restitch topstitching if necessary (11.2f).

8. Press the seams, clip the threads, and check the fit.

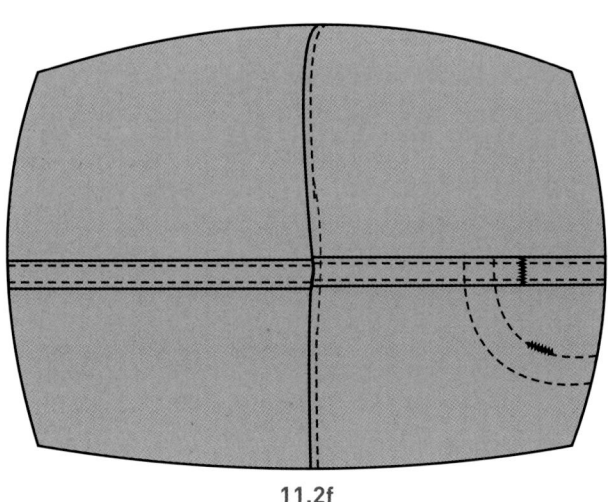

11.2f

184   CHAPTER 11 CROTCH SEAMS

LETTING OUT CROTCH SEAMS

1+ hour

If the client's pants are too tight in the crotch seam, you simply need to lower the "rise"/crotch seam, therefore lengthening it. This can only be done on pants with sufficient seam allowance.

1. Follow the instructions to measure how much to let out the crotch seams (see page 182) (11.3a).

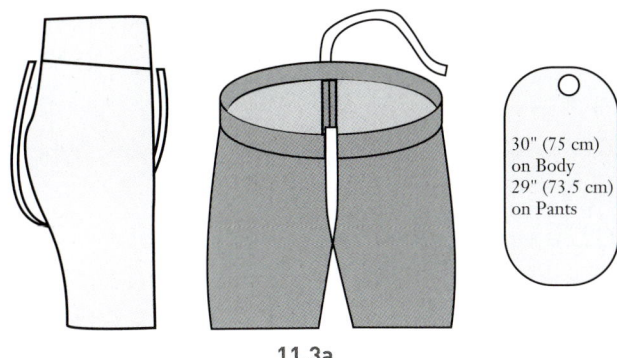

11.3a

2. From the measurements you noted previously, determine the extra length you will need to make the rise to fit the client and check to see if there is enough seam allowance on the pant to do the alteration. Typically, you can only do a maximum of about 1" (2.5 cm) if there is between ¼" (6 mm) to ⅝" (1.5 cm) of seam allowance (11.3b).

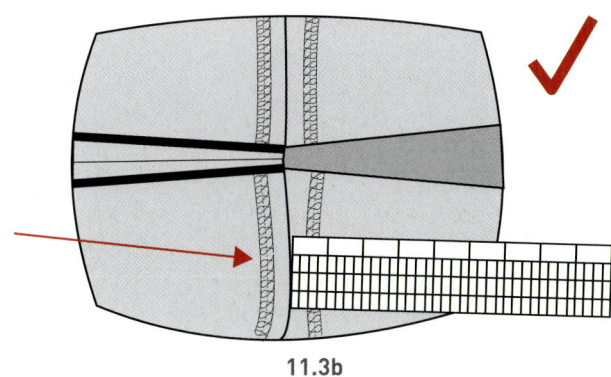

11.3b

3. If more than 1" (2.5 cm) needs to be let out, you cannot perform this alteration method (11.3c). Go to the alteration instructions for adding gussets (see pages 187–8).

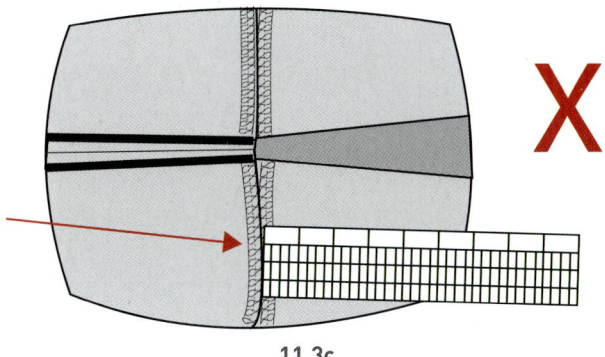

11.3c

4. Unpick any topstitching that might be in the way of your alteration at least 2" (5 cm) past either side of the inseams/rise/crotch seam. You will be stitching the inseams at the crotch point and depending on the order in which the garment was constructed you may need to unpick a little of the front and back rise/crotch seams before continuing this alteration (11.3d).

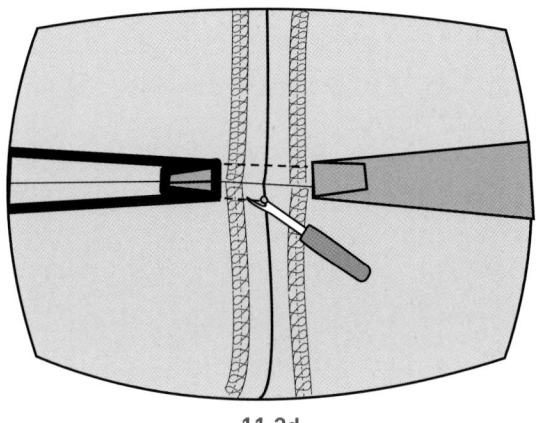

11.3d

5. Measure and mark the desired alteration amount tapering back to the original seam as quickly as possible while keeping a smooth line (11.3e).

6. Stitch the new line. Press the seam open.

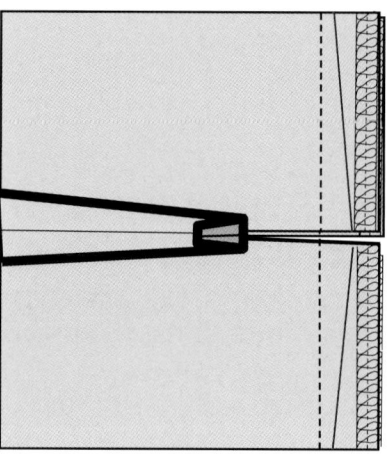

11.3e

7. Pin in the ditch in the inseams to stitch and reconnect the crotch seams (11.3f).

8. If necessary, restitch any topstitching on the inseams/crotch seams

9. Press the seams, clip the threads, and check the fit.

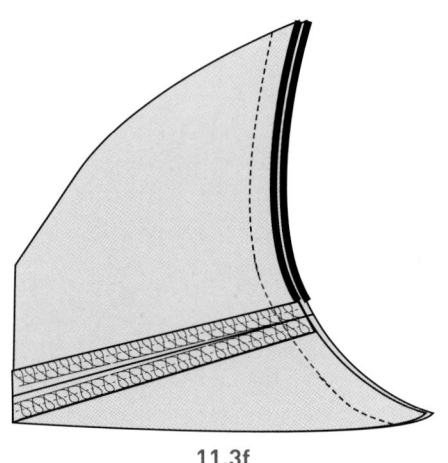

11.3f

ADDING GUSSETS

1+ hour

If you are constantly ripping out the crotch seam of your pants or the crotch seam needs to be let out more than 1" (2.5 cm), adding a gusset is a great option. A gusset is a football or diamond shaped piece of fabric that allows for a greater range of motion and can be seen most often in armscyes and crotch seams.

1. Follow the instructions to measure how much to let out the crotch seam (see page 182) (11.4a).

2. From the measurements you noted, determine how much longer you will need to make the rise to fit the client.

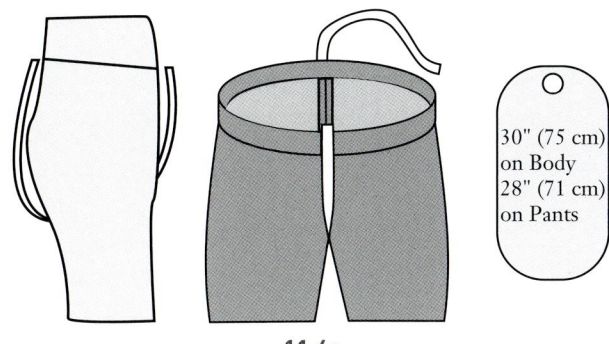

11.4a

3. Create the gusset by finding a fabric that is similar to the pant fabric. If you have woven fabric, use woven fabric to make the gusset. If you have knit fabric, use knit fabric to make the gusset. Aim to have the same fiber content, fabric weight, and stretch, if any. Make a pattern that is the desired new length plus ¼"–½" (6 mm–1.2 cm) seam allowance. Use the template on page 189 (figure 11.4i) for general shaping (11.4b).

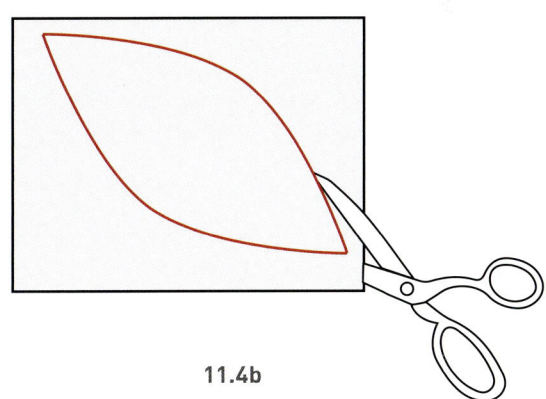

11.4b

4. Serge the raw edges of the gusset (11.4c).

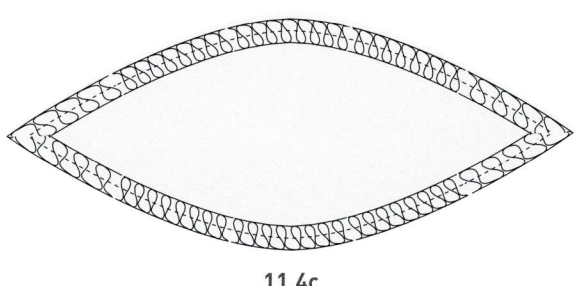

11.4c

5. Seam rip the inseam at the crotch of the pants for about 4" (10 cm) on either side of the center seam (11.4d).

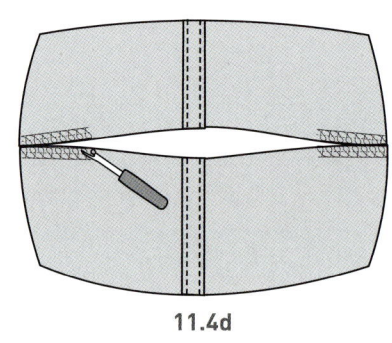

11.4d

6. Pin the center of the gusset to the front crotch seam and pin out from there. Stitch the gusset the front (11.4e).

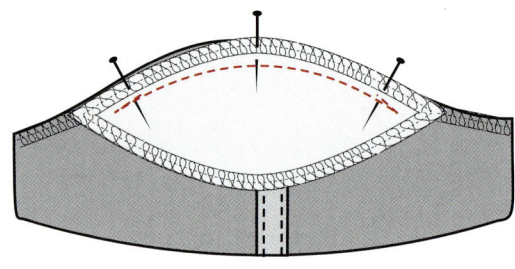

11.4e

7. Repeat step 6 on the on the back crotch seam (11.4f).

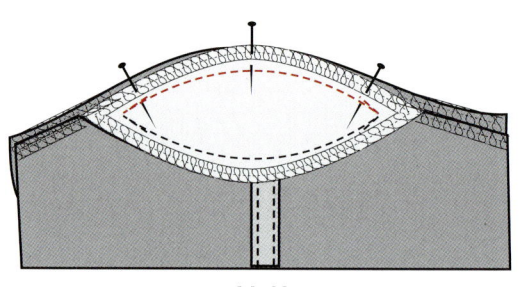

11.4f

8. Restitch the inseams to secure the stitch, getting as close to the gusset as possible (11.4g).

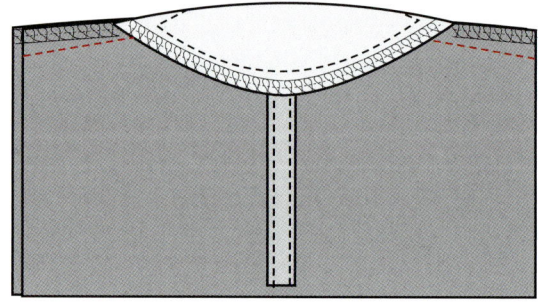

11.4g

9. Topstitch the gusset seam allowance to secure the gusset if desired (11.4h).

10. Press the seams, clip the threads, and check the fit.

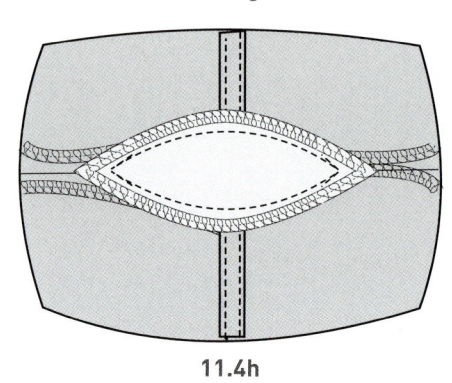

11.4h

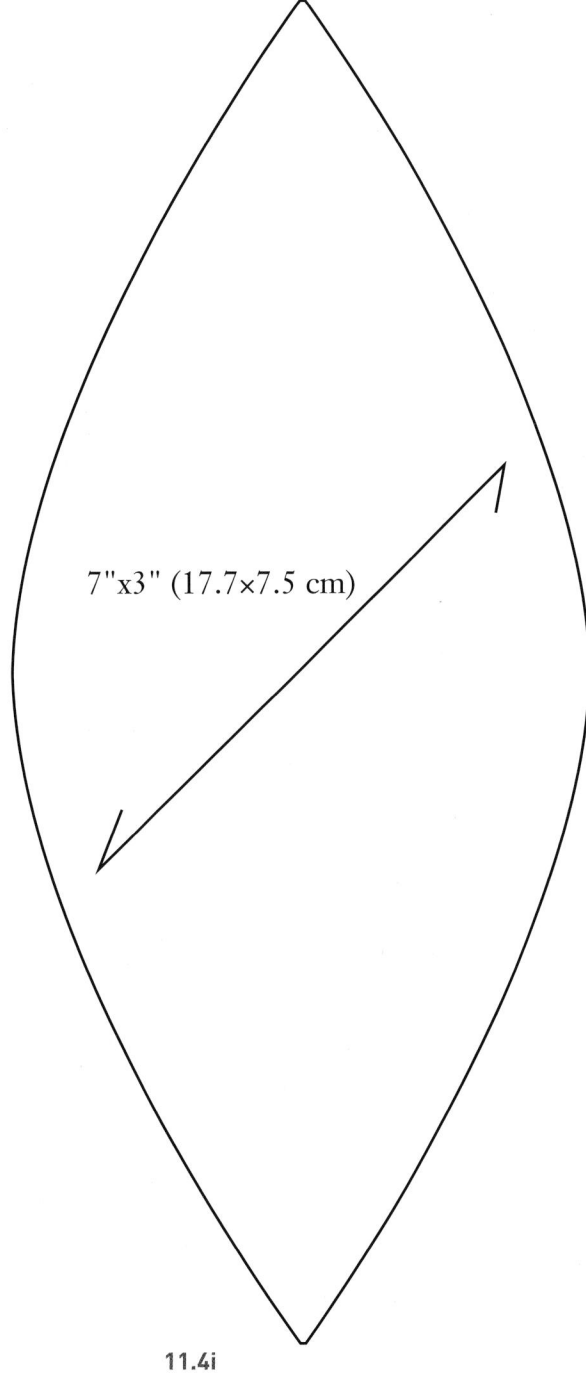

11.4i

ADDING GUSSETS

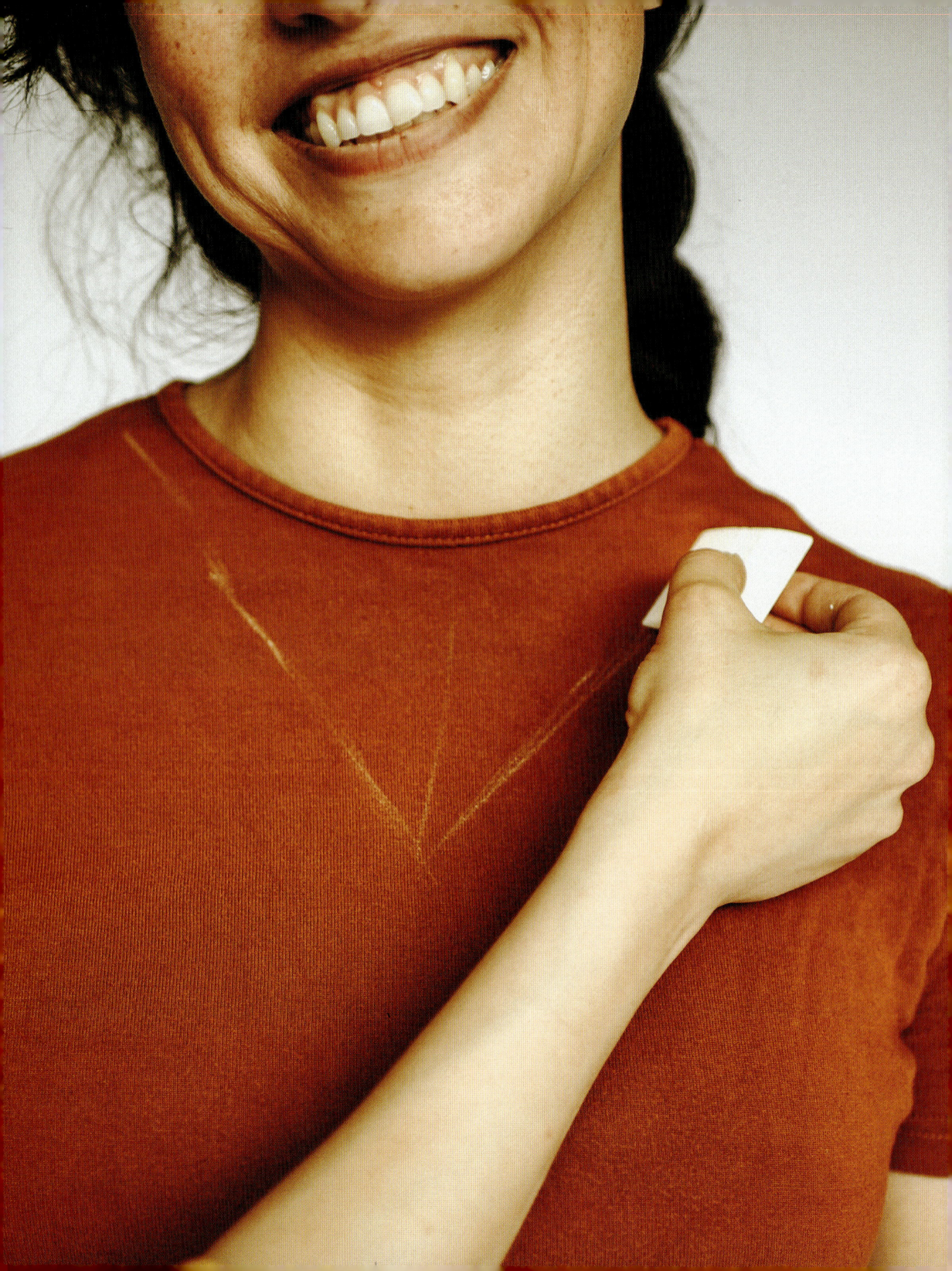

CHAPTER 12

Necklines and Collars

Collars and necklines can range from simple to complex. You will need to put some consideration into whether or not the alteration will be appropriate for your skill level, time, and how much the customer is willing to pay. Easy necklines are often single layered tops whereas complicated collars and necklines may include facings and linings like suit jackets. Gauge your time, skills, and abilities appropriately!

- Reshaping necklines
- Collars

COLLAR/NECKLINE TYPES

The world of collars and necklines is vast and exciting! A collar that is too tight or a neckline that is too revealing may cause someone to leave that garment untouched for years. Alternatively, a collar that makes someone feel powerful or like themselves can lead to a well-worn favorite. Below are just a few examples of collars and necklines that you may encounter in your wardrobe or that you may be asked to alter (12.1)!

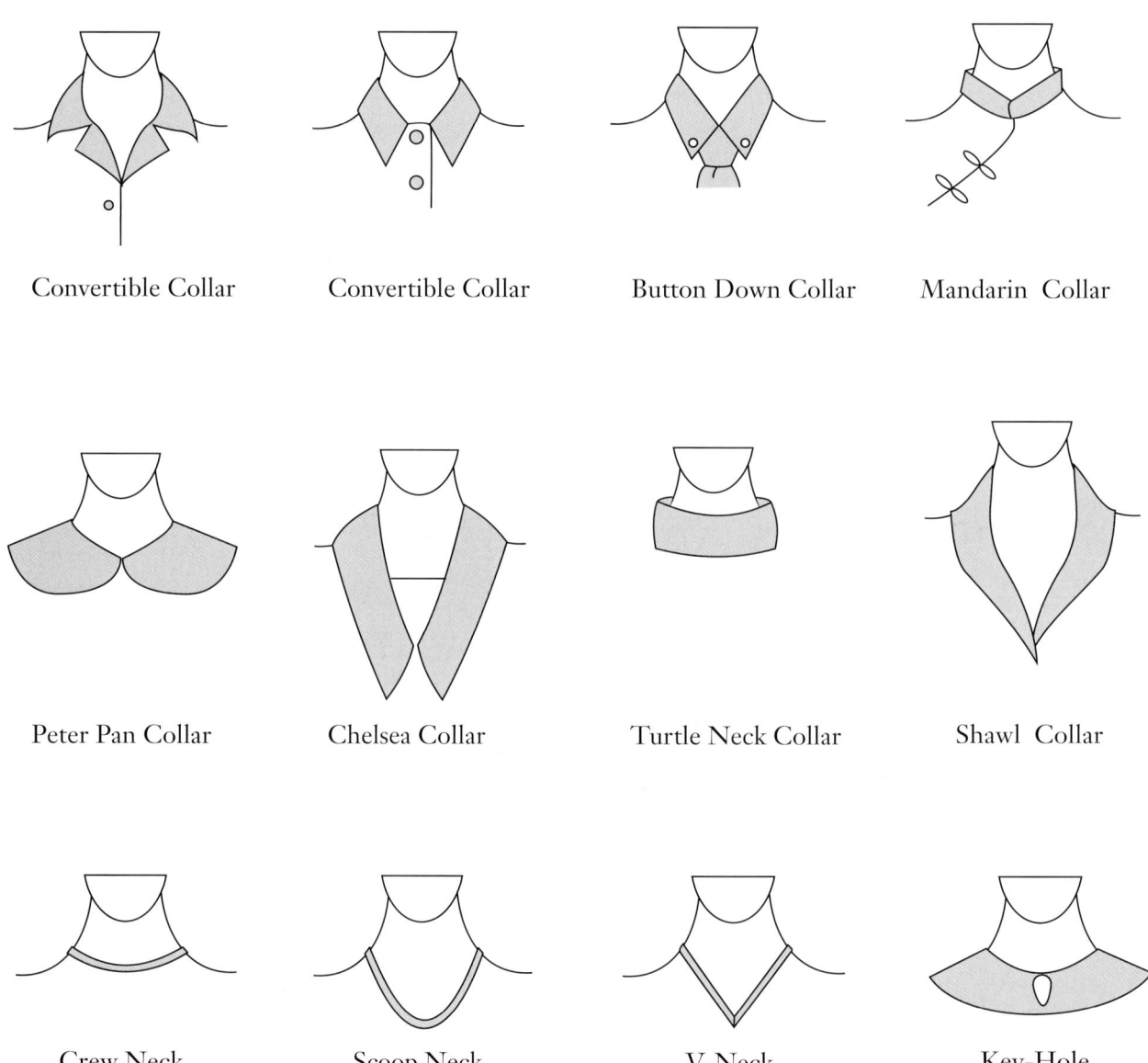

12.1

RESHAPING NECKLINES

30 minutes–1 hour

For this example, I have illustrated what it would look like to change a crew neck, knit t-shirt into a scoop neck by cutting off the original neckline and adding bias tape or rib-knit binding to finish the raw edge of the neck. Do not attempt to turn a neckline once or twice, it will pucker and look unprofessional. Use a facing, bias tape, or other appropriate neckline finish for professional results!

1. Have the client put on the garment and ask them how they would like the neckline changed. The most common request will be to turn a crew neck into a scoop or V-neck, AKA lowering the neckline. If the client would like a more modest or higher neckline, you will need to add fabric to the garment (12.2a).

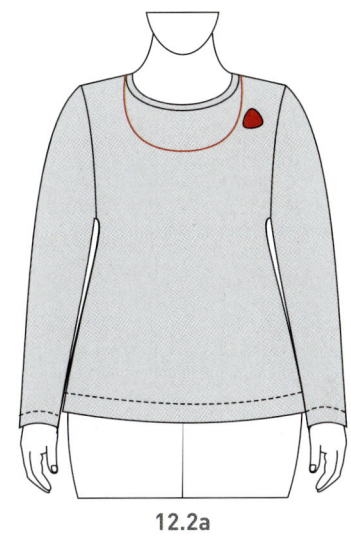

12.2a

2. Mark the new desired neckline, mark the seam allowance, and cut the new neckline (12.2b).

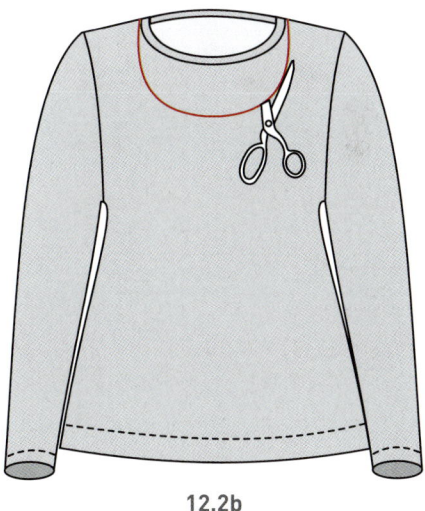

12.2b

RESHAPING NECKLINES | 193

3. Determine how the end will be finished: bias tape, facings, rib-knit neck band, etc. … Pin the new neckline finishing to the garment (12.2c).

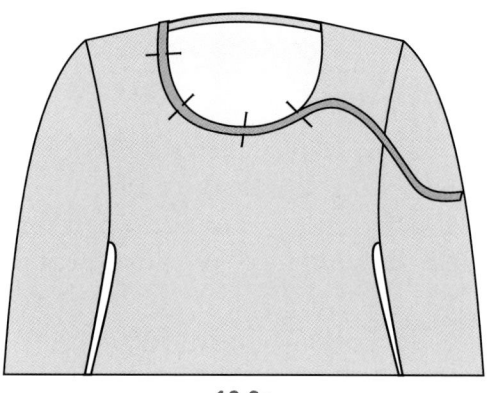

12.2c

4. Stitch the new neckline facing to the neckline (12.2d).

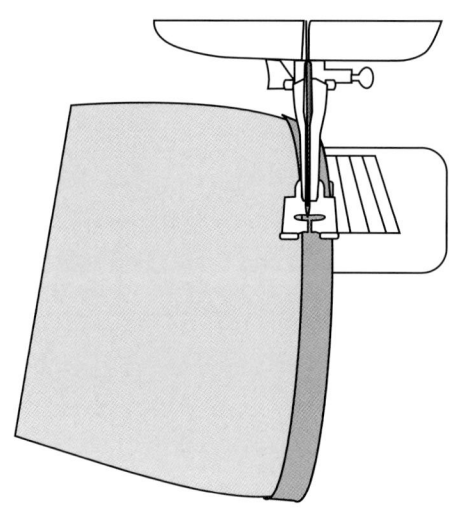

12.2d

5. Press the neckline, clip the threads, and check the fit (12.2e).

12.2e

COLLAR ADJUSTMENTS

1 hour

Is your client's collar a little too 1970s for them? Do they want to patch or replace a tattered collar? Most of the time, it is going to be easier to remove the collar, pattern a new one, and then stitch the new collar onto the garment. If making a new collar isn't the right course of action for a project, there are a couple of adjustments you can easily make for a collar.

1. If a collar is too big at the neck, pin out the amount that needs to be taken out (12.3a).

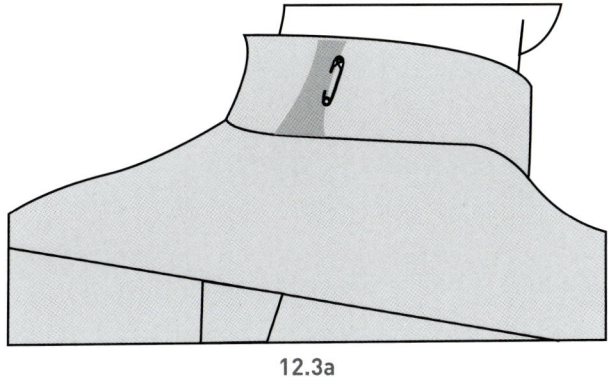

12.3a

2. Unpick the center back of the collar from the shirt (12.3b).

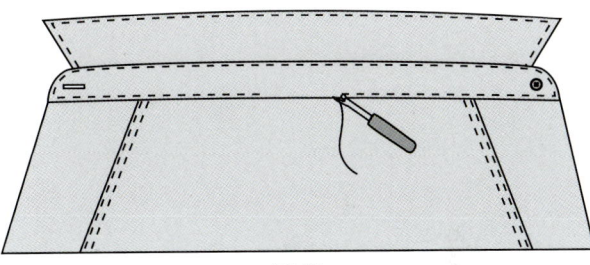

12.3b

3. Cut the center back of the collar to create a seam that makes the collar smaller. Unpick the stitching on all collar parts if you would like to have the seam allowance hidden in the collar. If you are looking for a fast fix, you can create the seam so it is on the outside of the collar so that when it is flipped down you do not see the seam. Mark the new stitch line (12.3c).

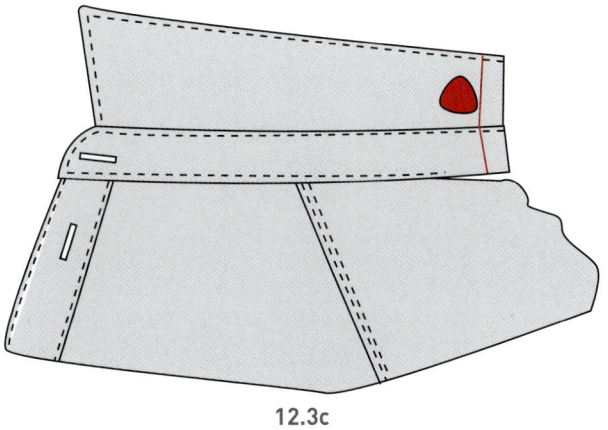

12.3c

4. Stitch and finish the raw edge of the seam OR if you unpicked the collar so that the seam is on the inside of the collar, press the seams open and then press the collar flat (12.3d).

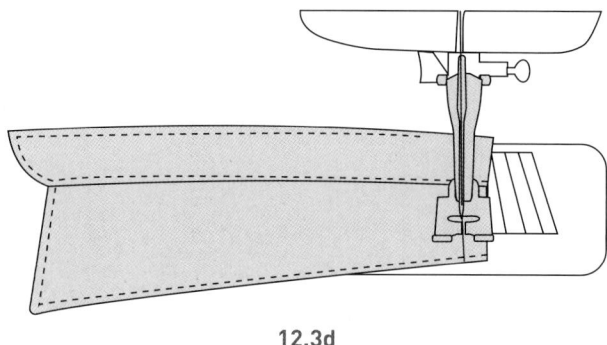

12.3d

5. Once the collar has been made smaller, you can then gather, ease, or create a pleat/tuck/dart in the center back of the shirt to fit the new size of the collar. Pin the shirt to the collar and stitch the raw edge into the collar with a topstitch (12.3e).

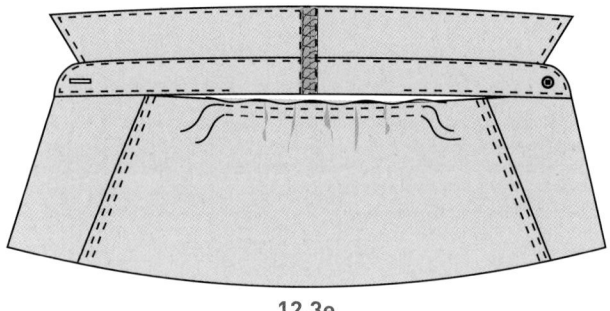

12.3e

6. Press the collar, clip the threads, and check the fit (12.3f).

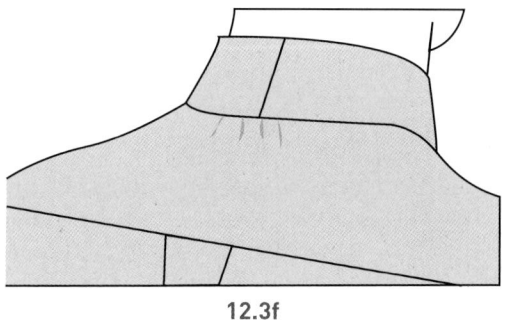

12.3f

COLLAR ADJUSTMENTS | 197

CHAPTER 13

Repairs

Repairs can range from quick/satisfying fixes like replacing a zipper head on a beloved winter coat to longer, and possibly messier, tasks like replacing the lining in an old leather jacket. This chapter will outline core repairs and further reading suggestions for creative repairs.

- Buttons
  - Button sizing
  - Replacing two-hole and four-hole buttons
  - Replacing shank buttons
- Patches
  - Iron-on
  - Visible mending
  - Fusible bonding web patch
- Darning
  - Machine darning
  - Hand darning
- Zippers
  - Anatomy
  - When to replace a zipper
  - When to fix a zipper
  - When to say "No"
- Linings
  - When to repair
  - When to replace
- Hook and loop tape
- Outdoor and waterproof gear repair

BUTTONS

Button Types

There are so many wonderful different button shapes, sizes, colors, and material types that you can select from. The most common buttons you will see are two-hole, four-hole, shank, and suspender buttons (13.1).

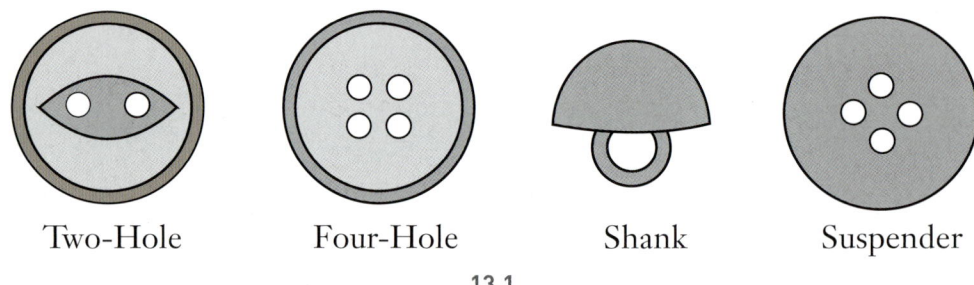

Two-Hole Four-Hole Shank Suspender

13.1

How to Determine Button Size Based on Buttonhole Length

1. Measure the diameter of the button and add the button height (not the shank height). This will be the measurement you need to determine how long your buttonhole should be (13.2).

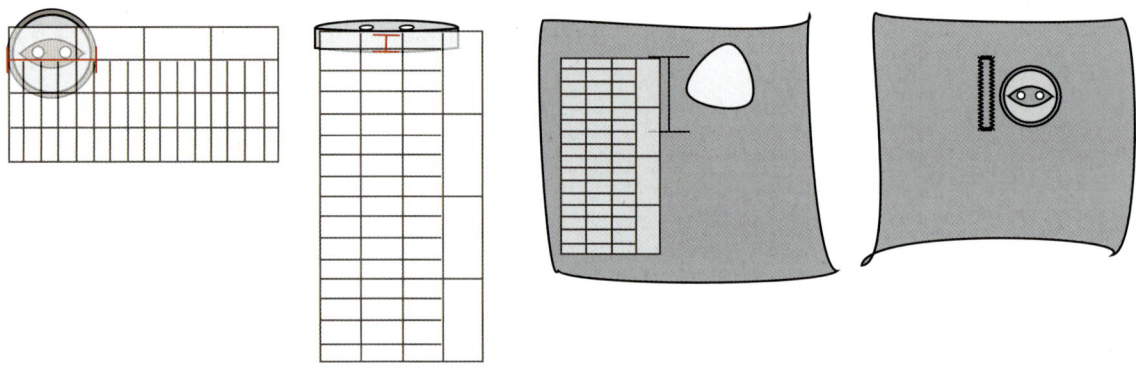

13.2

How to Sew on a Button That Has Fallen off or Is Loose on a Garment

Two- and Four-Hole Button

30 minutes △

1. Find the correct size of button based on other buttons on the garment or by measuring the buttonhole (see how to determine button size on page 200)

2. Use a length of thread as long as one of your arms stretched out to your suprasternal notch/center of your body. Anything longer than this can be challenging to work with. Either select a pre-treated thread such as silamide (2-ply waxed nylon thread) or treat the thread with beeswax, thread conditioner, or good ol' fashioned spit.

3. Thread the eye of a needle and match the cut ends at the bottom. Tie a knot at the end of your double thread. Clip the thread tails to ⅛" (3 mm).

4. Begin by stitching on the technical face/public side of the garment where the button will go so that the knot will be hidden under the button. I assure you that this method will produce the most beautiful button you've ever sewn! (13.3a).

5. On the technical back/private side of the garment, stitch ⅛" (3 mm) away from your previous stitch and come back up through to the public side of the garment (13.3b).

6. Next, put the thread through the back of one of the buttonholes. For a four-hole button, follow the diagram (13.3k) to determine which style of button threading you would like to use. Go down through the second hole of your liking and aim to have the needle go through exactly or very close to the original stitch you made (13.3c).

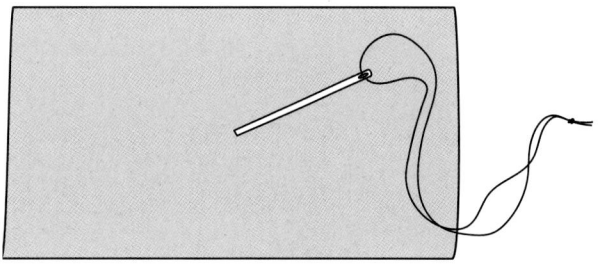

13.3a

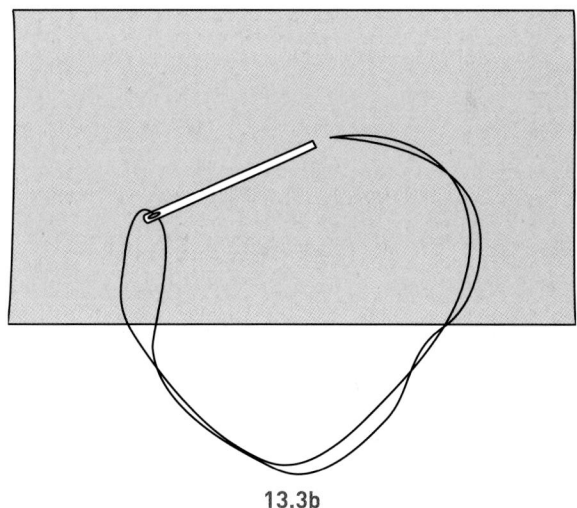

13.3b

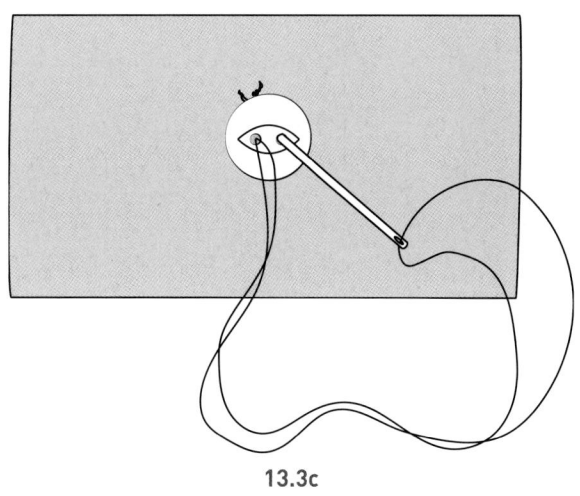

13.3c

7. Before continuing, slip a toothpick, pin, or end of a paperclip under the button so that you can create a thread shank. Due to the turn of the cloth, the height that is created through folding fabric, or working with multiple layers of fabric, you will need to create distance between the button and the fabric so that your button can actually get through the hole!

8. Once again, on the technical back/private side of the garment, stitch on or very close to the second stitch you made originally and come back up through to the public side of the garment through the first hole you went through (13.3d).

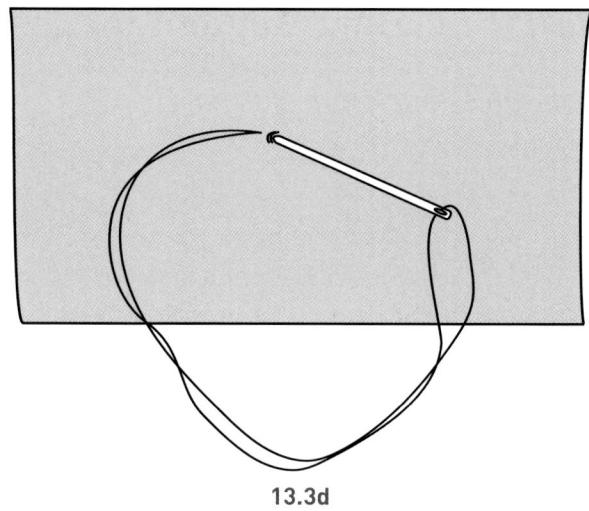

13.3d

9. Repeat that process three to five times and then switch to the next set of holes on the four-hole button, or go to step 11 for a two-hole button. You may remove the toothpick, pin, or end of a paperclip at this point as well as the shank should be established (13.3e).

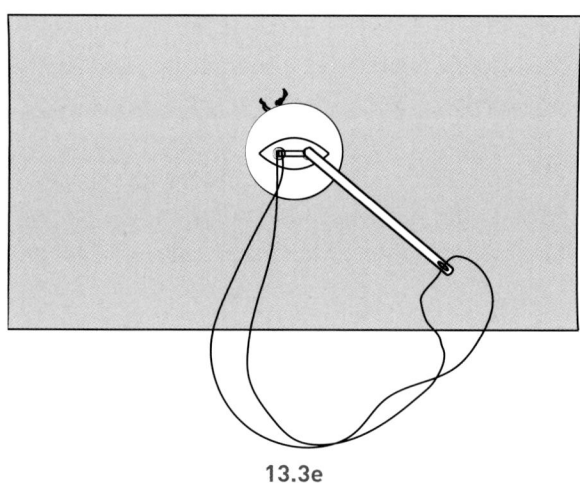

13.3e

10. Once again, on the technical back/private side of the garment, stitch on or very close to the second stitch you made originally and come back up through to the public side of the garment through the first hole you went through (13.3f).

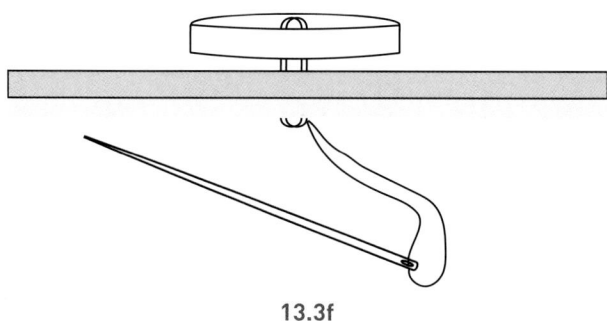

13.3f

11. After coming up from the back side for the last round, go through the holes but then do not go to the back side of the garment (13.3g).

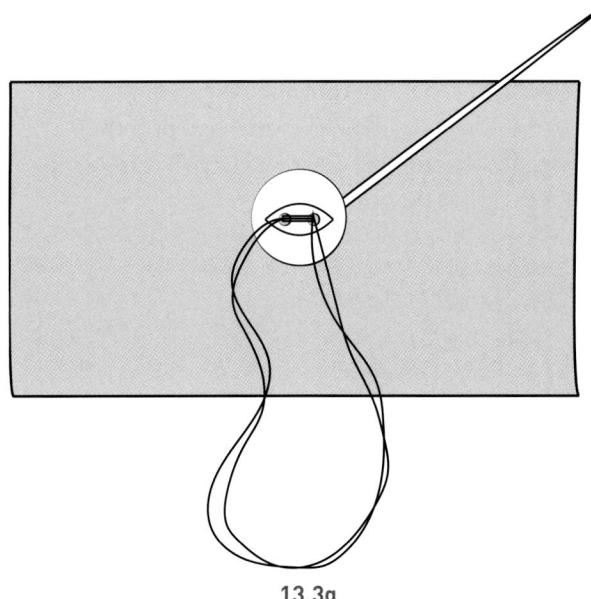

13.3g

12. Keep the needle and thread under the button and wrap the excess thread around the sewn threads to create the shank. I generally wrap the thread around about ten times or whatever it takes to get a sturdy shank! (13.3h).

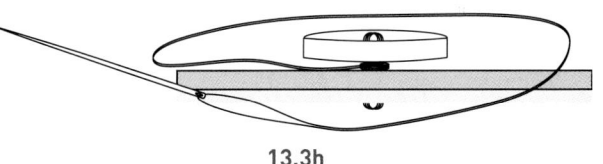

13.3h

13. On the last loop that you create around the button, wrap the thread around the button twice and pull the thread through to secure the thread shank (13.3i).

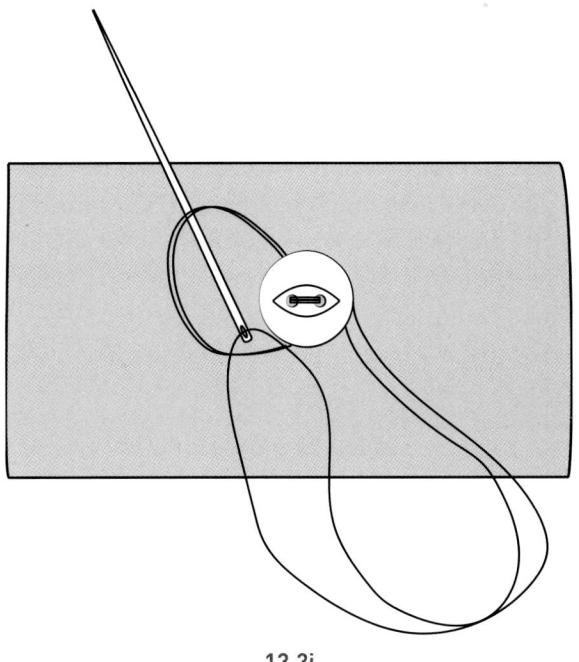

13.3i

14. Next, you will finish by taking a small "bite" of fabric under the button without pulling the needle all the way through. Wrap the thread around the needle 2–3 times and pull the needle through to create a knot that is at the base of the thread (13.3j).

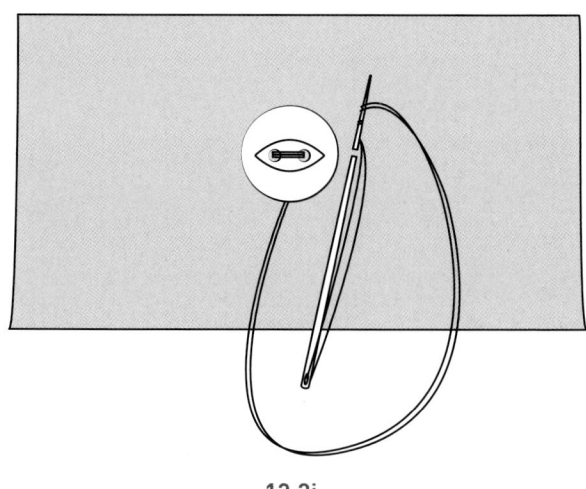

13.3j

15. For extra security, I like to put the needle through the technical back/private side of the garment and repeat the bite/knot process (13.3k).

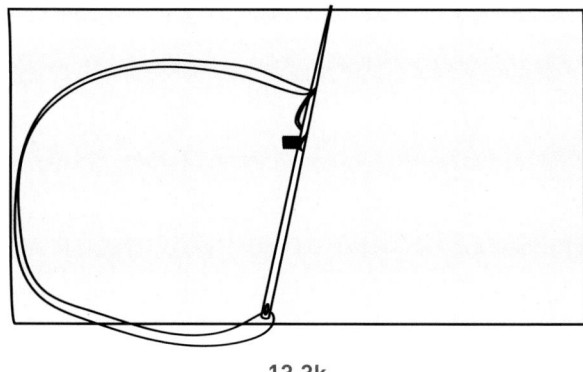

13.3k

16. Finally, you will hide your thread tails by taking a stitch in between the layers of fabric, pulling the tail out of the technical back/private side of the garment and then clipping the thread as close to the base as possible. The back threading of your button should look as clean and beautiful as the front! See figure (13.3L) for variations on how you can sew a four-hole button.

***Note on suspender buttons: these have a unique shape so that the suspender tab will not slip off the button. One side of the button is flat and the other is convex, like a tiny soup bowl. If you are sewing on buttons for suspenders, be sure to get a suspender button.

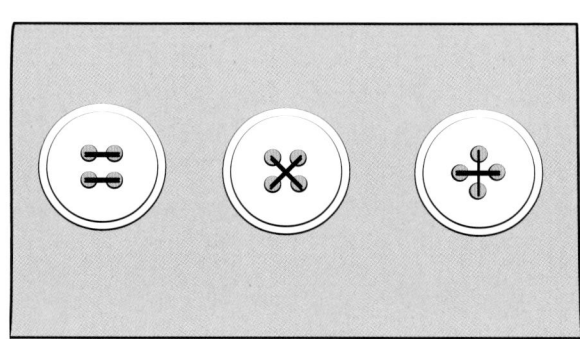

13.3l

Shank Button

30 minutes △

1. Find the correct size of button based on other buttons on the garment or by measuring the buttonhole (see how to determine button size on page 200).

2. Use a length of thread as long as one of your arms stretched out to your suprasternal notch/center of your body. Anything longer than this can be challenging to work with. Either select a pre-treated thread such as silamide (2-ply waxed nylon thread), or treat the thread with beeswax, thread conditioner, or good ol' fashioned spit (this will tickle!).

3. Thread the eye of a needle and match the cut ends at the bottom. Tie a knot at the end of your double thread. Clip the thread tails to ⅛" (3 mm). Begin by stitching on the technical face/public side of the garment where the button will go so that the knot will be hidden under the button (13.4a).

4. On the technical back/private side of the garment, stitch ⅛" (3 mm) away from your previous stitch and come back up through to the public side of the garment (13.4b).

5. Next, put the thread through the shank of the button and then out of the other side. Put your needle down into the fabric and aim to go through exactly or very close to the original stitch you made (13.4c).

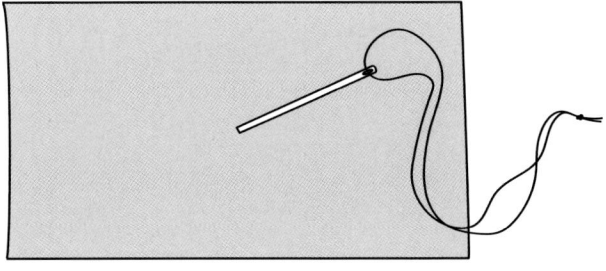

13.4a

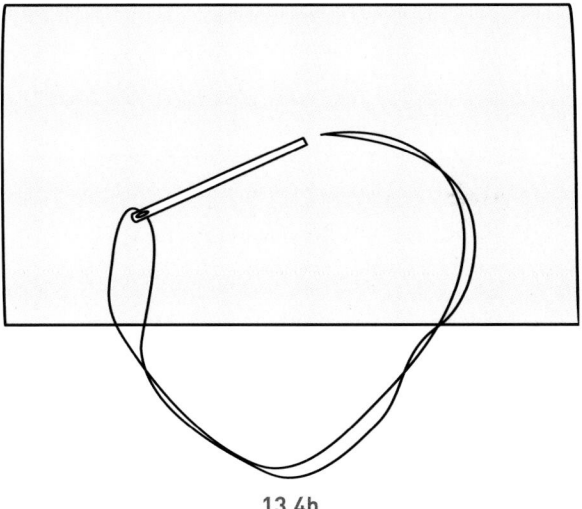

13.4b

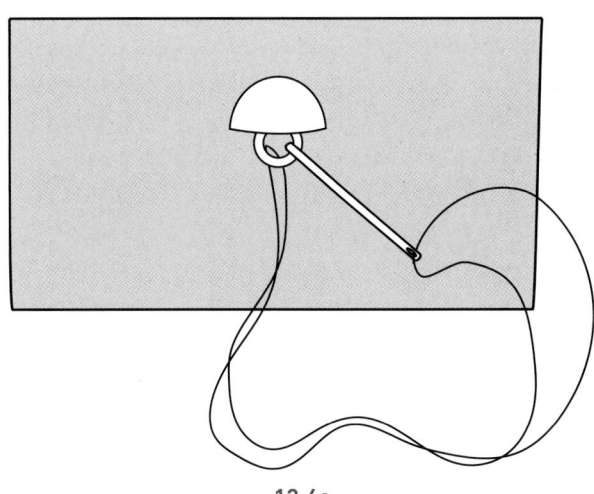

13.4c

6. Before continuing, if you need an additional shank, slip a toothpick, pin, or end of a paperclip under the button so that you can create a thread shank. Due to the turn of the cloth, the height that is created through folding fabric, or working with multiple layers of fabric, you may need to create extra distance between the button and the fabric so that your button can actually get through the hole! If you have a shank button that is sufficient and fits through the buttonhole already, the work is already done for you!

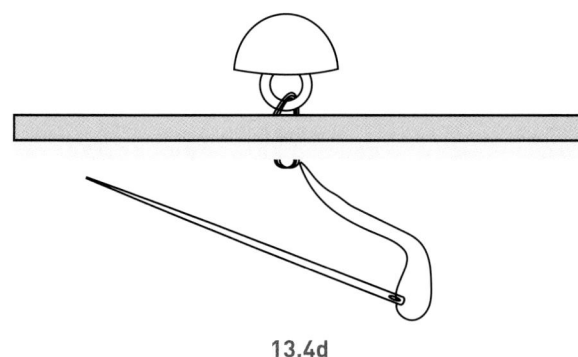

13.4d

7. Once again, on the technical back/private side of the garment, stitch on or very close to the second stitch you made originally and come back up through to the public side of the garment through the first hole you went through. At this point you can do it all by straddling the needle under the fabric (13.4d).

8. Repeat the process five to eight times or until the shank button isn't super wobbly.

9. After coming up from the back side for the last round, do not go through the hole. Keep the needle and thread under the button and wrap the excess thread around the sewn threads to create the shank. I generally wrap the thread around about ten times or whatever it takes to get a sturdy shank! (13.4e).

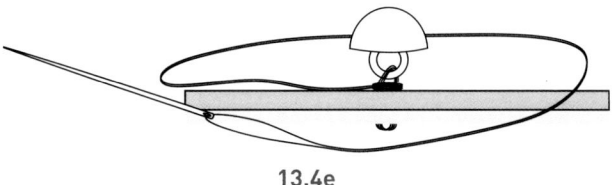

13.4e

10. For the final step, you will go on the backside of the garment and secure the button by taking a small "bite" of fabric without pulling the needle all the way through (13.4f).

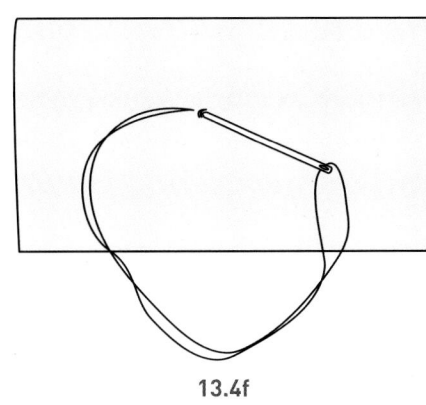

13.4f

11. Wrap the thread around the needle two to three times (13.4g).

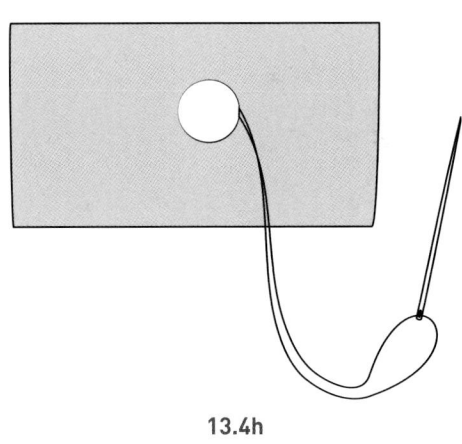

13.4g

12. Pull the needle through to create a knot that is at the base of the thread (13.4h).

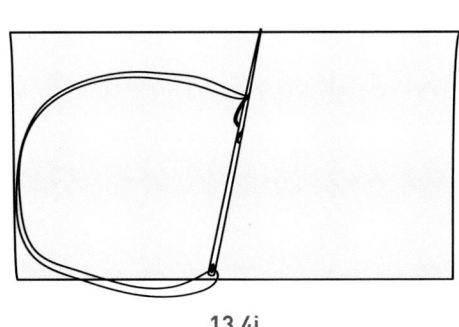

13.4h

13. Finally, you will hide your thread tails by taking a stitch in between the layers of fabric, pulling the tail out of the technical back/private side of the garment and then clipping the thread as close to the base as possible. The back threading of your button should look as clean and beautiful as the front! (13.4i).

13.4i

BUTTONS | 207

DECORATIVE PATCHES/VISIBLE MENDING

Patches can be as creative or simple as you would like! Visible mending has become popular in recent years and offers a way for your garment to take on a new life and for you to create little works of art. I enjoy these processes immensely, but did not commonly do them in my alterations shop. I have provided some examples of visible mending to inspire you, but will focus on the simpler options. Some resources you can use to create Sashiko-style visible mending, hand embroidery, etc. Here are some book recommendations for creative repairs and upcycling:

Mending Matters: Stitch, Patch, and Repair Your Favorite Denim & More by Katrina Rodabaugh

Make and Mend: Sashiko-Inspired Embroidery Projects to Customize and Repair Textiles and Decorate Your Home by Jessica Marquez

Mending Life: A Handbook for Repairing Clothes and Hearts by Nina Montenegro

Mend Patch: A Handbook to Repairing Clothes and Textiles by Kerstin Neumüller

ReFashioned: Cutting-Edge Clothing From Upcycled Materials by Sass Brown

Wear, Repair, Repurpose: A Maker's Guide to Mending and Upcycling Clothes by Lily Fulop

Iron-on Patches

30 minutes

Iron-on patches are readily available online and at craft and fabric stores. I generally do not use them as they leave a sticky residue if you forget to use a press cloth on the back side of the garment and tend to be a heavier weight than what I am working with. However, if you need a quick patch for work clothes, or for a garment that a child will grow out of in a couple of months, these patches are a wonder! Here are my tips for using them when it seems like the best option for your project.

1. Cut the patch at least ½" (1.2 cm) larger than the hole you are covering. If the patch is the same size as the hole, there will be nothing to hold the patch on, so make sure your patch is larger! (13.5a).

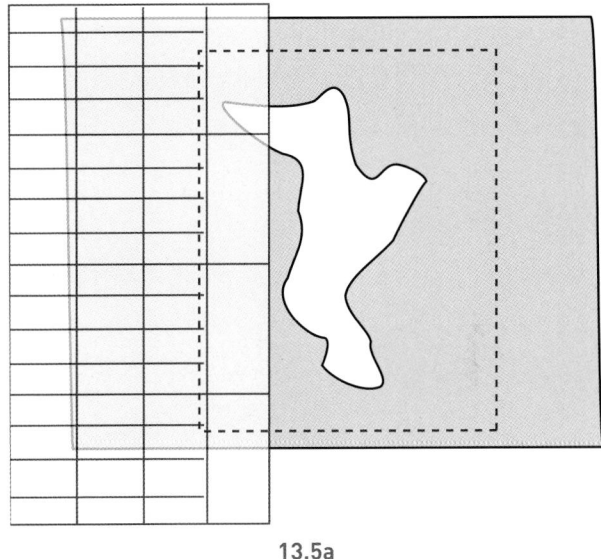

13.5a

2. Press the area that needs to be patched on the garment. If the fabric has stretched and warped, you can try spraying a bit of fabric sizing or run a basting stitch to gather the fabric back into shape. Place a scrap piece of fabric or press cloth under the patch so that you don't get glue on your ironing board. Once you are happy with the placement of the patch, press and hold the patch as long as the patch instructions recommend (13.5b).

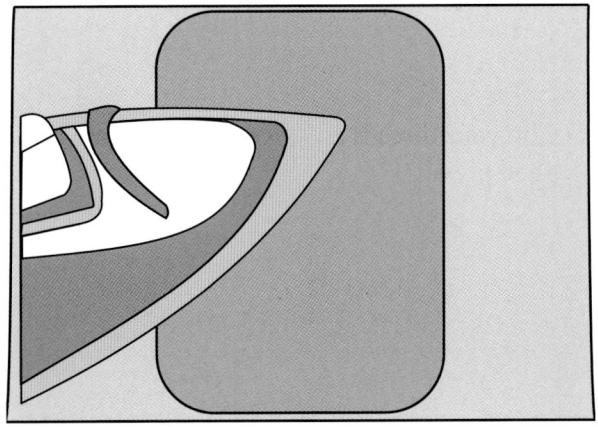

13.5b

DECORATIVE PATCHES/VISIBLE MENDING | 211

3. Carefully check that the edges of the patch have adhered to your garment. The next step is optional, however I would highly recommend stitching the edge of the patch as the iron-on patches tend to come unstuck after a few washes (13.5c). The glue will make your needle sticky, so grab some rubbing alcohol or an alcohol wipe to clean your needle as you go. Use a straight stitch, zigzag, decorative stitch, or hand stitch (like a blanket stitch or prick stitch) to secure the edge of the patch to the fabric (13.5d front of pant, 13.5e back of pant).

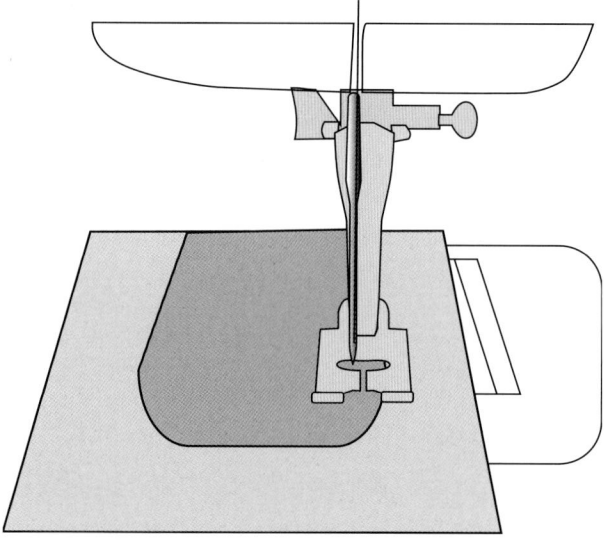

13.5c

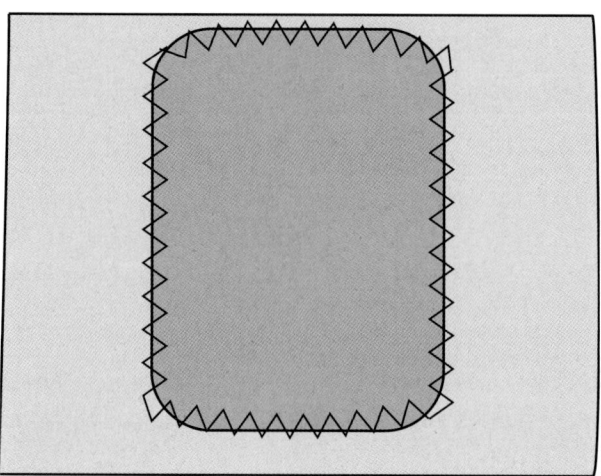

13.5d

4. Clip your threads and give that patch one more good press!

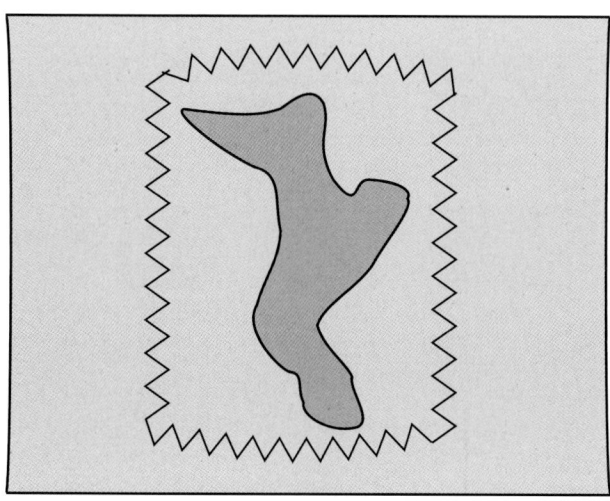

13.5e

Fusible Bonding Web Patches

30 minutes–1 hour

Imagine a fairy craft-spider decided to help you out by making a web of glue that isn't messy and is only sticky once pressed … that is the magic of fusible bonding web! Fusible bonding web, also known under the brand name Stitch Witchery, is spun glue that you can find by the yard (recommended!) or in small rolls. This is my favorite patch method as it is highly customizable and works well as a single- or double-layer patch. I don't recommend using it for hems, but I do recommend it for making custom patches!

1. Find a fabric that is similar in weight, structure, and fiber content to the garment that needs to be repaired and make sure to have fusible bonding web on hand (13.6a).

2. Determine whether the client needs a patch on the inside, outside, or both. Knees tend to need a double patch, whereas places like a crotch seam get a little bulky with internal and external patches. This is mostly based on preference and how rough the person will be in the area that is damaged.

3. Determine the shape and size of the patch(es). Make sure it is AT LEAST ½" (1.2 cm) larger on all sides of the patch. If you would like to have finished edges, allow another ¼" (6 mm) to the size in addition to the ½" (1.2 cm) + (13.6b).

4. Cut the patch(es) and cut the fusible bonding web to the same size (13.6c).

5. Serge or stitch the fusible bonding web to the fabric as close to the edge as possible. Do not iron the fusible bonding web yet! Place the fusible bonding web on the underside of the fabric that you would like to see on the outside up OR if you are doing an inner patch, with the fusible bonding web on the technical face/public side (13.6d).

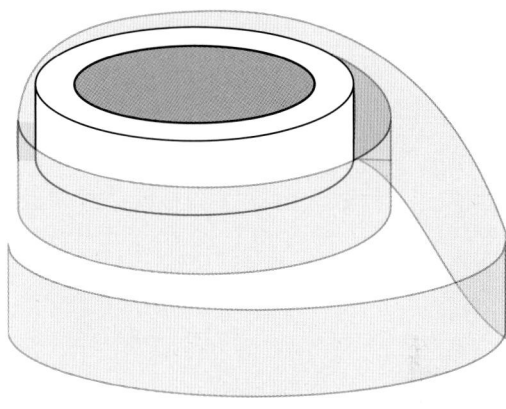

13.6a

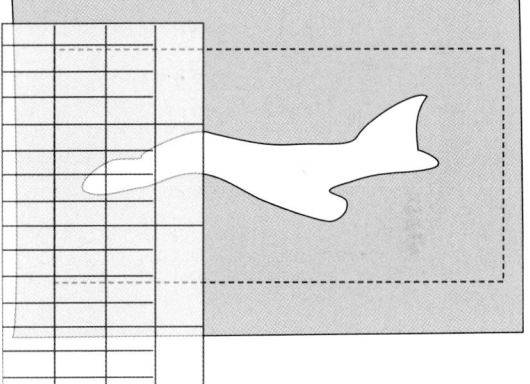

13.6b

13.6c

6. Press the area that needs to be patched on the garment. If the fabric has stretched and warped, you can try spraying a bit of fabric sizing or run a basting stitch to gather the fabric back into shape. If you are working on a curve, like a crotch seam, use a pressing ham or other pressing tool to maintain the correct shape.

7. At this point you have a few options. If you are looking for finished edges, you can CAREFULLY press the ¼" (6 mm) serged or stitched edge under making sure you don't melt the center of the patch (keep a pressing cloth under the patch just in case) OR you can stitch it down without pressing. If you are not pressing the ends under (great for inner patches) you can pin the patch(es) on to the garment and the edges and or center (13.6e).

8. If you are keeping a visible hole, cut away the fusible bonding web on that side of the patch. Press the patch(es) holding the iron directly on it for 30 seconds.

9. Carefully check that the edges of the patch(es) have adhered to your garment. If not, go back through and press until they stick. Keep in mind that the serge may be tight enough that the fusible bonding web is covered and will not adhere. Fear not! This is why we move to the next step!

10. Stitch the edge of the patch(es) as it will come unstuck after a few washes. The glue may make your needle sticky, so grab some rubbing alcohol or an alcohol wipe to clean your needle as you go. Use a straight stitch, zigzag, decorative stitch, or hand stitch (like a blanket stitch or prick stitch) to secure the edge of the patch to the fabric (13.6f).

11. Clip your threads and give that patch one more good press!

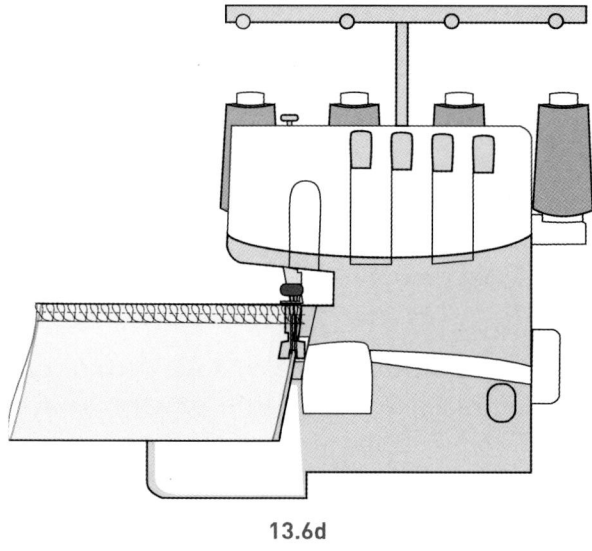

13.6d

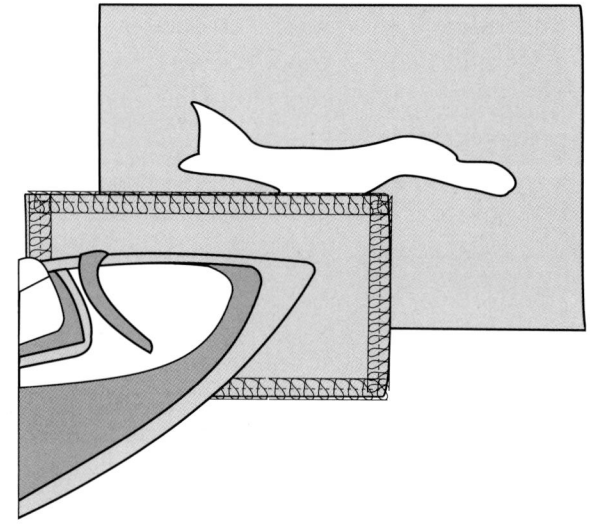

13.6e

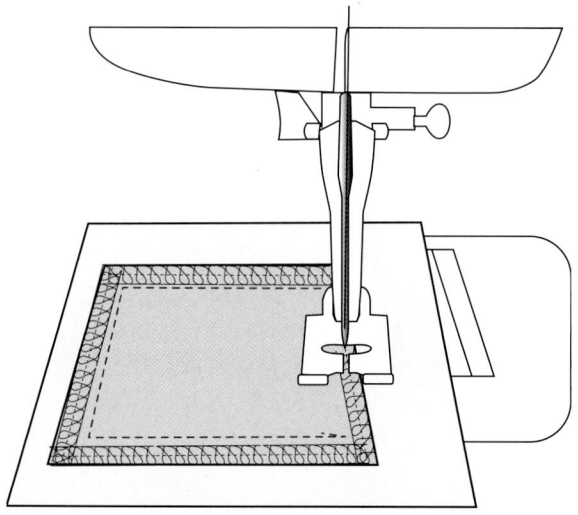

13.6f

214 | CHAPTER 13 REPAIRS

DARNING
About Darning
Darning is the art and act of repairing a hole or a worn area of fabric with needle and thread. This can be done on knits or wovens and by machine or by hand. Darning tools are often wooden, stone, or porcelain in various shapes so that you can stretch the fabric over them to stitch/weave the fabric back together without sewing multiple layers together. Some of the darning tools you may find are in the shape of an egg, mushroom, or gourd. Darning needles have a blunt tip and come in various sizes and lengths.

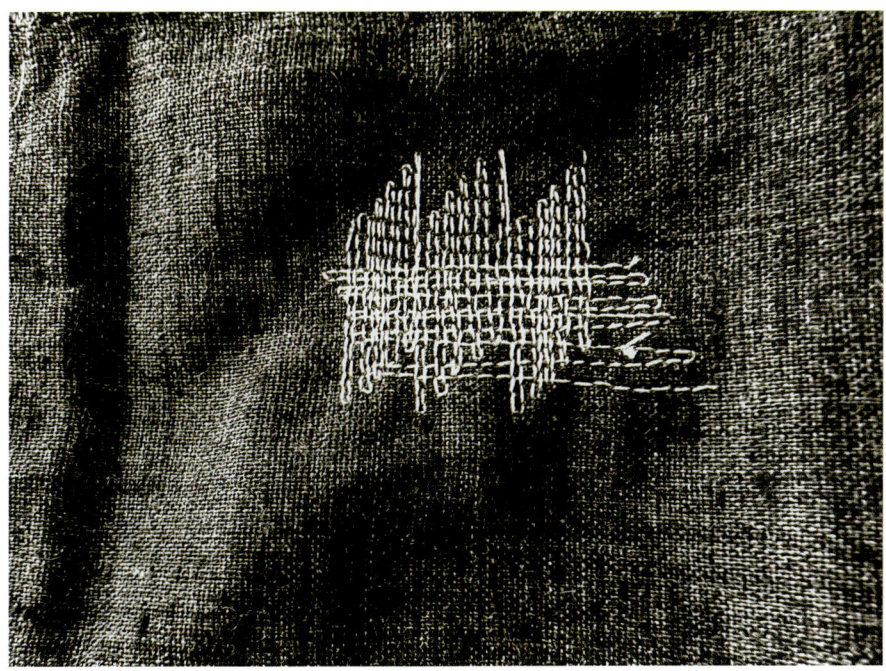

Machine Darning

30 minutes–1 hour

Some machines will have a darning stitch which essentially goes forward and backward slowly moving the needle position from left to right. I absolutely love using this feature on my Bernina. If you do not have this option, you can do this free hand on your machine with a little practice by simply stitching in alternating forward and backward stitches slowly inching over from one side of the tear to the other.

1. Place a piece of fabric under the fabric or follow instructions for making the patch (see pages 213–14) *and* then continue to this step (13.7a).

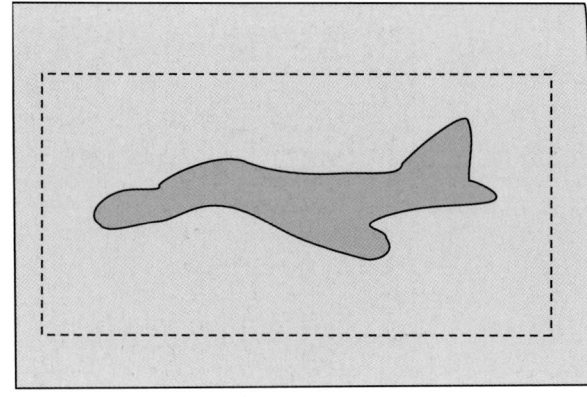

13.7a

2. First darn from top to bottom/vertically (13.7b).

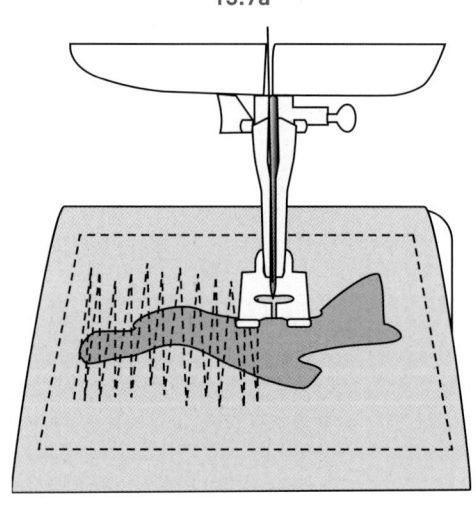

13.7b

3. Use the darning stitch on your machine to stitch from left to right/horizontally (13.7c).

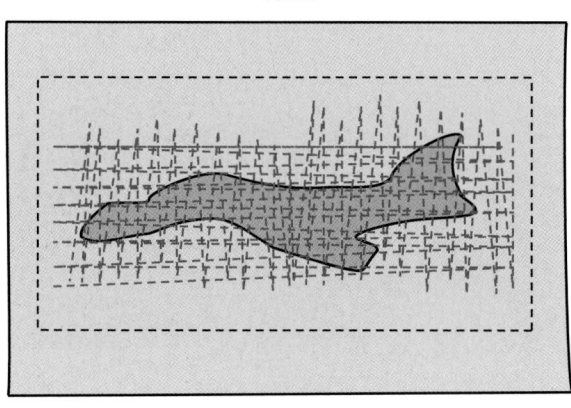

13.7c

Hand Darning

30 minutes–1 hour △

Hand darning can be a tedious, meditative, or a quick task depending on the repair and your time! To darn typically means to mend a knit garment by repairing the hole with weaving yarn up and down/warp and then left to right/weft. You may choose a yarn that is the same color and thickness (measured by WPI wraps per inch/Tex/yarn weight) as the fabric you are working with, or you can make a statement with visible mending, different colors, and thicker yarns. The most common items you will see that need to be darned are socks and knit sweaters.

1. Place the garment that needs to be darned over a darning tool (see page 215 for darning tool information).

2. Gently tug the garment over the darning tool to keep the natural stretch it has with the knit structure. If you do not stretch the garment, it will pucker and may become too small, so be sure to stretch the fabric a little while you darn (13.8a).

13.8a

3. Beginning ¼"–½" (6 mm–1.2 cm) away from the area that needs to be darned on all sides, begin weaving up and down/warp wise/vertically using yarn and a darning needle. Start your darning with a tailor's tack/backstitch. Avoid creating a knot with your yarn as you darn so that you don't have an uncomfortable/visibly noticeable bump on your work (13.8b).

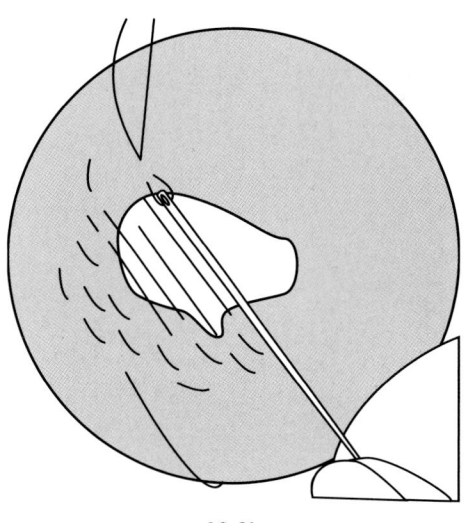

13.8b

4. Once you have covered the area that needs to be darned, begin darning left to right/weft wise/horizontally starting ¼"–½" (6 mm–1.2 cm) away from the area that needs to be darned on all sides (13.8c).

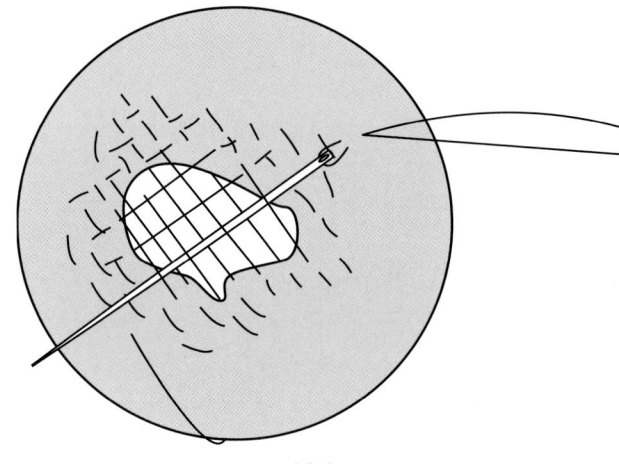

13.8c

5. Continue to gently stretch the garment so that it doesn't get too tight or bunch up. Darn ¼"–½" (6 mm–1.2 cm) past the edge of the hole (13.8d). End with a tailor's tack/backstitch.

6. Clip your threads and check to make sure you can still stretch the garment.

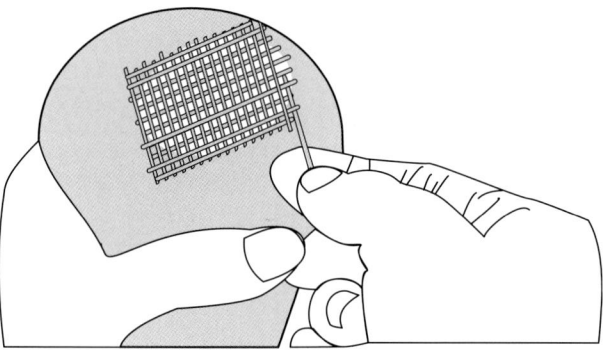

13.8d

ZIPPERS

Have you ever had a zipper break on your jacket, jeans, or backpack? Did you know that nine times out of ten you can fix that zipper for under $5? In this section, we will discuss the anatomy of a zipper, how to tell whether you need to replace an entire zipper, or if you can quickly replace one component of the zipper.

Anatomy of a Zipper

The zipper consists of four main parts: the zipper **tape** that is sewn into the garment that holds the teeth, the **teeth or coil** that are attached to the tape, **the slider/head** and pull that close the teeth/coil together, and the **hardware** that keeps the zipper slider/head from coming off the tape. The hardware can include top and bottom stops, insert pins, pins, and retaining boxes for separating zippers (13.9).

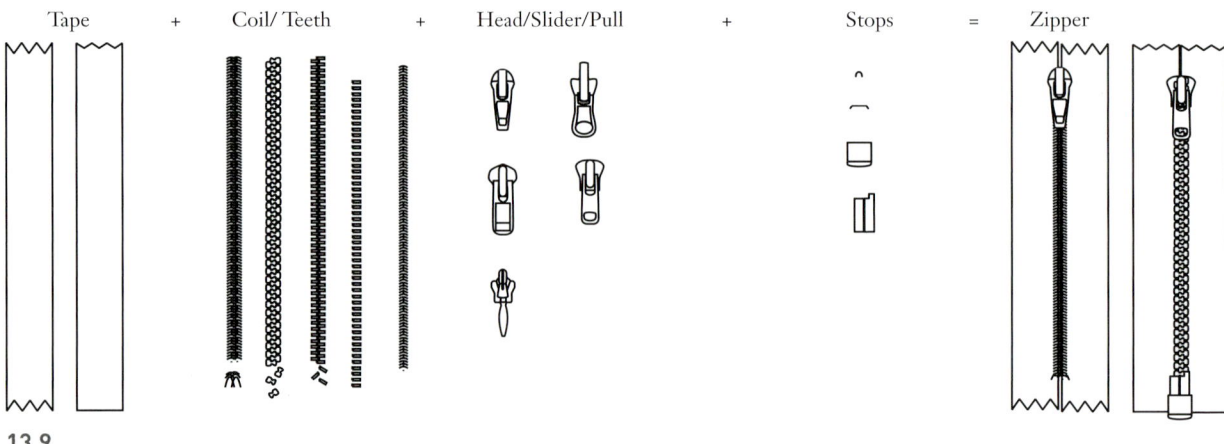

13.9

Types of Zippers

There are three main types of zippers: **metal, coil**, and **molded** plastic. Metal teeth zippers are most commonly used in jeans, leather jackets, and apparel that takes on a lot of wear and tear. Coil zippers include water-repellent zippers, invisible zippers, and reverse coil zippers. Coil zippers are made from polyester or nylon that has been shaped into a continuous coil that is wrapped around a cord and sewn to the zipper tape. Molded plastic zippers, commonly known as the YKK brand VISLON®, use plastic teeth and are used in bags and jackets. All zippers can have a closed bottom, open bottom, closed on both ends, or made continuously (13.10).

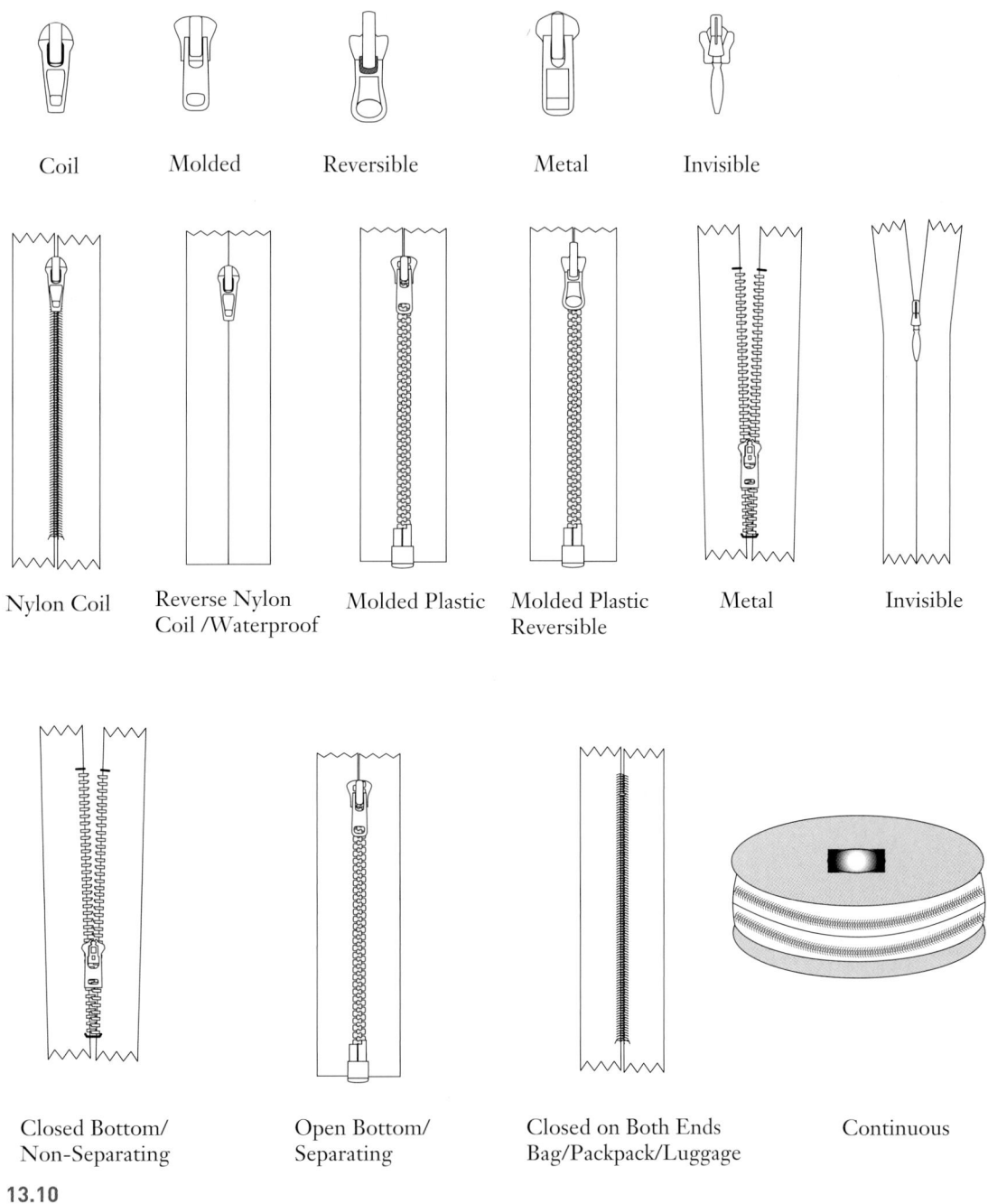

13.10

When to Replace a Zipper

When determining how to fix a zipper, you first need to establish whether you need to replace the zipper, replace the zipper head, or simply clean the zipper teeth. The following examples are what to look for if a zipper needs to be replaced rather than repaired.

- Teeth are missing from the insertion site on a separating zipper (13.11a)
- Teeth are missing from the midsection of a zipper (13.11b)
- The bottom of the zipper tape on a separating zipper has separated from the insertion pin (13.11c)
- The coil has been unraveled or has melted/warped (13.11d)

If none of the issues are present on the zipper, you can reference instructions on when to replace a zipper head (see page 226). If any of the issues are present, you will need to establish whether or not the zipper replacement is possible (see page 227).

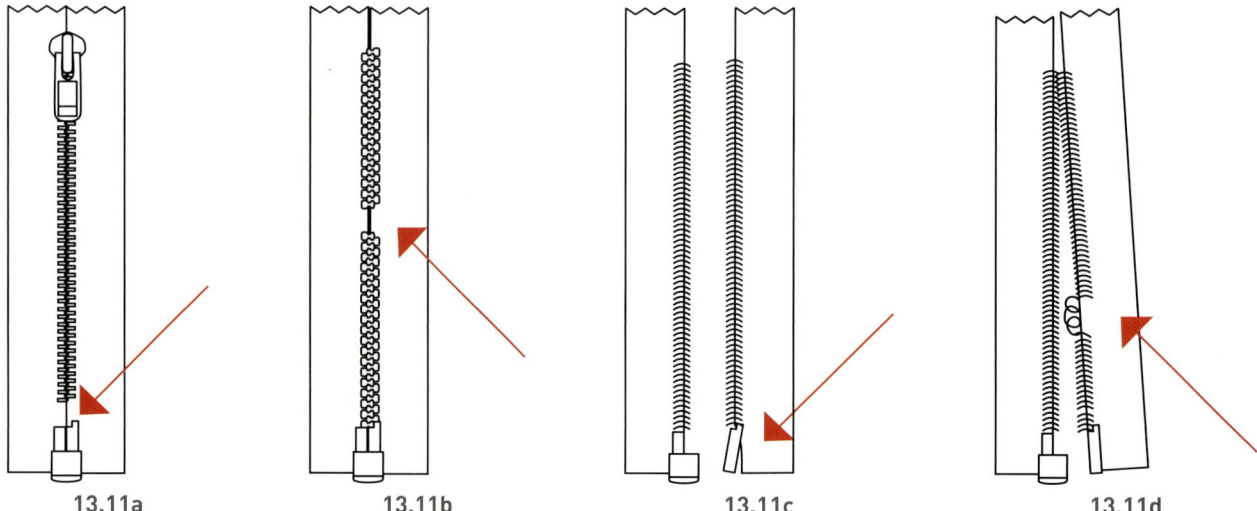

13.11a   13.11b   13.11c   13.11d

When to Fix a Zipper/Replace a Zipper Head

The majority of zippers can be repaired simply by putting a new slider/pull on. If the slider is still present, you can look on the back side to find a number and style type. If there isn't any text on the back side of the zipper, you can measure the millimeter distance from one side of the zipper teeth/coil to the other and that should give you an idea of what size you will need. For example, if the distance between a coil zipper is 5 mm, then you need a size 5 coil zipper coil. Once you have found the zipper pull that you need, you can take the following steps based on whether your zipper has a closed bottom, open bottom, is closed on both ends, or is made continuously.

Replacing a Zipper Head on Non-Separating/Closed/Closed at Both Ends/Continuous Zippers

30 minutes

1. For **coil zippers**, you can fix the zipper by sliding one end of the zipper head onto one side of the coil and then the other. I like to do this from the bottom and with one end of the zipper tape cut a bit shorter than the other, or you can sometimes attach the slider from the top depending on the zipper. It can be helpful to have one end of the zipper tape shorter than the other if possible (13.12a). If you do not have access to the end of the tape, you may be able to get the zipper on from the side of the coil with a little patience and practice!

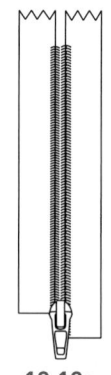

13.12a

2. For **metal zippers**, you almost always need to reattach the zipper head from the bottom of the zipper. This usually means that you have to remove the bottom stop and some of the zipper teeth with a pair of pliers so that you have a little tape to get your zipper head started on one side, and then the other (13.12b).

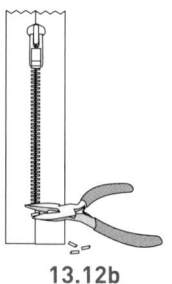

13.12b

3. **Plastic molded** zippers can be fixed from the top or bottom. Remove some of the teeth on either side of the tape with pliers so you have a little bit of space to attach the zipper head on one side, and then the other. Slide the new head onto tape so that the teeth interlock (13.12c).

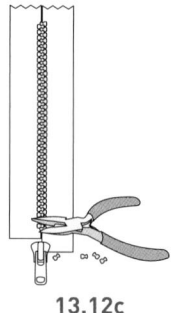

13.12c

4. **Invisible zippers** are the most challenging zipper heads to replace and often end up in a zipper replacement. If you want to attempt this, you will need to remove the plastic stop with pliers and without pulling out the coil at the bottom of the zipper. Next, roll the zipper tape on one side of the zipper into the groove of the zipper head and then the other. You may have to try several times to make sure the zipper will line up correctly at the top and bottom of the garment (13.12d).

13.12d

Replacing a Zipper Head on Separating Zippers

15 minutes △

1. For all separating zippers you begin by simply removing the top stop on the side of the tape with the zipper head with pliers (13.12e).

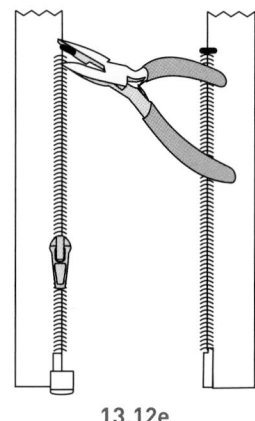

13.12e

2. Remove the damaged or broken zipper head and throw the zipper head away so you do not accidentally try to reuse a damaged zipper head (13.12f).

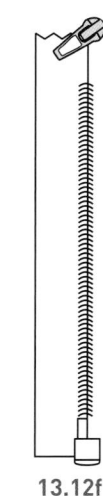

13.12f

3. Next, slide the new zipper slider on the tape and check that the zipper can connect and zip from the pin insertion point, and then secure the zipper by adding a top stop with pliers (13.12g).

   Sometimes it can be challenging to get the zipper head onto the zipper if the top of the tape has been folded down and stitched in. In this circumstance, you can try to seam rip the stitching where the tape has been folded, replace the zipper head, and then restitch the zipper in place. If you don't want to do that, you can carefully cut a small part of the fold in the middle of the zipper tape, slide the zipper head on, and then place the new top stop directly over the fold to prevent the cut from unraveling.

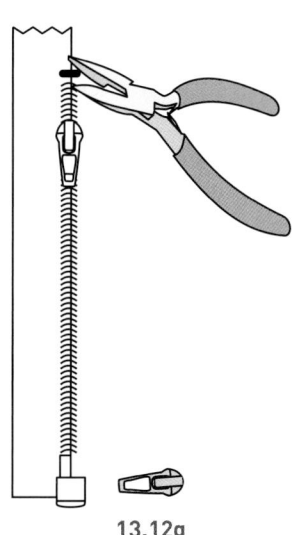

13.12g

When to Replace a Zipper Head

After establishing that a zipper does not need to be replaced, you can investigate to see if and when you can replace the zipper slider. The following are examples of when a zipper head/slider has been pinched or broken such that it no longer connects the teeth or coil of a zipper.

- When the zipper separates from the bottom after being zipped (13.13a)

- When the slider does not stay up (13.13b)

- When the teeth/coil are intact, but the slider does not connect them (13.13c)

- When the slider has come off the tape (13.13d)

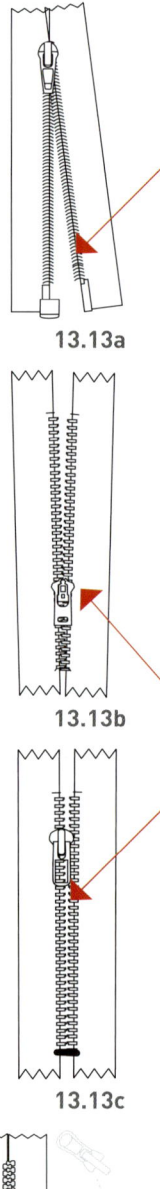

13.13a

13.13b

13.13c

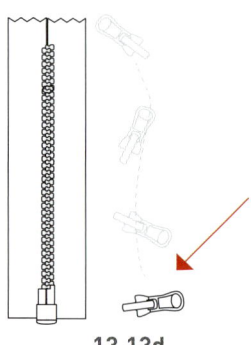

13.13d

When to Say "No"

As much as I would like to repair and replace every zipper possible to extend the life of the garment, sometimes it is more work and effort than it is worth saving. The following are circumstances in which it's time to thank the garment for its service, and upcycle it or use it for another purpose:

- When the zipper has been attached by a seam sealer. Unless you are skilled in this arena or the garment can stand to be smaller on the wearer, pass on this one.
- With delicate fabrics that will tear if you seam rip them.
- Fabrics with down fill. The down fill will come up through the textile every time you send the needle through the fabric. Again, if you are skilled in this, go for it! Otherwise, save yourself the headache and pass on this zipper replacement.
- With fabrics that you are uncomfortable working with like leather, sequin, mesh, etc.
- Garments with challenging fabric and zipper shields/plackets that need to be removed.

LININGS

A lining is a layer of fabric that covers the inside of a garment or product. You might commonly find clients who have a dress, skirt, pair of pants, leather jacket, or suit jacket that they love but the lining is shredded, or they may have issues with the lining being too small and tugging on the outer garment. Because this repair requires a broader understanding of garment construction and pattern-making, I suggest checking out Cabrera and Meyers' wonderful tailoring books *Classic Tailoring Techniques: A Construction Guide for Men's Wear* or *Classic Tailoring Techniques: A Construction Guide for Women's Wear*.

WHEN TO REPAIR A LINING

30 minutes–1+ hours

- Repair a lining if there are small sections that can be patched using the patch or darning techniques (see pages 208–18). Note that you do not want to attach the lining to the outer fabric unless it is already connected or quilted. You may need to open up the center back or often a sleeve where there is a bit of topstitching to get into the garment.
- Repair a lining that is not cracking or shredding. If the fabric falls apart when you gently tug on it, OR if the lining has shrunk and is starting to tug/bunch/warp on the outer fabric you may need to replace the lining.

REPLACING OR RETHREADING DRAWSTRINGS

30 minutes △

It is such a pain to lose one end of a drawstring on a hoodie or pair of pajama pants, and it can seem impossible to get it back into place! Follow these instructions to make quick, easy work of the task!

1. Attach a safety pin or elastic threader to one end of the drawstring (13.14a).

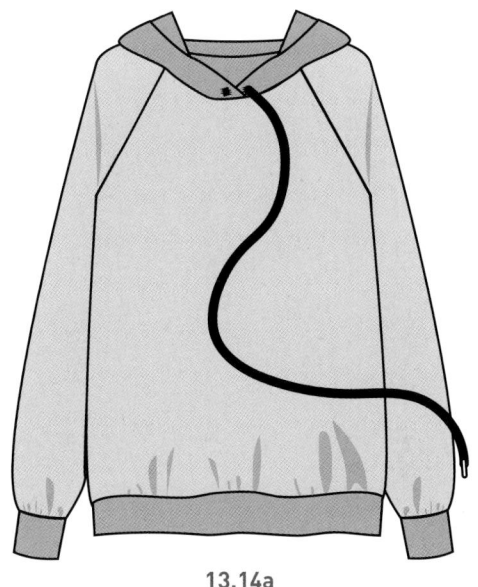

13.14a

2. Use the loose end of the drawstring with the safety pin or an elastic threader to feed the drawstring through the tunnel of the hood or waistband. Anchor the other end close to the buttonhole opening so you don't accidentally pull the entire drawstring out. When you get to seam allowance points, you may need to squeeze the top and bottom of the waistband to create a tunnel. It is common to get stuck in the seam! If you are struggling, pull the drawstring out away from the seam a bit and keep trying (13.14b).

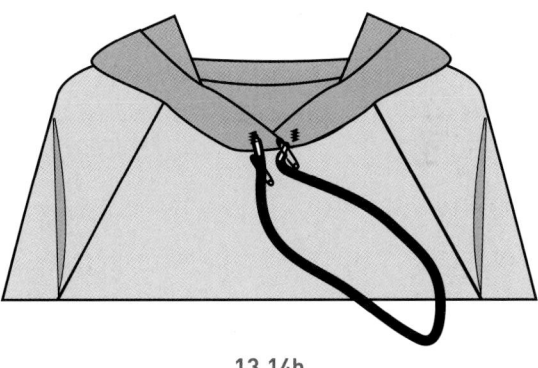

13.14b

3. Once you get all the way through, you may choose to stitch the drawstring at the center back so it does not come out as easily. Otherwise, creating a knot or turning and stitching the ends so they are too large to go through the buttonholes can save you in the future! (13.14c).

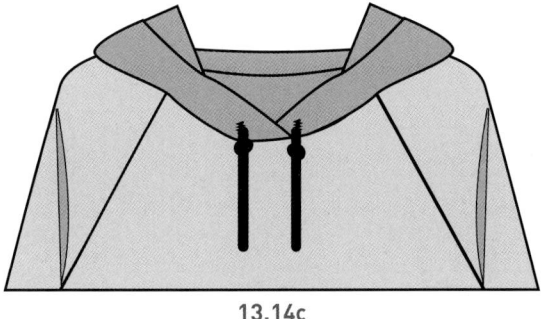

13.14c

HOOK AND LOOP TAPE

30 minutes △

Just like Kleenex is a brand name for facial tissues, Velcro is a brand name for your best friend, or worst thread enemy, hook and loop tape! It is characterized by one end that has loops (soft side) and the other that has hooks (prickly side). It is highly useful and is also infamous for picking up every thread, hair, and bit of fuzz that comes within a three-foot radius of the garment it is attached to.

Reviving or Replacing Hook and Loop Tape

- Sometimes you simply need to clean out hook and loop tape with a fine comb. If you can clean out the excavation site and the tape is still functional, you are done! Otherwise …
- You can replace hook and loop tape by simply unpicking the tape, cutting new tape to size, and top stitching it on as close to the edge as possible (13.15).

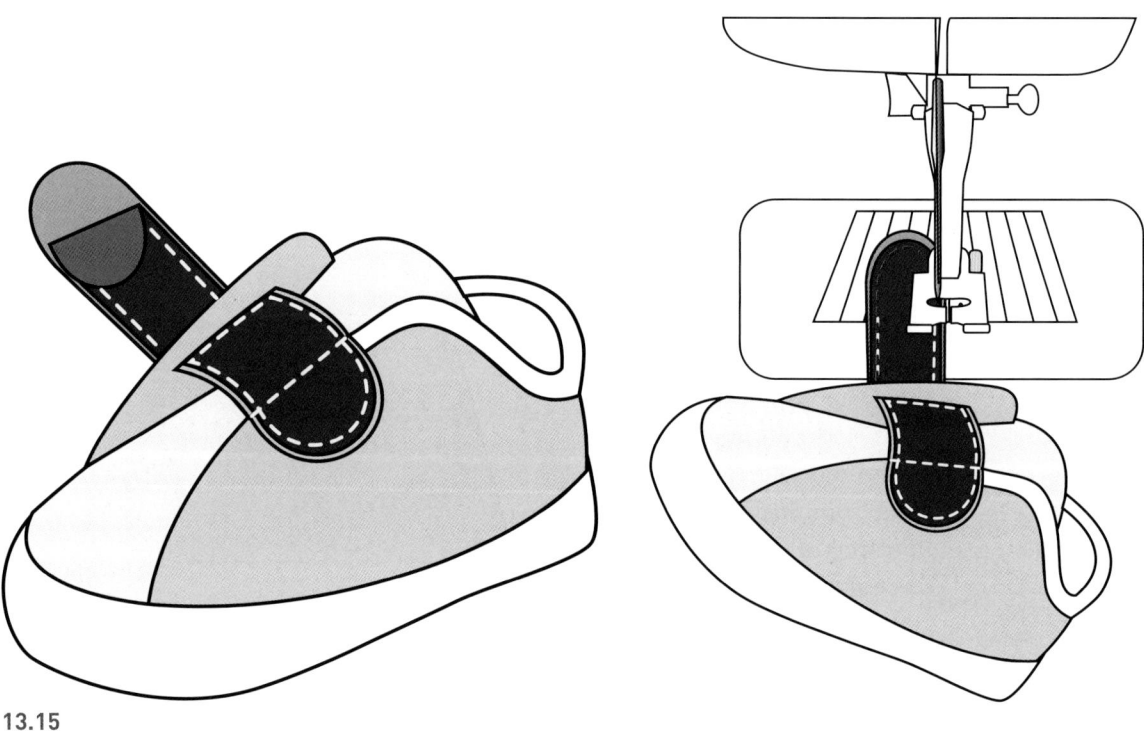

13.15

OUTDOOR/OTHER GEAR

Some of the most rewarding and daunting repairs you can take on are with the gear that gets you out of the house and into nature or your workplace. Whether you have a backpack zipper that is no longer functioning, a pair of gloves with holes in the fingertips, a tent with a hole, or waterproof gear that no longer keeps you dry, there is often a great solution that costs much less than purchasing new kit! This section won't cover every possible gear scenario, but it has some general tips for what you might encounter when repairing outdoor/other gear.

Patches

30 minutes

For any outdoor gear patching that needs to happen, I highly recommend self-adhesive, waterproof nylon patches. The patches come in sheets like a sticker with nylon fabric on one side, and adhesive on the other in a variety of colors. You simply cut them to size, prepare the garment by cleaning it and laying it flat, remove the paper backing on the patch, and place the patch carefully onto any rips or holes. I will occasionally stitch around the edge as I would in the patches listed earlier in this chapter (see pages 212 and 214), but if you don't plan to wash the item that you are patching, you can usually get away with using this very fancy sticker. For gear that needs to be waterproof, I put the patch on both sides of the fabric:

- Backpacks
- Tents
- Bags

Zippers

For outdoor gear, backpacks, fanny packs, bags, and sleeping bag zipper repair or replacement, see pages 222–6 for instructions.

- Note that one of the main reasons outdoor gear fails is due to debris in the zipper teeth or zipper head. If the gear you are repairing is dirty, use a toothbrush to brush out debris, if necessary clean the zipper with water, detergent, or a zipper cleaning solution and then lubricate the zipper teeth or coil with zipper lubricant.
- If you need to replace the zipper head, follow the instructions on page 223. Often there is a small tab of fabric or binding that needs to be unpicked in order to access the zipper teeth/coil. Carefully remove any tabs and seams, remove the old head, and then place the new head on. After the zipper head is on, you will need to reattach and sew any seams or tabs that prevented the zipper head from coming off.
- If you need to replace the zipper, really consider your time and the cost of the garment prior to committing to the repair. If the gear is near and dear to the client and they are willing to pay you for what your time is worth, wonderful! If not, consider upcycling the gear!

WATERPROOF GEAR

If you have gear that was once waterproof and no longer is, you may be able to treat the gear to be waterproof once again. Most fabric finishes that help make textiles become waterproof fade a bit after each wash, while some remain waterproof forever! There are several products on the market that you can apply to some fabrics to revive the waterproof coating, but you usually cannot make something waterproof unless it was specifically designed with the proper textile structure and fiber. Some of the products that can be used to revive your gear are toxic and bad for the environment, so be sure to do your research to see what is most appropriate for your gear. Commonly used products include Scotchgard, DWR or Durable Water Repellent (avoid C8 fluorocarbon-based DWR), and beeswax.

Resources

Fabric, Sewing Supplies and Equipment

B. Black and Sons
https://www.bblackandsons.com/
Wholesale wool and lining fabrics for apparel and fashion, tailoring and sewing supplies.

Denver Fabrics
https://denverfabrics.com/
Quality fabric, deadstock, and generous sized swatches.

Etsy
https://www.etsy.com/
Global marketplace for fabrics, trims, notions and sewing supplies.

Gold Star Tools
https://www.goldstartool.com/
Online international supplier for fashion and sewing supplies.

JoAnn Fabrics
https://www.joann.com/
Fabric and sewing tools/ supplies.

Mood
https://www.moodfabrics.com/
Premium fabrics by the yard sold online.

Sewing Parts Online
https://www.sewingpartsonline.com/
Sewing supplies, notions/ trims, and sewing machine replacement parts.

Spoonflower
https://www.spoonflower.com/
On-demand, online digital fabric printing.

Wawak
https://www.wawak.com/
Online sewing supplies, equipment, interfacings, repair products.

Machines

I get asked all the time what machines I recommend for sewists, so I have included a list below of the machines that I use and have experience with. Please note that there are many machines that will be great for your studio that may not be listed below!

Home Sewing Machines:
Bernina 1008
Classic workhorse machine, not computerized, easy to maintain.

Bernina 300 Series
Quality, computerized machines, easy to use, can be used without foot pedal.

Industrial Lockstitch Machines:
Juki DDL 8100 or 8700
Affordable, not computerized, easy to maintain.

Brother S7300
Computerized industrial machine, auto thread trimmer, programmable.

Serger/ Overlock Machines
Brother 1034D
Easy to use, affordable, 4-thread serger.

Bernina 1300 MDC2
Quality 4-thread serger.

Coverstitch Macines
Brother Coverstitch 2340CV
A little finicky, as all coverstitch machines are, but gets the job done.

Juki MF-7523 Coverstitch
Industrial coverstitch with a steep learning curve and beautiful results.

Glossary

Alterations Adjustments that are made to custom fit a garment to an individual body.

Backstitch The process of stitching backwards over the loose threads at the beginning and end of a project to secure the threads so stitches do not come undone.

Bar Tack Zigzag stitches sewn closely together to reinforce a component or part of a garment such as the bottom of a zipper, the top and bottom of a button hole, or a belt loop.

Baste Hand or machine sewing long stitches that can be easily removed. This stitch can be used to hold a zipper in place prior to stitching, mark a delicate fabric, or hold two fabrics in place together.

Bias A 45 degree angle on fabric that provides stretch without elastic fiber properties. A true bias is 45 degrees, and 30 degree or 60 degree angles may be used in some cases.

Bias Tape Pre-made or handmade strips of fabric cut on the bias/45 degree angle of a fabric. Bias tape comes in various sizes and is a great way to finish edges, especially on curves like necklines.

Blind Hem/Invisible Hem A hem finish created on a blind hem machine, home machine with a blind hem foot/stitch, or via hand sewing that is not visible on the outside of a garment.

Break How much the hem on bottoms breaks over a shoe or foot. Breaks can range from no break, meaning the fabric does not fold over the shoe, to a full break, meaning one full fold above the shoe.

Bring Up To shorten a length of a garment or part of a garment like shoulder seams or hems.

Coverstitch A common method of finishing knit hems using a coverstitch machine.

Cross Grain/Crosswise Grain The yarns of woven fabric that run perpendicular to the selvedge. Also called the weft.

Cuff A layer of fabric at the bottom of a sleeve at the wrist or a fold of fabric at the bottom of a pant leg.

Darning Mending a hole by interweaving yarn on fabric.

Darts Fabric that is folded together and then stitched in a triangle or fisheye/diamond shape that adds shape to a garment. Darts can be added to garments to make them smaller/more fitted to the body.

Ease The amount of extra fabric in a garment to allow for ease of motion or the act of stitching the edge of a garment in order to make it fit another piece of fabric, like setting sleeves.

Facing A pattern piece cut into fabric used to finish raw edges of necklines, armholes, and waistbands.

Gather/Gathering Stitch A row or multiple rows of stitching used to make a larger/longer piece of fabric fit a smaller piece of fabric resulting in a ruffled effect. Used on skirts attached to waist bands, puff sleeves, yokes, etc.

Grain/Straight of Grain The yarns of woven fabric that run parallel to the selvedge edge. Also called the warp.

Gusset A triangular piece of fabric inserted into a seam to add fullness. Often used in crotch seams and armscyes.

Hem The raw or finished edge of a garment at the bottom edge of a garment.

Inseam The seam on the inside of the leg.

Interfacing Fusible or sewn in materials applied to fabrics that give garments stability or structure. Common parts of garments that contain interfacing include cuffs, collars, lapels, and facings.

Ironing The act of using an iron in a back and forth motion to remove wrinkles from finished garments.

Lining An inner layer of fabric that encloses raw edges of the outer garment and provides comfort for the wearer.

Outseam The outseam is the outer seam on a pant, dress, or skirt.

Placket An opening in sleeves, pants, and skirts that allow garments to be put on or easily removed. Plackets are commonly closed with buttons or hook and eyes/bars and can be found above button down/up sleeves or waistbands.

Pleat A fold of fabric that is stitched down to make a garment smaller/shorter or for decorative purposes.

Pressing The act of using an iron to press fabric, seams, and hems flat or to press a crease in place.

Repairs Fixing clothing by darning, mending, patching, or fixing/replacing hardware.

Right Side/Technical Front The public side of a fabric.

Seam The line where two pieces of fabric are sewn together.

Seam Allowance The distance between the raw and finished edge of a garment.

Seam Ripper A sewist's best friend! A tool used to unpick and rip stitches out of fabric.

Selvedge The finished edge of a woven fabric parallel to the straight of grain.

Serging/Overlocking A common method of finishing raw edges of knit and woven fabrics fabric using a serger/overlock machine.

Stay Stitch Pre-sewing along the raw edge of a curve to help prevent fabric from stretching out on a curve. Commonly used on necklines and waistbands.

Stitch-in-the-Ditch Stitching in the center of an existing seam in order to secure layers of fabric together. Commonly used in waistbands, with original hems, and in quilting.

Take in Removing fabric or stitching further away from a seam allowance in order to make a garment smaller or more fitted to the body.

Taper To narrow a garment.

Topstitching/Edge Stitching Stitching near a fold or seamed edge on a garment to keep the fabric in place. Topstitching can also be decorative.

Understitch Sewing a line of stitching close to the seam that goes through the seam allowances and lining of a garment to prevent the fabric from showing on the public side of the garment. Commonly used in necklines, armscyes, waistbands, and with facings.

Vent A slit or opening on a garment that allows for movement of the body.

Warp The vertical yarns on a woven fabric.

Weft The horizontal yarns of a woven fabric.

Wrong Side/Technical Back The side of the fabric that is not typically visible on a apparel.

Zipper A garment fastener.

Acknowledgements

Writing and illustrating a book was never on my radar and proved to be more challenging and humbling than I could have imagined. I wish to sincerely extend my gratitude to the people who held my metaphorical seams together and also to those who have been teachers, mentors, and friends. Thank you to Bloomsbury Publishing and the kind, thorough, and supportive team including Georgia Kennedy, Rosie Best, Faith Marsland, Mandy Collison, and Joanne Rippin. Thank you to Lea Black for beautifully capturing and editing the photographs in this book, and for the models/stylists who agreed to be photographed: Kevin/Matilda/Charlie Lewallen, Emily Mower, Josh Hartung, Melanie-Angela Neuilly, Rochelle Smith, Yimin Chen, Maggie Zee, and Luis Garcia Hernandez. Thank you to my colleagues/teachers/mentors Lori Wahl, Sonya Meyer, Sandra Evenson, Erika Iiams, Shelley McGuire, Carrie Lawrence, Ellen Bredehoft, and Lee Hodgson—you have taught me everything that led me to creating this book! Thank you to my friends and students who helped me visualize and execute this project including Maggie Zee and Jaeda Schnuerle. Thank you to my friends and cheerleaders Olivia Warren, Chelsea Feeney, Kristine Petterson, and David Lee-Painter for our weekly check-ins that helped me stay on track and sane through this process. A special thank you to Yimin Chen for being my accountability buddy and zooming with me every Tuesday and Thursday for two years to chip away at the book illustrations.

Extra special recognition needs to be made to my former business partner and "work wife" Sara Holden who started Altered Ego with me and continued to carry the torch when I transitioned to academia—our community is so lucky to have you and the services you provide to them.

My deepest appreciation goes to my family who endlessly support me and who also hope I never decide to get my PhD or write another book! My children Matilda and Charlie, my sister Candace, my mom Patty, and my dad Bruce. Finally, the person who deserves the most praise during this process—my patient, kind, loving, supportive husband Kevin—thank you for everything.

Index

A

alterations
    deviations in manufactured garments 30
    goals of 6
    identification of problems 32–5
    marking methods 31
    methods 6–7
    position of client when pinning 30
    pre-washing, drying and pressing of garments by client 30
    seam allowances 35
    top-downwards working 33
    uneven sides 30
    working with clients 36–7
    workspace organization 28–9
    see also bottom hems; letting out; taking in
awls 23

B

back gap 94–5, 129–31
ball head pins 10
ball point pins 10
beeswax 13
bias tape, lengthening hems and 69–70
blind hem 46–7
blind hemming machine 46–7
boned bodices 154–5, 162–3
bottom hems
    bias tape 69–70
    cadet cut hem 49–50
    cross/catch stitch 63, 64
    fabric, adding 71–3
    hand stitch hems 63–6
    jeans 132–9
    knitwear coverstitch hem 51–2
    knitwear faux coverstitch using a twin needle 55–6
    lace, adding 74–5
    lengthening 67–75, 90–1
    maxing out seams 68
    measuring 44–5
    napkin roll hem 61–2
    prick/pick stitch 63, 66
    serge and blind hem 46–7
    shortening 44–66
    suit jackets 90–1
    twice turn hem 48–9, 57–60
    vertical hem stitch 63, 65
bottoms
    back gaps 94–5
    darts/pleats/tucks 105–7
    ease/gathers 108–9
    elastic in waistbands 121–2
    gussets/panels 123–4
    inseams 102–3, 116–17
    letting out 113–24
    outseams 98–101
    seam allowance 119–20
    side seams 98–101, 114–15
    side zippers 110–11
    taking in 93–111
    waistbands 96–7, 118–24
    see also crotch seams; jeans
buckles 23
bulky/woolly nylon thread 17, 54
buttons 24, 200–7

C

caddies 29
cadet cut hem 49–51
catch stitch 63, 64
chairs 29
chalk marking tools 12
clay chalk 12
clients
    estimates, giving 36
    uneven sides of 30
    working with 36–7
collars 191–6
communication with clients 36
cone thread 17
content of fiber 38, 39
coverstitch machines 18, 29, 53
creativity in problem-solving 67
cross/catch stitch 63, 64
crotch seams
    gussets, adding 187–9
    letting out 182, 185–6
    measuring 181–2
    taking in 181, 183–4
cuffs 171, 176–7
curved machine needles 14

D

darning 215–18
    as repair method 8
    tools 29
darts 105–7, 148–51
decorative head pins 10
decorative patches 208–14
denim/jeans machine needles 14
deviations in manufactured garments 30
distressing jeans 135
dorcas pins 10
drag lines 32
drawstrings 229
dresses
    shortening 46–9, 51–3, 55–62, 64
    see also bottom hems

E

ease/gathers 108–9
elastic in waistbands 96–7, 121–2
estimates 37
eveningwear
    shortening 57–60, 66
    twice turn hem 57–60
eyelets 23

F

fabric/ fiber
    fabric structure 38, 40–1
    fiber content 38, 39
    knit fabrics 15, 40
    natural fiber 39

nonwoven fabrics 41
semi-synthetic fiber 39
synthetic fiber 39
woven fabrics, identifying 40
woven fabrics, needles and 15
fabric, adding, to lengthen hems 71–3
fabric markers and pencils 12
fashion rulers 11
fasteners 24
flat head pins 10
fluff thread 17, 54
formalwear
boned bodices 154–5, 162–3
shortening 57–60, 66
twice turn hem 57–60
French curves 11
fusible bonding web patches 213–14

G
gathers 108–9
glass head pins 10
gravity feed irons 22
grommets 23
gussets 33, 123–4, 187–9

H
hammers 23
hand darning 217–18
hand sewing needles 13
hand stitching
blind hem 46–7
bottom hems 63–6
cross/catch stitch 63, 64
prick/pick stitch 63, 66
vertical hem stitch 63, 65
hand tools 25–6
hardware 23–6
hems and hemming *see* bottom hems; top hems
hip curves 11
home machine blind hem 46–7
home machine needles 14
home machines 17
hook and loop tape 230

I
identification of problems 32–5
industrial machine needles 14
industrial machines 17–18
inseams 102–3, 116–17, 140–2

ironing
irons and ironing boards 29
tools 29
iron on patches 211–12

J
jeans
back gap 129–31
bottom hems 132–9
distressing 135
inseams 140–2
machine needles 14
outseams 140–2
shortening 133–40
taking in 129–31, 140–2
topstitching thread 17

K
knit fabrics 15, 40
knitwear coverstitch hem 51–2, 78–9
knitwear faux coverstitch using a twin needle 55–6, 80–1

L
lace, adding, to lengthen hems 74–5
landfills, textile waste in 1
lengthening
bias tape 69–70
bottom hems 67–75
fabric, adding 71–3
lace, adding 74–5
maxing out seams 68, 88–9
as method of alteration 7
suit jackets 90–1
top hems 88–91
letting out
boned bodices 162–3
bottoms 113–24
crotch seams 182, 185–6
elastic in waistbands 121–2
gussets/panels 123–4
inseams 116–17
measurement 118
as method of alteration 7
panels 160–1
seam allowance 119–20
side seams 114–15, 158–9
tops 157–63
waistbands 118–24
linings 57, 228
L squares 11

M
machine darning 216
machines *see* sewing machines
marking methods 31, 58–9
marking tools 12
maxing out seams 33, 68
measurement
bottom hems 44–5
crotch seams 181–2
letting out 118
shortening 44–5
methods of alteration 6–7

N
napkin roll hem 61–2
natural fiber 39
necklines and collars 191–6
needles
beeswax/thread conditioner 13
changing 15
hand sewing 13
knit fabrics 15
machine 14–15
sizes 14
thimbles 13
threaders 13
twin needles 55–6
universal v. ballpoint 14
woven fabrics and 15
no, saying
suit jackets 166
zippers 227
nonwoven fabrics 41

O
outdoor gear 231–2
outseams 98–101, 140–2
overlock machines 18, 29
overlock thread 17

P
panels 33, 123–4, 160–1
pants
shortening 44, 46–50, 65
see also bottom hems; bottoms
patches 208–14, 231
patching as repair method 8
pegboards 29
pick stitch 63, 66
pinning, position of client and 30
pins 9–10

plackets 176–7
pleats/tucks 105–7, 152–3
point turners 24
position of client when pinning 30
pressing and ironing 21–2
pre-washing, drying and pressing of garments by client 30
prick/pick stitch 63, 66
princess seams/darts 148–51
problem-solving, creativity in 67
pulling, areas of 32

R
rasps 23
repairs
    buttons 200–7
    darning 8, 215–18
    drawstrings 229
    hook and loop tape 230
    linings 228
    methods 7
    outdoor gear 231–2
    patches 8, 208–14, 231
    zippers 220–7, 232
rulers 11

S
safety pins 10
sandpaper 23
seam gauges 11
seams
    allowances 35, 68, 88–9
    crotch seams 181–9
    inseams 102–3, 116–17, 140–2
    maxing out 33, 68
    outseams 98–101, 140–2
    princess seams/darts 148–51
    side seams 98–101, 114–15, 146–7, 158–9
semi-synthetic fiber 39
serge and blind hem 46–7
serger machines 18, 29
serger thread 17
sewing machines
    coverstitch 18, 29
    home 17
    industrial 17
    needles 14–15
    overlock 18, 29
    serger 18, 29
    workspace organization 29
sewing space organization 28–9
shank buttons 200, 205–7
shirttail hem 82–3
shortening
    bottom hems 44–66
    cross/catch stitch 63, 64
    eveningwear 57–60, 66
    formalwear 57–60, 66
    jeans 133–40
    knitwear coverstitch hem 78–9
    knitwear faux coverstitch using a twin needle 80–1
    measurement 44–5
    as method of alteration 7
    prick/pick stitch 63, 66
    shirttail hem 82–3
    suit jackets 84–7
    top hems 77–87
    vertical hem stitch 63, 65
shorts
    shortening 44
    see also bottom hems
shoulders 167–9
side seams 98–101, 114–15, 146–7, 158–9
side zippers 110–11
silamide/2-ply waxed nylon thread 16
silk pins 10
skirts
    shortening 51–2, 55–6
    see also bottom hems
sleeves 170–5
slow fashion 1
space for sewing, organization of 28–9
special machine needles 14
steamers 22
structure of fabric 38, 40–1
suit jackets
    lengthening 90–1
    lined, shortening hems 84–5
    saying no to altering 166
    sleeve hems 172–5
    unlined, shortening hems 86–7
suspender buttons 200, 204
sustainability, alteration and repair and 1
synthetic fiber 39

T
taking in
    back gaps 94–5
    boned bodices 154–5
    bottoms 93–111
    crotch seams 181, 183–4
    cuffs 171, 176–7
    darts 148–51
    darts/pleats/tucks 105–7
    ease/gathers 108–9
    elastic in waistbands 96–7
    inseams 102–3
    jeans 129–42
    as method of alteration 6
    outseams 98–101
    pleats/tucks 152–3
    princess seams/darts 148–51
    side seams 98–101, 146–7
    side zippers 110–11
    sleeves 170–1
    tops 145–55
    waistbands 96–7
taking up shoulders 167–9
tape measures 11
Tex number 17
textile waste in landfills 1
thickness of thread 17
thimbles 13
thread
    bulky/woolly nylon/fluff 17
    conditioner 13
    cone 17
    fuzz factor 17
    hand sewing 16
    jeans/topstitching 17
    machine sewing 16
    overlock 17
    serger 17
    silamide/2-ply waxed nylon 16
    strength, testing 17
    Tex number 17
    thickness 17
    woolly nylon/bulky nylon/fluff 54
threaders 13
thread marking 12
toolboxes 29
tools
    hand 23–6
    hardware 23–6
    ironing 29
    machines 17–18
    marking 12
    needles 13–15
    pins 9–10
    pressing and ironing 21–2

rulers 11
thread 16–19
top-downwards working 33
top hems
    knitwear coverstitch hem 78–9
    knitwear faux coverstitch using a twin needle 80–1
    lengthening 88–91
    maxing out seams 88–9
    shirttail hem 82–3
    shortening 77–87
    suit jackets 84–7
tops
    backs 150–1
    boned bodices 154–5, 162–3
    cuffs 171, 176–7
    darts 148–51
    fronts 148–9
    letting out 157–63
    necklines and collars 191–6
    panels 160–1
    pleats/tucks 152–3
    princess seams/darts 148–51
    shoulders 167–9

side seams 146–7, 158–9
sleeves 170–5
taking in 145–55
topstitching thread 17
T-pins 10
tucks 105–7, 152–3
twice turn hem 48–9, 57–60
twin machine needles 14
twin needles, knitwear faux coverstitch using 55–6
2-ply waxed nylon thread 16

U
uneven sides of clients 30

V
Velcro/hook and loop tape 230
vertical hem stitch 65
visible mending 208–14

W
waistbands 96–7
    darts/pleats/tucks 106–7
    ease/gathers 108–9

elastic 121–2
letting out 118–24
seam allowance 119–20
waterproof gear 232
wax chalk 12
woolly nylon/bulky nylon/fluff thread 17, 54
workspace organization 28–9
woven fabrics, identifying 40
woven fabrics, needles and 15

Y
yard sticks 11

Z
zippers
    anatomy of 220
    fixing/replacing zipper heads 223–6
    issues with, identifying 222
    outdoor gear 232
    repair kits 23, 29
    saying no 227
    types 221